Audio 🔊 Included

150 KEYBOARD TIPS & LESSONS

150 KEYBOARD TIPS & LESSONS

TAKE YOUR PLAYING FROM ORDINARY TO EXTRAORDINARY!

BY MARK HARRISON

PLAYBACK+
Speed • Pitch • Balance • Loop

To access audio, video, and extra content visit:
www.halleonard.com/mylibrary

"Enter Code"
8099-4587-7802-6627

ISBN 978-1-5400-1445-0

Visit Hal Leonard Online at
www.halleonard.com

Contact Us:
Hal Leonard
7777 West Bluemound Road
Milwaukee, WI 53213
Email: info@halleonard.com

In Europe contact:
Hal Leonard Europe Limited
42 Wigmore Street
Marylebone, London, W1U 2RN
Email: info@halleonardeurope.com

In Australia contact:
Hal Leonard Australia Pty. Ltd.
4 Lentara Court
Cheltenham, Victoria, 3192 Australia
Email: info@halleonard.com.au

T0071258

CONTENTS

INTRODUCTION

Welcome to 150 KEYBOARD TIPS & LESSONS. This book/audio package is chock full of techniques and tricks to help your playing become more professional. Just dive into the alphabetic list of "tips" to learn what you need to know, from Styles (Blues, Boogie-Woogie, Funk, Gospel, Jazz, Rock, and more) to Keyboard Techniques (Arpeggios, Crossover Licks, Left-Hand Patterns, Neighbor Tones, Target Notes, and more) to Music Theory (Diatonic Chords, Triads, Seventh Chords, Downbeats and Upbeats, Voice Leading, and more) to Synthesizer Terms (Attack, Envelope, Filter, Glide, Waveform, and more). You get the idea!

Good luck with learning your *Tips and Lessons*!

– Mark Harrison

ABOUT THE AUDIO

On the accompanying audio tracks, you'll find recordings of almost all the music examples in the book. Most of the tracks feature a full band, with the rhythm section on the left channel and the keyboard on the right channel. To play along with the band on these tracks, simply turn down the right channel. For the solo keyboard tracks with separate left- and right-hand parts, the left-hand piano part is on the left channel, and the right-hand piano part is on the right channel, for easy hands-separate practice as needed.

ABOUT THE AUTHOR

Mark Harrison is a professional keyboardist, composer/arranger, and music educator/author based in Los Angeles. He has recorded three albums as a contemporary jazz bandleader (with the Mark Harrison Quintet) and plays regularly on the Los Angeles club and festival circuit with the Steely Dan tribute band Doctor Wu. Mark's TV music credits include *Saturday Night Live*, *The Montel Williams Show*, *American Justice*, *Celebrity Profiles*, *America's Most Wanted*, *True Hollywood Stories*, and many others.

Mark has held faculty positions at the Grove School of Music and at the University of Southern California (Thornton School of Music). He currently runs a busy online teaching studio, catering to the needs of professional and aspiring musicians worldwide. Mark's students include Grammy winners, hit songwriters, members of the Boston Pops and Los Angeles Philharmonic orchestras, and first-call touring musicians with major acts. He has also written Master Class articles for *Keyboard* and *How to Jam* magazines, covering a variety of keyboard styles and topics.

For more information on Mark's educational products and online lessons, please visit *harrisonmusic.com*.

ADD9 CHORDS

Adding ninths (sometimes referred to as seconds) is a great way to spice up major and minor chords in pop and rock styles. The ninth is the highest extension in a five-part chord—for example, a Cmaj9 chord would be spelled C-E-G-B-D, so D would be the ninth. However, in contemporary styles we will often want to add the ninth but exclude the seventh, which is what the chord symbol C(add9) is telling us to do. The ninth is often played (or voiced) a whole step above the root of the chord, which is why it is sometimes called a second. Let's see how to apply the add9 chords to some comping patterns.

TRACK 1

Pop Ballad – Basic Triads

Notice that we are just using simple major or minor triads in the right hand, with voice leading (inverting the triads to move smoothly between successive chords) and octave doubling (duplicating the top note of the right hand an octave lower). As in most piano ballad styles, we depress the sustain pedal for the duration of each chord. This groove uses an alternating-eighths right-hand technique (alternating between the chords played on the downbeats, and the thumb notes played in between on the upbeats). Now we'll vary this pattern by adding ninths to the chords.

TRACK 2

Pop Ballad – Triads with Added 9ths

Notice that the ninth often moves (or resolves) to the root of the chord—the movement from D to C in measure 1, for example. Although the chord symbols have been upgraded to reflect the added ninths, in practice you'll often apply this technique to chord charts with only basic triad chord symbols (when stylistically appropriate, of course). Next we'll look at a pop/rock comping pattern.

TRACK 3

Pop/Rock – Basic Triads

Again, we are using basic major and minor triads, with voice leading. In this pop/rock style, the right hand is playing a steady driving eighth-note rhythmic pattern, and the left hand is playing the root of each chord, with an anticipation (landing an eighth note ahead) of beat 3 in each measure. Now we'll upgrade this pattern with added ninths.

TRACK 4

Pop/Rock with Added 9ths

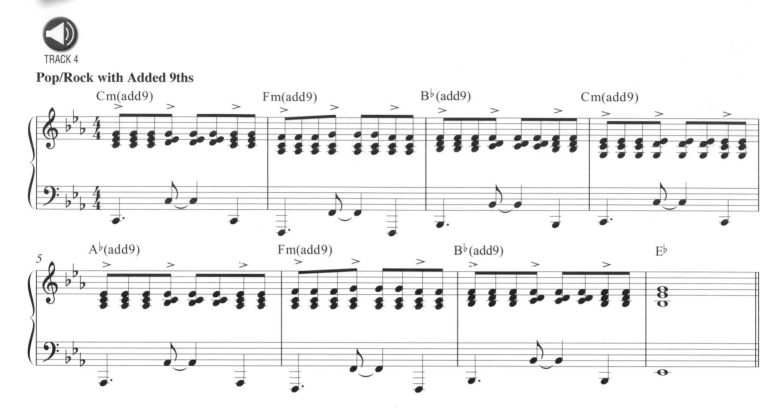

Again, notice how the ninth resolves to the root of each chord (i.e., the motion from D to C in measure 1). Have fun with your added ninths. As with any harmonic device, don't overdo it; but in the right context, it will make your piano parts sound very hip!

AFTERTOUCH

Aftertouch is the act of exerting pressure on a key of a synthesizer keyboard after the note is first played. This can then trigger a particular musical effect, such as changing the volume or tone color, or adding vibrato or tremolo. This is normally a programmable function, meaning that the aftertouch can be programmed to change the volume, tone color, etc., within a particular sound (or program) on a synthesizer. If your synth has aftertouch capability, you'll likely find that some of the presets have already been programmed in this way.

Our first music example uses aftertouch to create vibrato (a regular variation in pitch) on a lead synth sound played over a funk groove. The vibrato is indicated by the wavy lines following each of the longer notes:

TRACK 5

Funk

Listen to this track and you'll hear that the lead synth sound is on the right channel, and the rest of the band is on the left channel. Fire up a lead synth (with aftertouch vibrato) on your axe, and try playing along! This lead synth part was played using the ES2 "virtual" software synthesizer within Logic. The other instrument sounds in the backing band also come from Logic software instruments: the electric piano is played using the Vintage Electric Pianos plug-in and the "fingerstyle" electric bass is played using the EXS24 software sampler.

Note that aftertouch can be programmed and performed using either a "real" physical keyboard synthesizer, or a virtual software synthesizer being played from a keyboard controller.

Harmony/Theory Notes

The progression on Track 5 is in the key of C minor, but the lead synth part uses a C Dorian mode (which is a B♭ major scale displaced to start on the note C). The C Dorian mode contains the note A, which is why we have natural signs before the A's in measures 3–4 (as these contradict the A♭ in the key signature). Using Dorian modes within minor keys in this way, is commonly done across a range of funk and jazz styles.

TRACK 6

Blues Shuffle

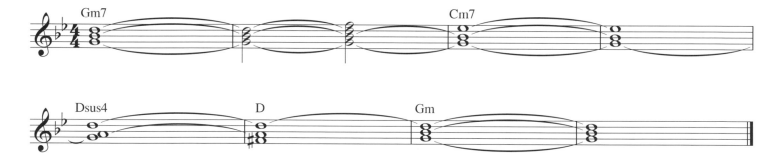

Listen to the track and you'll hear that the organ sound is on the right channel, and the rest of the band is on the left channel. You'll also notice that during measures 3–4 the rotating speaker effect starts to speed up, and during measures 7–8 the rotating speaker slows down again. This was triggered by using aftertouch on a controller keyboard. The organ part on the track is played using the Vintage Electric Organs virtual instrument, a plug-in within the Logic digital audio workstation software. The sound has the lower drawbars pulled out (selecting the lower frequencies) and the higher drawbars pushed in (muting the higher frequencies). This results in a mellower, more rounded sound. Try playing along with this track using your favorite organ patch, and experiment with the rotary speaker effect if your instrument has that capability.

Harmony/Theory Notes

The above organ example uses an upper structure triad, which is a vital voicing technique in many contemporary styles. The right-hand notes on the Cm7 chord form an E♭ major triad (E♭ G B♭). These are the 3rd, 5th, and 7th of the Cm7 chord, and can be thought of as a major triad (E♭ major in this case) built from the 3rd of the chord (Cm7 in this case). Otherwise we're using simple major and minor triads based on the chord symbols, with the 7th of the Gm7 chord being added during measure 2. The Dsus4 chord symbol signifies that the 4th (G in this case) has replaced the 3rd of the chord (F♯ in this case). This then resolves to the D major triad (containing the F♯) in the following measure.

ALTERNATING EIGHTH NOTES

Alternating eighths is a term I use to describe a comping style where the right hand alternates between the upper notes of a chord (played with the 2nd, 3rd, 4th, and/or 5th fingers) and the lowest note of that chord (played with the thumb), using an eighth-note rhythmic pattern. We saw some examples of this technique in *Add9 Chords* (p. 6), employed in a pop ballad style. Next we'll apply this concept to a pop/rock shuffle groove.

TRACK 7

Pop/Rock Shuffle

Note the "swing-eighths" symbol above the music (telling you to treat each pair of eighth notes as a quarter-eighth triplet): this is how we create the shuffle feel for this example. Listen to the audio track to make sure you're comfortable with this swing-eighths rhythmic subdivision. Also, in this groove both the right- and left-hand parts are anticipating beat 3 (landing an eighth note before the beat).

Chord Voicing Tips

This is another example using upper-structure triads, a vital voicing technique in many contemporary styles. The right-hand notes on the Cm7 chords form an E♭ major triad (E♭-G-B♭). These are the third, fifth, and seventh of the Cm7 chord, and can be thought of as a major triad (E♭ major in this case) built from the third of the chord (Cm7 in this case). In a similar fashion, an F major triad has been built from the third of all the Dm7 chords.

We've also used a couple of different upper structures on the major chords. On the E♭maj7 chords, the right-hand notes form a G minor triad (giving us the third, fifth, and seventh of the E♭maj7 chord), a minor triad built from the third of the chord. On the B♭maj7 chord, the right-hand notes form an F major triad (the fifth, seventh, and ninth of the B♭maj7 chord), a major triad built from the fifth of the chord. This upgrades the chord symbol by adding the ninth (and removing the third), giving a transparent, modern sound.

The F11 chord is a suspended dominant, where the fourth or eleventh has replaced the third. For this we have built a major triad from the seventh of the chord (E♭ in this case), giving us the seventh, ninth, and eleventh of the chord. The Dsus2 chord indicates that we have replaced the third of a D major triad with the second (or ninth). The resulting voicing in the last measure can be thought of as an inversion of a double 4th, which is a three-note shape built using intervals of a 4th (here E-A-D). We'll return to these very hip double-4th voicings later!

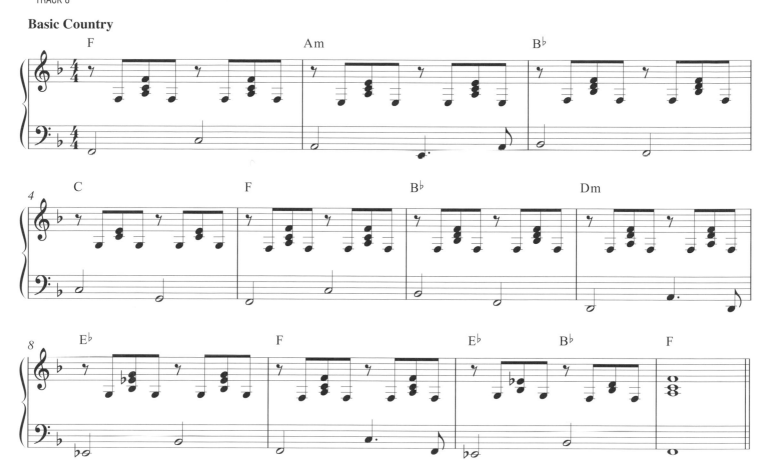

Our next alternating-eighths pattern is in a basic country style, played with straight eighths.

TRACK 8

Basic Country

Here, the right hand plays a triad on beats 2 and 4 of each measure, alternating with the thumb note (an octave below the top note of each triad) on each upbeat. Note that the left hand plays on beats 1 and 3 (moving from the root to the fifth of each chord), while the right hand rests on these beats; this creates the back-and-forth motion between the hands that is typical of country comping styles. The right-hand part is voiced with basic major and minor triads derived from the chord symbols, using inversions to voice lead smoothly through the progression.

ANALOG SYNTHESIZER

An **analog synthesizer** uses analog circuits to generate sound electronically. This is the earliest and most classic synthesizer technology, and the enduring quality and warmth of analog sounds ensure that these synths (and, more recently, their digital and software-based clones) are still widely used in the 21st century.

The earliest widely available analog synths were large modular systems that emerged in the 1960s. These were followed in the early 1970s by "all-in-one" analog synthesizers that were integrated into a single unit, rather than using separate physical modules. The most famous and successful of these was the Minimoog (see p. 117). At the time, the processing required to generate just a single note was rather complex, so most synthesizers remained monophonic, meaning they could play only one note at a time.

Polyphonic analog synthesizers then emerged, with the ability to play more than one note simultaneously. Around this time, the use of microprocessor technology enabled sound programs (or "patches") to be stored in the synthesizer's memory, for instant recall during a performance. The first synths of this type were manufactured by Sequential Circuits, notably including their ground-breaking five-voice synthesizer, the Prophet-5 (see p. 152).

By the late 1980s, analog synths had fallen out of favor, being replaced by digital synthesizers and samplers. However, in the 1990s analog sounds and synths began to have a big resurgence, fueled in part by electronic dance music and hip hop styles. Into the 21st century, analog synths are alive and well, with new "hardware" analog synths being manufactured alongside virtual (computer-based) instruments.

Now we'll look at some musical examples of analog synth sounds. First up is an R&B/pop groove using a classic Minimoog-style bass sound:

TRACK 9

R&B/Pop

Listen to the track and you'll hear that the synth bass is on the right channel, and the rest of the band is on the left channel. Try playing along with this example, using your favorite synth bass sound. The fat and rounded sound of the Minimoog is ideal for synth bass lines in various styles. This example was produced using a Moog bass sample within the Omnisphere virtual instrument (see p. 133). This particular Moog bass uses a pulse waveform (see p. 153), which has a somewhat hollow yet warm sound characteristic. The sounds in the backing band include a staccato synth comping part and a soft analog synth pad, both from the Kontakt software sampler and synthesizer (see p. 103).

Harmony/Theory Notes

The above synth bass part uses the root, 5th, and 7th of the E5 chord, which are common note choices for this type of R&B/Pop bass line. All the bass notes in this example come from the E Dorian mode, a typical choice within this implied key of E minor. The 16th-note rhythms (in particular, landing on the 2nd and/or 4th 16th notes with the beat) give this bass line a funky, syncopated effect.

Next we have a rock groove using a Roland Jupiter-style synth pad. The Roland Jupiter-8, introduced in 1981, remains one of the classic analog synths of all time. (For more on this important synth, see p. 99.)

TRACK 10

Rock

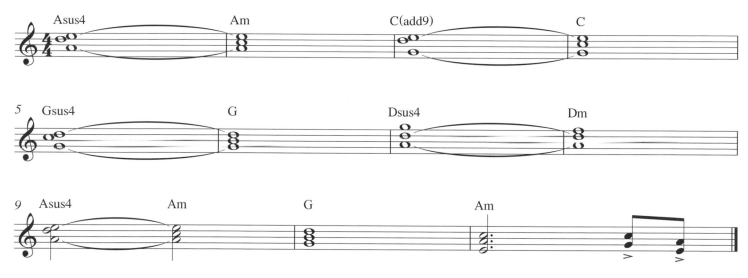

Listen to the track and you'll hear that the synth pad is on the right channel, and the rest of the band is on the left channel. This example uses a Roland Jupiter-8 synthesizer sample, again within the Omnisphere virtual instrument. In the backing band, the Kontakt software sampler provides the rhythm section (bass and drums) sounds.

Harmony/Theory Notes

Notice the above synth part has some linear motion, or "interior resolutions." For example, the D in the first measure (the 4th of the Asus4 chord) resolves to the C in the second measure (the 3rd of the Am chord). Similarly, the D in the third measure (now the 9th of the Cadd9 chord) again resolves to the C in the fourth measure (the root of the C chord), and so on. This type of motion is an effective way to spice up your synth pads and chordal parts.

ANTICIPATIONS

An **anticipation** occurs when a rhythmic event lands before the beat, and is then held over (or followed by a rest on) the beat. An example of an eighth-note anticipation would be a chord landing on an upbeat (say, halfway through beat 2) and then holding through the following downbeat (beat 3 in this case). The pop/rock shuffle groove of Track 7 (p. 10) is a good example of this. An example of a 16th-note anticipation would be a chord landing on the last 16th note within the beat, and then held through the following beat. Here we will focus on 16th-note anticipations, beginning with an R&B ballad.

TRACK 11

Note how the right-hand voicings are often anticipating (landing a 16th note ahead of) beat 3. Also, the left-hand pattern frequently anticipates beats 2 and/or 4. This all combines to create a rhythmic conversation between the hands that is typical of R&B ballad styles.

Chord Voicing Tips

This R&B ballad example also uses upper-structure triads and four-part chord shapes as follows:

- The Bm7 and Gm7 chords are voiced by building major triads from the third: D/B and B♭/G.

- The A11 chord in measure 6 is voiced by building a major triad from the seventh: G/A.

- The Dmaj9 and B♭maj9 chords are voiced by building minor-seventh shapes from the third: F♯m7/D and Dm7/B♭.

- The A11 chord in measure 10 is voiced by building a minor-seventh shape from the fifth: Em7/A.

- The A7♭9 chord is voiced by building a diminished-seventh shape from the third: C♯dim7/A.

We also have some added ninths on the major chords in measures 2 and 3. And the left hand is using some root-fifth, root-seventh, and open-triad arpeggio patterns.

The next example uses anticipations within a swing-16ths rhythmic framework, often found in today's funk shuffle and hip-hop styles. Note the "swing-16ths" symbol above the music (telling you to treat each pair of 16th notes as an eighth-16th triplet); again, check out the audio track to get comfortable with this rhythmic feel. The right-hand voicings are often anticipating beat 1 by a 16th note, which together with the downbeats used in the left-hand part (whole notes in measures 1–4, and quarter-note octaves from measure 5 onward) is characteristic of funk piano styles.

TRACK 12

Chord Voicing Tips

This R&B/funk shuffle example also uses upper-structure triads and four-part chord shapes as follows:

- The G7 chords are voiced by building a diminished triad from the third: Bdim/G.

- The C11 and F11 chords are voiced by building major triads from the seventh: B♭/C and E♭/F.

- The Cm7 chord is voiced by building a major triad from the third: E♭/C.

- The G11 chords are voiced by building a minor-seventh shape from the fifth: Dm7/G.

- The D7(♯5, ♭9) chords are voiced by building a minor-seventh-flatted-fifth shape from the seventh: Cm7♭5/D.

- The D7(♯5, ♯9) chords are voiced by building a major-seventh-flatted-fifth shape from the third: F♯maj7♭5/D.

- The E♭maj9 chord is voiced by building a minor-seventh shape from the third: Gm7/E♭.

On the G7 chords (as well as the B diminished triads), we are also adding some passing triads (C major and D minor). These come from the G Mixolydian mode.

ARPEGGIATOR

An **arpeggiator** is a synthesizer function that generates arpeggios (broken chords) from chord voicings played on the keyboard. For example, if you play and hold a C major triad on a typical workstation keyboard and hit the Arpeggio button, you will hear a sequence of the individual notes C, E, and G over one or more octaves, depending on the range and pattern selected. Depending on the particular device, you can also control the speed of the arpeggios, and whether they play downward, upward, or in a random sequence.

Arpeggiators are also often implemented in software sequencers or computer-based digital audio workstations (see p. 39), as well as virtual instruments or softsynths. Coming up we have an example of an arpeggiator being used in Reason, which is a leading digital audio workstation commonly used for electronic dance music production. Reason has an internal arpeggiator plug-in called RPG-8; it was used for this example, which is in a techno style (see p. 178). The synth voicings you see below in measures 1–8 were also played in measures 9–16, but during these measures the RPG-8 arpeggiator was applied to this synth part, turning the voicings into the series of three-note ascending arpeggios you see in measures 9–16 of the notation:

TRACK 13

Techno

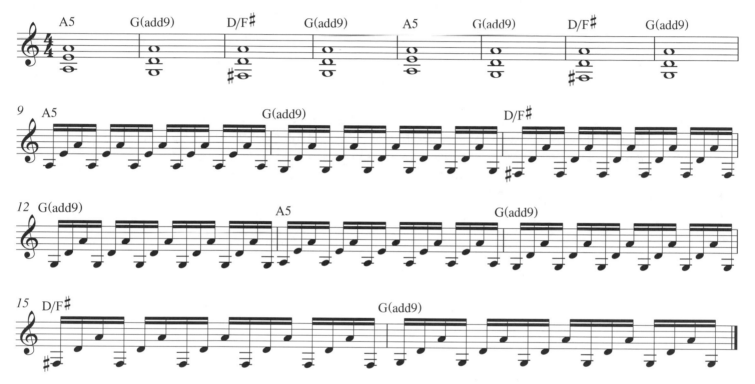

Listen to the track and you'll hear that the synth chords and arpeggios are on the right channel, and the rest of the band is on the left channel. The synth sound on the right channel is an analog/wavetable blend from the Thor plug-in synth within Reason; this bright synth sound is particularly suitable for electronic dance music styles. Note that the tempo of the arpeggio is synced (matched) with the tempo of the overall sequence. This is normal for arpeggiators working inside digital audio workstation "hosts."

In the backing band, Thor is also providing the analog lead fills and techno-bass sounds that you hear on the left channel. Note that the delay (echo) effect applied to the lead synth is also tempo-synced to the main sequence. This is a common and effective technique across a range of contemporary and electronic styles.

A

ARPEGGIOS

An **arpeggio** is the result of playing the notes of a chord one at a time, or "broken chord" style. This technique has many applications in both classical and popular music. Our first example is an excerpt from Mozart's Piano Sonata in C Major, which uses an arpeggio accompaniment in the left hand below the melody in the right hand.

TRACK 14

In the first measure, the left-hand notes C-G-E-G outline a C major triad. In the second measure, the left-hand notes D-G-F-G (together with the B in the right-hand melody) outline a G7 chord, and so on. This is a common type of accompaniment figure in classical music, and is referred to as "Alberti bass." Next we will look at a pop/rock comping example that uses arpeggios in the right hand.

TRACK 15

Pop/Rock

In the first measure, the right-hand notes C-E-G-E outline a C major triad. In the second measure, the right-hand notes C-E-A-E outline an A minor triad, and so on. Notice that the right-hand arpeggios anticipate beat 3 in each measure. The left hand, meanwhile, is playing the root of each chord using a repeated eighth-note pattern. This is all typical of pop/rock comping styles.

ARTICULATION

The **articulation** of a note describes how it is played—whether the note is short, long, accented, and so on. Applying the correct articulations to a piece of music is very important, whether it is an 18th-century Bach fugue, or a 21st-century neo-soul ballad. The following example of a D major scale shows some commonly used musical articulations.

We can analyze the articulations at the bottom of page 18 as follows:

- The dot underneath the first D means *staccato* (play the note short).
- The dash underneath the E means *tenuto* (play the note long).
- The arrow underneath the F# is an *accent* (play the note hard).
- The arrow-with-dot underneath the G is a *staccato accent* (play the note short and hard).
- The arrow-with-dash underneath the A is a *tenuto accent* (play the note long and hard).
- The curved line connecting the B, C#, and D is a *slur* (play *legato*, meaning smooth and connected).

ATTACK

In a synthesizer, the **attack** is the first stage of a envelope generator (see p. 58), which is a modifer normally applied to the filter (see p. 67) to control the timbre, or to the amplifier to control the volume. The attack is the time taken for the envelope to reach its peak, before the decay time (see p. 36) begins.

In musical terms, a slow attack applied to a (conventional low-pass) filter means that the sound will be darker at the beginning, and then become brighter during the attack time up until the peak. By contrast, a fast attack applied to the filter means that all the harmonics/frequencies will be present right from the beginning. A slow attack applied to the amplifier means that the sound will be quieter at the beginning, and then become louder during the attack time up until the peak. By contrast, a fast attack applied to the amplifier means that the full volume of the sound will be present right from the beginning.

The recorded example on Track 16 demonstrates these principles, playing a single repeated note and using a simple sawtooth waveform (see p. 165) generated by the ES2 synth plug-in within Logic (see p. 111).

The first group of four notes uses different attack times applied to the filter:

- 0 ms (milliseconds), 500 ms, 1500 ms, and 5000 ms.

TRACK 16

The second group of four notes uses different attack times applied to the amplifier:

- 0 ms, 500 ms, 2000 ms, and 5000 ms.

In the first group of four notes, you can hear that, as the attack time increases, the sound is darker at the beginning and takes progressively longer to reach the brightness peak. In the second group of four notes, you can hear that, as the attack time increases, the sound is quieter at the beginning and takes progressively longer to reach the volume peak (without the brightness or tone color changing).

Understanding the role of the attack stage in the envelope generator is important when programming your synth. To mimic a brass sound you might typically apply a slower attack to the filter, as it takes a moment for the upper harmonics to emerge on a note played on a trumpet, for example. By contrast, to mimic a string sound you might apply a slower attack to the amplifier, as it takes a moment for the full volume to emerge on a note played on a cello.

One more thing… If you're on a recording session and the producer asks you for a shorter attack on your synth sound (with no other qualification), assume that he or she means the attack time within the amplifier envelope; i.e., they want the sound to "speak" right from the beginning. It's surprising how many indifferent-sounding presets on today's synths can be improved just by tweaking the attack times.

BALLADS

The term **ballad** is used to describe any song played at a slow tempo. In contemporary styles, ballads typically have either an eighth-note rhythmic subdivision (as in classic pop or rock ballads, and country ballads) or a 16th-note rhythmic subdivision (as in modern rock and R&B ballads). Our first example is an eighth-note pop ballad pattern, using an alternating-eighth right-hand comping style.

TRACK 17

This example includes several inverted chord symbols, where a major or minor triad is placed over its third or fifth in the bass. For example, the D/F♯ is a D major triad placed over its third (F♯) in the bass, and the B/F♯ is a B major triad placed over its fifth (again F♯) in the bass. This is a common sound in pop styles, and is often done to enable the bass line to move in a stepwise manner. The right hand is mostly using basic triads in measures 1–4, and is then embellishing with some added ninths in measures 5–8. Next we'll see the same chord progression used with a 16th-note R&B ballad comping pattern.

TRACK 18

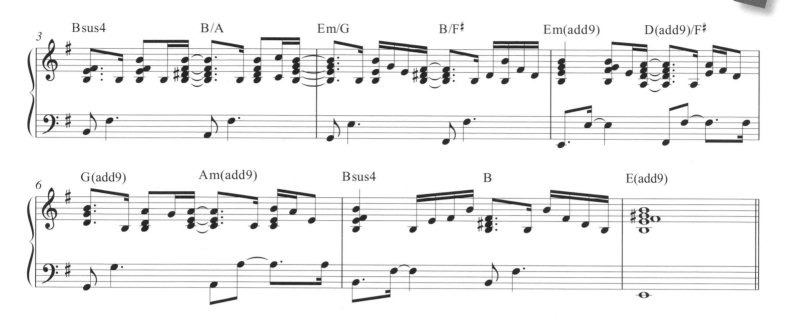

Here the right-hand voicings anticipate beat 3 by a 16th note in most measures, which is typical of R&B ballad styles. Also, the right hand is embellishing with arpeggios on beat 4 in some measures (don't overdo this!). Meanwhile, the left hand frequently anticipates beats 2 and/or 4, again normal for the style. As in the previous eighth-note ballad example, we are mostly using basic triad voicings in the first half, with some added ninths to spice things up in the second half.

In **Open Triads** (p. 135), we use this same chord progression to illustrate another very common left-hand technique for ballads.

BASS LINES

One of the most important musical uses of synthesizers is to play **bass lines** in a variety of contemporary styles. You may know that synth bass is overwhelmingly used in most forms of electronic dance music. But synth bass is also heard across a diverse range of styles such as rock, old-school R&B/funk, new age, and smooth jazz.

Our first example of a synthesizer bass line is in a funky house style (see p. 87) and uses some glide (a more gradual, rather than sudden, change in pitch between successive notes; see p. 77).

TRACK 19

Funky House

Listen to the track and you'll hear that the synth bass sound is on the right channel, and the rest of the band is on the left channel. Fire up a funky synth bass sound on your axe and try playing along! This synth bass sound is from the ES2 softsynth, a synth plug-in built into Logic. The electric piano in the backing band is played using Vintage Electric Pianos, another great Logic plug-in instrument.

Harmony/Theory Notes

As with all bass lines shown in this book, this example sounds an octave lower than written. This is for consistency with regular (i.e., non-synth) bass writing, as the bass is a transposing instrument (by one octave). Notice also that this bass line mostly uses the roots and 7ths of these minor 7th and dominant 7th chords, with some use of minor pentatonic scales. (For example, the A♭, F, and E♭ at the end of measure 1 come from the B♭ minor pentatonic scale.) This is an effective bass line technique across a range of funk/R&B and electronic dance music styles.

Our second example of a synthesizer bass line is in a synth-pop style (see p. 175) and is typical of the more keyboard-centric pop music of the 1980s:

TRACK 20

Synth-Pop

Again the synth bass sound is on the right channel, and the rest of the band is on the left channel. This is another synth bass sound from the ES2 softsynth, this time using an analog pulse waveform (see p. 195), which has a bright yet "hollow" sound characteristic.

The ES2 synth is also providing most of the backing band on the left channel, notably the staccato synth clavinet, the synth bells (during the first repeat i.e. measures 1–8) and the synth strings (during the second repeat; i.e., measures 9–16). By the way, the drum loop used is in the style of the classic LinnDrum machine, a staple of many synth-pop and dance hits of the 1980s.

BLUES

Blues is an indigenous American music style that emerged in the late 19th century, flourished and developed in the 20th century, and laid the foundations for modern-day R&B and rock 'n' roll styles. A number of regional blues styles have developed, including Chicago and New Orleans blues. Most blues music uses a swing-eighths rhythmic feel, and a 12-measure progression consisting of three four-measure phrases, which start with the I, IV, and V chords of the key (chords built from the 1st, 4th, and 5th degrees), respectively. The blues does not normally use diatonic chords, instead favoring dominant chords built from these scale degrees (for example, C7, F7, and G7 chords for a blues in C). Most piano blues uses driving, propulsive left-hand patterns, as in this Chicago Blues example.

TRACK 21

Note the repetitive nature of the left-hand pattern, with the root and fifth of each chord during beats 1 and 3 of each measure, and the "♭3–3" movement within beat 2. The right-hand part then plays off of this foundation, using various rhythms and syncopations.

Chord Voicing Tips

This Chicago Blues example uses upper-structure four-part chord shapes as follows:

- The F7 and C9 chords are voiced by building minor-seventh-flatted-fifth shapes from the third: Am7♭5/F and Em7♭5/C.

There are also various other right-hand blues devices being used as follows:

- On the C7 and G7 chords, we use 6ths (the third up to the root of the chord), embellished with a grace note a half step below the third of each chord.
- We approach measures 4 and 8 with parallel 3rds (moving by half steps), which lead into descending crossover licks.
- In measure 11, on the C7 chord, we use a repeated upper note (the root of the chord) against the moving half-step line underneath.

Next we will examine a New Orleans Blues pattern. This regional blues style is somewhat different from the others in that it often uses an eight-measure form (instead of the standard twelve measures), with a straight-eighths rhythm and anticipations of beat 3, as in the following example.

TRACK 22

New Orleans Blues

This time the left-hand pattern is derived from the root, third, fifth, and sixth (thirteenth) of each dominant chord.

Chord Voicing Tips

This New Orleans Blues uses some upper-triad movement on each chord: the B♭-F major triad movement on the F7 chord, the E♭-B♭ major triad movement on the B♭7 chord, and so on. This type of IV-I triad movement is known as "backcycling," and is a staple sound in blues, gospel, and rock styles.

Further Reading

For more info on blues piano, please check out my *Blues Piano: The Complete Guide with Audio!*, published by Hal Leonard LLC.

BLUES SCALE

The **blues scale** is a six-note scale that is widely used in blues, rock, R&B, funk, and gospel styles. Here is a C blues scale.

TRACK 23
Part 1

The C blues scale contains the following notes (with intervals above the tonic C in parentheses): C, E♭ (minor 3rd), F (perfect 4th), F♯ (augmented 4th), G (perfect 5th), and B♭ (minor 7th). This scale is equivalent to the C minor pentatonic scale, with an added F♯.

The following example shows a blues melody over a twelve-measure blues progression in C. The melody breaks down into three similar four-measure phrases, each starting on an upbeat, which is typical of blues phrasing. The entire C blues scale shown above is used over the C7, F7, and G7 chords. You can probably hear that some of these notes sound tense over these chords; we get away with this because of the unique melodic character of the blues scale—in fact, these tensions are one of the defining characteristics of the blues.

TRACK 23
Part 2

Basic Shuffle Blues

Note that the left-hand pattern is alternating between the root-plus-fifth and root-plus-sixth of each chord. This pattern sounds great on many blues and blues/rock songs, and works within both swing-eighths and straight-eighths rhythmic feels.

BOOGIE-WOOGIE

Boogie-woogie styles emerged in the early part of the twentieth century, and featured fast tempos and driving left-hand patterns. Both the left and right hands often play single-note lines, as opposed to the more chord-based patterns used in later blues styles. The eighth notes are almost always swung. This example features a classic boogie-woogie left-hand pattern, using octaves to outline the notes in each chord.

TRACK 24

Boogie-Woogie

The left-hand octaves outline the root, third, fifth, sixth (thirteenth), and seventh of the chords in measures 1–8, and just the root, third, and fifth of the chords in measures 9–11 (with the sixth added in measure 10). Meanwhile, the right hand is playing melodic runs using half steps and whole steps: the E-F-F♯-G run (connecting the third to the fifth on the C7 chord), the E♭-F-F♯-G run (connecting the seventh to the ninth on the F7 chord), and so on. The right hand also leads into some basic chord tones with grace notes a half step below: into the third of C7, and into the sevenths of F7 and G7. We're also using some 6ths: from the C Mixolydian mode in measure 4, approaching the fifth and seventh of the C7 chord by half step in measures 2 and 8, and approaching the third and fifth of the F7 chord by half step in measure 6.

Chord Voicing Tips

This boogie-woogie example uses upper-structure four-part chord shapes as follows:

- The D♭9 and C9 chords are voiced by building minor-seventh-flatted-fifth shapes from the third: Fm7♭5/D♭ and Em7♭5/C.

CHART

A **chart** is a notated version of a song, showing the melody and chord symbols, or just the chord symbols without the melody. A chart should also show the overall form and sections of the song (intro, verse, chorus, etc.), as well as any road map instructions, which can include repeats of sections, D.C. (meaning go back to the beginning), D.S. (meaning go back to the "sign"), when to go to the coda (end section), and so on.

If the chart has melody and chord symbols, it is also referred to as a lead sheet. If a chart just has chord symbols, it is also referred to as a **chord chart**. A fake book is a collection of lead sheets, normally in a particular style (i.e., pop/rock, jazz standards, etc.). Chord charts are not normally found in books, but are prepared by musicians and bands as needed for rehearsal or performance. When presented with a chord chart or lead sheet, the musician needs to improvise the part, based on an understanding of the style. See *Faking It* (p. 64).

A chord chart might consist only of chord symbols and slashes. This tells the musician to comp (accompany) according to the style, as in the following example.

Sometimes the chord chart might include rhythmic information (in which case the slashes are given precise rhythmic values), with the specific voicings still being left up to the player.

A lead sheet, then, will include the melody as well as the chord symbols.

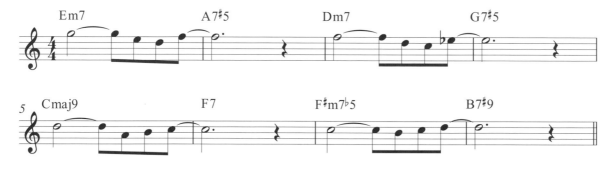

Many experienced keyboardists prefer to see a lead sheet rather than a chord chart even when accompanying (especially in jazz styles), to help ensure that the part they play is complementary to and supportive of the melody.

CHORD INVERSIONS

All triads and seventh chords can be **inverted** (i.e., re-arranged so that the root is no longer on the bottom). This may be done for several reasons, including:

- To voice lead smoothly between chords, avoiding unnecessary skips;
- To place a desired melody note on top of a chord;
- To accommodate a desired register or range for a particular keyboard sound, or to combine better with other instruments.

Any triad can be inverted, as shown in the following examples.

TRACK 25
Part 1

Triad Inversions

We can analyze the C major triads in the first measure as follows:

- The first triad is in root position, with the root on the bottom.
- The second triad is in first inversion, with the third on the bottom.
- The third triad is in second inversion, with the fifth on the bottom.
- The last triad is again in root position, an octave higher than the first.

Similar logic and terminology applies to minor, augmented, and diminished triads.

Any seventh chord can also be inverted. The following example shows inversions of three types of seventh chord (major seventh, minor seventh, and dominant seventh).

TRACK 25
Part 2

Seventh Chord Inversions

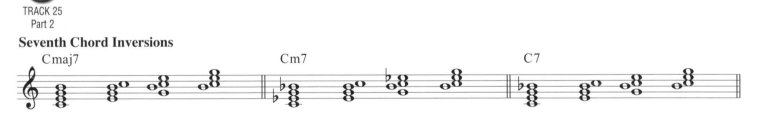

We can analyze the C major seventh chords in the first measure as follows:

- The first chord is in root position, with the root on the bottom.
- The second chord is in first inversion, with the third on the bottom.
- The third chord is in second inversion, with the fifth on the bottom.
- The fourth chord is in third inversion, with the seventh on the bottom.

Similar logic and terminology applies to the minor seventh and dominant seventh chords.

CHORD PROGRESSIONS

A **chord progression** is the sequence of chords used in a song. If the player is reading from a chart, the chord progression is normally the minimum level of information required, together with the form and road map of the song.

Being able to spell the chords in a given progression is, of course, important, but it is only the first step to interpreting and performing a song at a professional level. More experienced players will have different voicing choices to interpret chord symbols and progressions, as well as rhythmic patterns appropriate to the style.

Subject to many variations, there are three broad categories of chord progressions used in today's music.

1) **Diatonic**: all chords contained within a key.

2) **Chromatic unaltered**: chords borrowed from other keys, but still not altered (i.e., no sharped or flatted fifths and/or ninths).

3) **Chromatic altered**: chords borrowed from other keys, and with sharped or flatted fifths and/or ninths; normally indicative of jazz styles.

Another important variable is the size of the chords used: simpler pop styles favor triad progressions, whereas four-part (and larger) chords are normally found in R&B and jazz-influenced styles. Here are some examples of these different categories of chord progression.

Diatonic

In this progression of simple triads, all the chords are diatonic to (contained within) the key of G. This is typical of a simple pop ballad or rock song.

Chromatic unaltered

In this progression, all the chords are major sevenths, and they move between different keys. This is typical of more advanced rock or R&B styles.

Chromatic altered

This more sophisticated progression uses altered dominant chords in different keys, typical of jazz and Latin styles.

Further Reading

For more information on the different types of chord progressions used in pop, rock, and jazz styles, please check out my *Contemporary Music Theory: Level Two*, published by Hal Leonard LLC.

CHORD SYMBOL

A **chord symbol** is a symbol placed above the staff, telling you which chord is being used at that point in the music. Chord symbols normally have two components.

• A root note, telling you what the root of the chord is

• A suffix, telling you the type of chord

For example, the chord symbol "Cmaj7" has a root note of "C" and a suffix of "maj7," which tells you this is a C major seventh chord. If a chord symbol consists of only a root note with no suffix, then the chord is a major triad (for example, the chord symbol "C" signifies a C major triad).

When looking at a chord symbol, more experienced players will know what overall chord type it indicates (major, minor, dominant, diminished, etc.) For example, C, Cmaj7, Cmaj9, and C(add9) are all chords of the major type. Recognizing this helps with voicing choices, and in understanding the function of the chord within the progression.

The chord symbols that you see on charts will normally fall into one of the following categories.

- Triads: i.e., C, Cm, Caug, Cdim
- Seventh chords: i.e., Cmaj7, Cm7, C7
- Add9 chords, which add the 9th but exclude the 7th: i.e., C(add9), Am(add9)
- Ninth chords: i.e., the Dmaj9 and B♭maj9 chords used on Track 11 (p. 14)
- Eleventh chords: i.e., the Dm11 chords used on Track 126 (p. 157)
- Thirteenth chords: i.e., the A13 chord used on Track 75 (p. 94)
- "Slash" chord symbols, most often used to indicate an inverted chord (a chord with a tone other than the root in the bass): i.e., the Em/G and B/F♯ chords used on Tracks 17 and 18 (pp. 20-21)
- Suspended chords, which replace the third with another note—either the fourth/eleventh (sus4) or the second/ninth (sus2): i.e., the sus4 chords on Track 139, part 1 (p. 173).
- Altered chords, which flat or sharp the fifth and/or ninth of the chord: i.e., the D7(♯5,♭9) and D7(♯5,♯9) chords used on Track 12 (pp. 15-16).

Unfortunately, the world of chord symbols is rather "unregulated," meaning that the same chord may be indicated with several different chord symbols. For instance, this book uses the symbol "Cm7" for a C minor seventh chord, but you may also see this written as "Cmi7," "Cmin7," or "C-7."

Further Reading

This page is only a brief summary of a rather large subject! For much more information on all chord types and functions, commonly used chord symbols, scale sources, and all possible chord extensions and alterations, please check out my *Contemporary Music Theory: Level Three*, published by Hal Leonard LLC.

COMPING

Comping is a musical slang term for accompaniment. For synth players: if you're not playing a bass part or lead line on a song, you're likely to be playing a "comping" part based on your understanding of harmony and style. This involves creating stylistically appropriate voicings or figures from the chord symbols, and then playing them with a suitable rhythmic pattern. The choice of synth sound is also important, as it needs to fit the style being played.

Our first synthesizer comping example is in a funk style, and contains two different synth parts: a staccato (short and separated) comping part in measures 1–8, and a more sustained chordal part in measures 9–16.

TRACK 26

Funk

Listen to the audio track and you'll hear that the synth comping parts are on the right channel, with the rest of the band on the left channel. Both comping synths were played using the FM8 softsynth, from Native Instruments. The FM8 uses frequency modulation or FM synthesis (see p. 70), a digital synthesis method which is great for creating bright, edgy sounds rich in harmonic content. The FM8 is the computer-based successor to the popular Yamaha DX7 synthesizer (see p. 50). The sound in measures 1–8 is spiky and clavinet-like and is suited to the sparse two-note intervals and rhythmic syncopations used in this part. By contrast, the sound in measures 9–16 is a full and bright synth pad, suitable for larger and more sustained voicings.

The rhythm section on the left channel includes the Native Instruments Scarbee Red Bass, and the BFD virtual drum instrument.

Harmony/Theory Notes

Note that in measures 1–8 (the synth clav part), we are mostly playing the roots and 5ths of the chords (creating 4th and 5th intervals), with some double-4th three-note voicings (two perfect 4th intervals stacked one on top of the other). This is typical for clavinet and staccato synth comping in funk styles.

Then in measures 9–16 (the sustained synth part), we are using more double-4ths, frequently inverted. For example, the A-B-E voicing on beat 1 of measure 9, is actually a B-E-A double-4th, but inverted (rearranged) to place the E on top. This B-E-A double-4th is built from the 5th of the Esus4 chord, giving us the 5th, root and 4th of the chord respectively. Similarly, double-4ths have been built from the 2nd or 9th of the C(add9) chords, and from the 4th or 11th of the Am7 chords. Using double-4ths in this way is a great alternative to triads, if you want your synth comping to have a more hip and transparent sound.

Further Reading

For more information on funk keyboard and synth comping styles, please check out a couple of my other books: *R&B Keyboard: The Complete Guide with Audio!* and *The Pop Piano Book*. And for more information on all types of chord voicings including double-4th shapes, take a look at my *Contemporary Music Theory, Level Three*. All these books are published by Hal Leonard LLC.

Our next synth comping example is in a pop/rock style, and again contains two different synth parts: a chordal comping part with some arpeggios in measures 1–8, and a busier arpeggiated part in measures 9–16:

TRACK 27

Pop/Rock

Again, the comping synth is on the right channel, and the rest of the band is on the left channel. This time the comping synth is using the same analog brass synth throughout, from the ES2 softsynth (within Logic). This big, fat synth sound is perfectly suited to 1980s-style pop/rock. On the left channel, as well as the Native Instruments Scarbee bass and BFD drums we heard on the previous track, we've added a guitar part played using the RealStrat virtual guitar instrument from MusicLab.

Harmony/Theory Notes

In measures 1–8, this synth part uses a common pop-rock voicing technique called alternating triads. For example, during measure 1 we move from D major to G major triad and back again: the G major triad moving back to the D major triad can be thought of as a IV-to-I alternating triad movement, with respect to the D in the bass. Similarly, in measure 2 the F triad moving to the C triad is a IV-to-I with respect to the C in the bass, and so on. In measures 9–16, these upper triads are now arpeggiated (played "broken chord" style), reinforced by two-note intervals at the points of chord change.

Further Reading

For much more information on alternating triad voicing techniques, and pop/rock comping styles, please check out my *Pop Piano Book*, published by Hal Leonard LLC.

COUNTRY

Country is an American music style that emerged in the 1920s and continues to evolve into the twenty-first century. Traditional country music uses basic chord progressions (i.e., I-IV-V), swing-eighths rhythms, and simple song forms. More modern country styles frequently borrow from pop and rock music, using straight-eighths rhythms and more sophisticated harmonies. Our first example is in a traditional country style, using a I-IV-V triad progression in the key of G.

TRACK 28

Traditional Country

The right hand is playing basic triads derived from the chord symbols, and is using alternating eighths with rests on beats 1 and 3, which is typical of basic country comping. Walkups and walkdowns are being used to connect chords with roots a 4th apart; for example, there is a walkup in measure 2 (from the G chord up to the C chord), and a walkdown in measure 4 (from the C chord back down to the G chord). Walkups and walkdowns normally have three different components:

- A bass line that walks up the scale (i.e., the left-hand G-G-A-B in measure 2, leading to C in the next measure)

- A line moving a 10th (octave plus a 3rd) above the bass line (i.e., the right-hand B-C-D in measure 2)

- A drone (repeated note) above the line moving in 10ths with the bass (i.e., the repeated G in measure 2 in the right hand)—the drone note is normally the root of the chord when walking up, and the fifth of the chord when walking down.

Elsewhere, the left hand is playing the root of the chord on beat 1, and the fifth of the chord on beat 3. Next we'll look at a more modern country/rock example.

TRACK 29

Country/Rock

This time the right-hand part is based on pentatonic scales built from the root of each chord. For example, in measure 1 on the A major chord we are using the A pentatonic scale (A, B, C♯, E, F♯). The note E (the fifth of the chord) is being used as a drone, and below the drone we are alternating (sometimes referred to as "hammering") between B and C♯ (the next two notes below in the pentatonic scale) using grace notes. The intervals between these notes and the drone note create that characteristic country sound. The drone note is normally either the root or fifth of the chord, and sometimes both of these may be used within a phrase (for example, both A and E are used as drones in measure 15 on the A major chord).

On the A major chords in measures 2 and 10, we move between the 3rds D-F♯ and C♯-E, implying a D major-to-A major triad movement. This type of IV-I triad movement within a chord is called "backcycling," and is used across a range of contemporary styles. Similar movements occur on the G major chords, and on the E major chord in measure 14 (here with the 3rds inverted to become 6ths).

Further Reading

For more information on country and country/rock styles, please check out my *Country Piano: The Complete Guide with Audio!*, published by Hal Leonard LLC.

CROSSOVER LICKS

Crossover licks or phrases are an indispensable part of the blues piano vocabulary. They are descending right-hand phrases (normally including arpeggios) that require the upper fingers of the right hand to cross over the thumb on the way to the lower notes in the phrase. These are also sometimes referred to as "resolving" licks, as they normally end with a half-step resolution into the third of the chord. All of the following examples work over a C or C7 chord. You should learn them in as many keys as possible—they come in really handy!

TRACK 30

DECAY

In a synthesizer, the **decay** is the second stage of a envelope generator (see p. 58), which is a modifer normally applied to the filter (see p. 67) to control the timbre, or to the amplifier to control the volume. The attack is the time taken for the envelope to move from its peak, to the sustain level (see p. 173).

In musical terms, a longer decay time applied to a (conventional low-pass) filter means that the sound will become darker more slowly after the attack peak, until the sustain level (frequency) is reached. By contrast, a shorter decay time applied to the filter means that the sustain level (frequency) occurs right after the attack peak, which may cause a more abrupt change in the timbre. A longer decay time applied to the the amplifier means that the sound will more slowly become quieter after the attack peak, until the sustain level (volume) is reached. By contrast, a shorter decay time applied to the amplifier means that the sustain level (volume) occurs right after the attack peak, which may cause a more abrupt change in the volume.

The recorded example on Track 31 demonstrates these principles, playing a single repeated note and using a simple sawtooth waveform (see p. 165) generated by the ES2 synth plug-in within Logic (see p. 111).

> The first group of four notes uses different decay times applied to the filter (with the attack time set to 730 ms in each case):
>
> - 0 ms (milliseconds), 500 ms, 1500 ms, and 3000 ms.

TRACK 31

> The second group of four notes use different decay times applied to the amplifier (with the attack time set to 1000 ms in each case):
>
> - 0 ms, 500 ms, 1500 ms, and 2000 ms.

In the first group of four notes, you hear the same attack time (i.e., the time taken for the sound to get to its maximum brightness). You can also hear that, as the decay time increases, the sound takes progressively more time (after the attack peak) to become darker, i.e., to reach the sustain level of "brightness." In the first of these examples, you can hear the timbral change very abruptly after the attack peak (as the decay time is set to zero).

In the second group of four notes, you hear the same attack time (i.e., the time taken for the sound to get to its maximum loudness). You can also hear that, as the decay time increases, the sound takes progressively more time (after the attack peak) to become quieter, i.e., to reach the sustain level of "loudness" (which in this case is zero). In the first of these examples, you can hear the sound cut out very abruptly after the attack peak (as the decay time is set to zero, and the sustain level is also zero).

DIATONIC SEVENTH CHORDS

The word "diatonic" means "belonging to a major scale or key"; therefore, **diatonic seventh chords** are all found within the key being used. Simpler contemporary styles often stay within the restriction of a single key, and in this case the two most common sources of chords are diatonic triads and diatonic seventh chords. Compared to diatonic triads, these four-part chords are fuller and sound a little more sophisticated. Here are the commonly used diatonic seventh chords in the key of C major.

TRACK 32
Part 1

TRACK 32
Part 2

Next we will use these chords in a simple R&B ballad setting.

R&B Ballad

This example uses the chords in root position, though they can, of course, be inverted. Normal R&B ballad rhythmic stylings are being used: the right hand is anticipating beat 3 of each measure by a sixteenth note (and arpeggiating the chord during beat 2), and the left hand is playing a root-fifth pattern on each chord, landing on beats 1 and 3 and anticipating beats 2 and 4.

Further Reading

For more information on diatonic seventh chords, please check out my *Contemporary Music Theory: Level One*, published by Hal Leonard LLC.

DIATONIC TRIADS

The word "diatonic" means "belonging to a major scale or key"; therefore, **diatonic triads** are all found within the key being used. Simpler contemporary styles often stay within the restriction of a single key, and in this case the two most common sources of chords are diatonic seventh chords and diatonic triads. Compared to diatonic seventh chords, these three-note chords are less dense and sound more basic. Here are the diatonic triads in the key of C major.

TRACK 33
Part 1

Next we will use these triads in a simple pop/rock setting.

TRACK 33
Part 2

This example uses the chords in root position, though they can, of course, be inverted as needed. Normal pop/rock rhythmic stylings are being used: the right hand is playing a two-measure rhythmic phrase with eighth-note anticipations and the left hand is playing the root of each chord in octaves, with the lowest note on beats 1 and 3 and the highest note on beats 2 and 4 (with eighth-note pickups leading into beat 3).

Further Reading

For more information on diatonic triads, please check out my *Contemporary Music Theory: Level One*, published by Hal Leonard LLC.

DIGITAL AUDIO WORKSTATION

A **digital audio workstation (DAW)** is a piece of software running on a Mac and/or Windows PC platform (or a tablet/mobile device) that enables you to record, edit, and produce music. Many DAWs started out as MIDI sequencing programs some years ago, then added audio recording facilities as computer processing power increased. Here are some leading examples of computer digital audio workstation software in 2018:

- *Cubase*, manufactured by Steinberg. Runs on Mac and Windows platforms. Good all-round DAW for MIDI and audio editing, with virtual instruments included. Originally based on Steinberg's top-of-the-line Nuendo post-production software.

- *Digital Performer* or DP (see p. 40), manufactured by MOTU. Runs on Mac and Windows platforms. A widely-used DAW, popular with touring musicians and film composers, with excellent MIDI and audio capabilities.

- *FL Studio*, manufactured by Image Line Software. Originally a basic entry-level Windows program, FL Studio has matured into a popular and capable DAW, offering the typical combination of MIDI sequencing, editing, and audio tracking/mixing.

- *Garageband* (see p. 75), manufactured by Apple. Runs on Mac platform only. A streamlined and basic DAW that is pre-installed on newer Mac computers. A fun entry-level program for beginners and hobbyists.

- *Live*, manufactured by Ableton. Runs on Mac and Windows platforms. A loop-based DAW favored by electronic musicians and DJs. Designed from a live performance point-of-view, with a compact and easy-to-use interface.

- *Logic Pro* (see p. 111), manufactured by Apple. Runs on Mac platform only. Excellent "workflow" and ease-of-use. Comes with top-of-the-line virtual instruments, including a great interactive Drummer feature. Modestly priced for such a powerful software package.

- *ProTools*, manufactured by Avid. Runs on Mac and Windows platforms. The industry standard for audio recording, editing, and mixing. Also competing strongly for the MIDI/composer studio market, against other established DAWs such as Logic, Cubase, and DP.

- *Reason*, manufactured by Propellerhead. Runs on Mac and Windows platforms. An expandable DAW with a unique rack-style interface, favored by electronic musicians. Good range of softsynths also included.

- *Sonar*, manufactured by Cakewalk. Runs on Windows platform only. Another good all-round DAW for MIDI and audio editing, with virtual instruments included.

- *Studio One*, manufactured by PreSonus. Runs on Mac and Windows platforms. Very clean user interface and a useful "scratchpad" arranging function. A relative newcomer to the market, competing strongly against more established DAWs.

A MIDI recording session, with a DAW and using a keyboard controller, typically involves the following steps:

1. Open the DAW and launch (instantiate) a virtual instrument. This may be a softsynth that comes bundled with the DAW, or a third-party instrument from another manufacturer. This then generally appears as an audio or instrument track in the main arrange window of the DAW.

2. Record-enable the MIDI track, and check that you hear the desired sound when you play the keyboard controller. Then set up the click track and countoff (if necessary), hit record on the DAW, and play the part on your keyboard. The MIDI data should now be recorded in the appropriate MIDI track.

3. Do any necessary editing/fixing of the Midi data within the DAW.

4. Repeat steps 1–4 for other the tracks/instruments within your song arrangement.

5. When all the tracking and editing is finished, you'll switch over to the DAW's mixer page, to mix the final product to a single stereo track (or surround-sound if you prefer). Then it's done!

DIGITAL PERFORMER

Digital Performer (DP) is a music production and recording program, manufactured by MOTU. It is one of the leading DAW (digital audio workstation; see p. 39) software programs currently available. DP runs on the Macintosh and Windows computer platforms. Thanks to its good integration with video, it has become a firm favorite among film and media composers. Live sound engineers also like it, because its Chunks feature allows for easy re-arrangements of songs.

Now we'll listen to a couple of musical examples that were created in DP. Our first example is in an electronic dance style and uses only the softsynths bundled with DP (i.e. no third-party instruments). On this example we'll spotlight the synth comping part:

TRACK 34

Electronic Dance

Listen to the audio track and you'll hear that the synth comping sound is on the right channel, with the rest of the band on the left channel. The synth comping is a simple single-oscillator synth produced from DP's Polysynth instrument plug-in. The instruments on the left channel are also produced from DP plug-ins: the bass is from Bassline (a monophonic analog synth) and the drums are an emulation of a Roland TR-808 drum machine, from the Model 12 drum synthesizer. Also, the rhythmic arpeggio synth you hear starting in measure 9 on the left channel is from the Modulo synth plug-in.

Harmony/Theory Notes

Note that this synth part is mostly contained within the B minor pentatonic scale (B D E F♯ A), which is in turn built from the tonic of the minor key (B minor in this case). These two-note voicings project well and are often more effective than playing a full chord for this type of synth part.

Our next DP example is in a dramatic/film score style, and uses third-party (non-DP) softsynths/instruments. On this example we'll spotlight the cello ensemble part:

TRACK 35

Dramatic/Film Score

Listen to the track and you'll hear that the cello sound is on the right channel, with the remaining instruments on the left channel. The cello part uses a cello ensemble sound from the Kontakt software sampler/synth (see p. 103). Also on the left channel the low drone note (a common device used in suspenseful movie and TV writing) is a combination of an orchestral bass from Kontakt 3, and the famous "Hollywood String Section" patch from the Omnisphere softsynth (see p. 133). The remaining cellos, horns, and percussion on the left channel are also from Kontakt.

DIGITAL SYNTHESIZER

A **digital synthesizer** uses digital signal processing (DSP) techniques to create sounds. In the 1980s, digital synthesizer technology became widely available, in the form of Yamaha's wildly successful DX7 synthesizer (see p. 50). The clean, bright sound of this classic synth was a marked contrast to the other (analog) synthesizers available at the time.

Under the umbrella of digital synthesis, there are various synthesis methods, each of which use microprocessors and DSP technology. Here is a quick overview of these methods:

- *Additive synthesis* combines multiple harmonic (partials) to create detailed waveforms.

- *Frequency modulation* or *FM synthesis* (see p. 70) takes a simple waveform and "modulates" it with another waveform in the audio range, to create complex sounds. The Yamaha DX7 is the best-known synth to use this technology.

- *Granular synthesis* (see p. 81) splits sounds into small "grains" and then re-combines them in many different ways. Great for "soundscapes" and effects.

- *Phase distortion synthesis* modifies ("distorts") the phase angle of sine waves, to create different waveforms.

- *Physical modeling synthesis* (see p. 141) uses equations and algorithms to simulate a physical instrument's characteristics (or to create a new instrument).

- *Sample-based synthesis* uses digital recordings of acoustic and electronic instruments.

- *Wavetable synthesis* plays different sounds (from "wavetables") in quick succession, creating complex and evolving sounds.

So you can see that the term digital synth encompasses a lot of different methods and models. Next we have two music example using digital synthesis. First, we have an R&B ballad groove with an electric piano sound that uses FM or frequency modulation synthesis:

TRACK 36

R&B Ballad

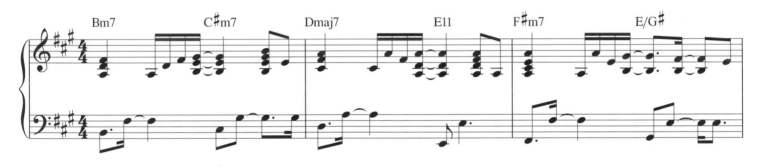

Listen to the track and you'll hear that the electric piano is on the right channel, and the rest of the band is on the left channel. Try playing along with this example, using your favorite electric piano patch. One of the most common uses of FM synths such as the DX7, was to provide this type of bright, bell-like electric piano sound, a staple R&B ballad ingredient in the 1980s. This electric piano example was produced using the FM8 softsynth from

Native Instruments, a computer-based successor to the venerable DX-7. The FM8 is also providing the "light digital synth pad" you hear in the backing band, on the left channel.

Harmony/Theory Notes

The above electric piano part again makes use of upper structure triads. For example, the right-hand notes on the Bm7 chord form a D major triad (D, F♯ and A). These are the 3rd, 5th, and 7th of the Bm7 chord, and can be thought of as a major triad (D major in this case) built from the 3rd of the chord (Bm7 in this case). Other upper structure triads are also used in this example, as follows:

- the right-hand notes on the C♯m7 chord form an E major triad (built from the 3rd of the chord)

- the right-hand notes on the F♯m7 chord form an A major triad (built from the 3rd of the chord)

- the right-hand notes on the Dmaj7 chord form an F♯ minor triad (built from the 3rd of the chord)

- the right-hand notes on the E11 chord form a D major triad (built from the 7th of the chord)

Also, the Amaj9 chords make use of an upper structure four-part chord: the right-hand notes form a C♯m7 four-part chord, which is built from the 3rd of the Amaj9 chord.

Further Reading

For much more information on R&B keyboard and synth comping styles, please check out a couple of my other books: *R&B Keyboard: The Complete Guide with Audio* and *The Pop Piano Book*. Both books are published by Hal Leonard LLC.

Next up is a synth-pop example using a sampled horn sound. Sampled instruments use actual recordings ("samples") of real instruments, for greater realism:

TRACK 37

Synth-Pop

Listen to the track, and you'll hear that the horn "stabs" are on the right channel, and the rest of the band is on the left channel. The horns in this example were produced using the EXS24 sample-based synth (within Logic). In the backing band, the FM8 softsynth is helping out again, providing the pulsating eighth-note synth comping, as well as the hard-edged synth bass (another typical FM-type sound).

Harmony/Theory Notes

Notice that the horn lines are mostly contained within the F♯ minor pentatonic scale (F♯ A B C♯ E), which is in turn built from the tonic of the minor key (F♯ minor in this case). This is a common technique in minor-key pop and R&B songs. Also, the horns are using an arranging technique known as "one-part density," which means that only one pitch is sounding at one time (in octaves). For the majority of pop applications, your synth horn parts will sound more realistic with one-part density, as opposed to playing thicker chords.

DORIAN MODE

A mode (or modal scale) is created when we take a major scale and displace it to start on another scale degree. An example of this is the **Dorian mode**, created when the major scale is displaced to start on the 2nd degree. The following example shows a C major scale displaced to create a D Dorian mode.

If you compare these two scales, you'll see that the notes are the same; they just begin and end in a different place. Thus, each has a different tonic and a different pattern of whole and half steps. You can also think of the Dorian mode as a major scale with flatted 3rd and 7th degrees (1-2-♭3-4-5-6-♭7). This mode has a minor sound and is a basic scale source for a minor seventh chord. We could say that C major is the relative major scale of D Dorian, as C major was the scale originally displaced to create the mode.

To use a Dorian mode harmonically, we would simply put the tonic of the mode (D in the above example) in the bass, and then place notes and/or chords from the mode (or from its relative major) above this bass note. A common tactic is to use diatonic triads from the relative major. For example, the diatonic triads in C major are C, Dm, Em, F, G, Am, and Bdim. Placing any of these—particularly IV and V (i.e., F and G)—above the tonic D is an effective way to create Dorian harmony.

Our first example is in the '60s cool-jazz style of Miles Davis and Wynton Kelly, and uses the E and F Dorian modes. When using E Dorian (measures 1–8 and 13–14), we play G and A triads in the right hand, which are IV and V of the relative major scale (D major). These triads can also be thought of as ♭III and IV with respect to the root of the implied Em7 chord. Similarly, when using F Dorian in measures 9–12, we use A♭ and B♭ triads in the right hand.

TRACK 38

Cool Jazz

This is a typical modal jazz example from the period, with the left hand outlining the roots, fifths, and sevenths of the Em7 and Fm7 chords (and staying within the E and F Dorian modes, respectively).

Next up we have a '70s-style jazz/funk groove using Dorian modes and triads.

TRACK 39

Jazz/Funk

This example uses the C Dorian mode in measures 1–4 and 7–9, with Eb and F triads in the right-hand part (IV and V of Bb major, the relative major scale of C Dorian). Similarly, when using Eb Dorian in measures 5–6, we have Gb and Ab triads in the right hand (from the Db major scale). Note the sixteenth-note anticipations, and the rhythmic conversation between the right- and left-hand parts—all very typical of funk keyboard styles.

Also notice that both these Dorian examples use a lot of inverted triads in the right-hand parts. Modal triads tend to sound better when inverted. Second-inversion triads are used the most, due to their strong and powerful sound.

For another important mode, see **Mixolydian Mode** (p. 120).

DOTTED NOTES

Whenever a dot is placed after a note, it adds half as much again to the rhythmic value or length (in other words, it multiplies the existing length by 1.5), as in the following example.

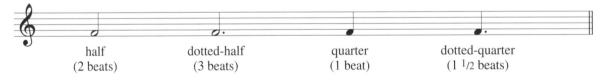

Without the dot, the second note above would just be a half note (lasting for 2 beats). But with the dot added, we add half as much again to the original length, so the note now lasts for 3 beats. Likewise, without the dot the fourth note would just be a quarter note (lasting for 1 beat). But the dot adds half as much again to the original length, so the note now lasts for 1½ beats.

Next we will see some ways in which these dotted notes can be used in a melody. If we use a dotted half note (3 beats) together with a quarter note (1 beat), the resulting total of four beats will fill a 4/4 measure. If we use a dotted quarter note (1½ beats) together with an eighth note (1/2 beat), the resulting total of two beats could occupy the first or second half of a 4/4 measure. These are common rhythmic combinations, as shown in this melody example.

Notice the eighth-note counting (1 & 2 & 3 & 4 &, etc.) in this example. It's good to be able to count through rhythmic figures in this way when necessary. Although experienced readers will recognize most rhythms at sight, they'll still need to count out rhythms once in a while!

DOWNBEATS

A **downbeat** falls on the beat (i.e., on beat 1, 2, 3, or 4 in a 4/4 measure)—as opposed to an **upbeat**, which falls in between the beats. This is illustrated as follows:

When we count eighth-note rhythms this way (1 & 2 &, etc.), we can see that the downbeats fall on 1, 2, 3, and 4, and the upbeats fall on the &s in between (referred to as the "and" of 1, "and" of 2, etc.).

Basic rock styles often emphasize downbeats, as in the following example:

TRACK 40

In case you haven't seen it before... a chord symbol with a "5" suffix means "root and fifth only" (equivalent to a triad with the third omitted). This is a common sound in hard rock and metal styles.

Chord Voicing Tips

This hard rock example mostly uses open root-fifth-root or fifth-root-fifth voicings in the right hand, with some variations as follows:

- The Esus4 chords are voiced as fourth-root-fourth (the fourth, A, being the suspension).
- The D(add9) and C(add9) chords are voiced as fifth-ninth-fifth (a very useful modern rock sound).

Also, the single eighth notes on the "and" of 2 and the "and" of 4 are adding the following chord extensions:

- The ninth of the chords in measures 1–2 and 5–6.
- The suspended fourth/eleventh of the chords in measures 3, 7, and 9.

DRUM AND BASS

Drum and Bass is an electronic dance music style, also known as **jungle**, that emerged in the early 1990s. The term "drum and bass" is often abbreviated to "D&B" or "DnB." This style typically uses "broken beat" drums at fast tempos (usually 155–180 beats per minute) and heavy bass lines that are sometimes quite complex. Although the drums and bass are not the only instruments used in this style, they are by far the most important and they are usually to the forefront in a D&B mix. The style heavily features both sampled and synthesized bass sounds, and classic drum machines such as Roland's TR-808.

Now we'll look at a couple of drum and bass examples, and spotlight the synth bass part on each. Our first example was created in Logic (see p. 111), using Logic's internal sounds and plug-ins:

TRACK 41

Drum and Bass

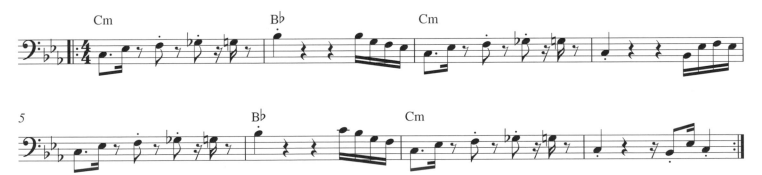

Listen to the track and you'll hear that the synth bass is on the right channel, with the other instruments on the left channel. The bass has a hollow quality, typical of an analog synth using a square waveform (see p. 170). On the second repeat, a "gated" synth part is added on the left channel, from the ES2 synth plug-in within Logic. This part is synced to the tempo of the track, a common effect in electronic dance music styles.

Harmony/Theory Notes

Note that the above bass line is derived from a C blues scale (C Eb F Gb G Bb). There is normally not much harmony at work in drum and bass styles; however, the simple root-and-5th synth voicings on the second repeat, together with the bass line, are implying the chord symbols shown.

TRACK 42

The next drum and bass example was created in Reason, using Reason's internal sounds and plug-ins:

Drum and Bass

Listen to the track and you'll again hear that the synth bass is on the right channel, with the other instruments on the left channel. This time the synth bass is produced using Thor, a noted plug-in synth within Reason, with some extra bite due to resonance (see p. 160) being applied to the filter. The synth comping that starts in measure 9 on the left channel is also produced from Thor.

DRUM MACHINE

A **drum machine** is an electronic musical instrument that produces drum sounds and rhythmic patterns. Early commercially available drum machines used analog synthesis, rather than samples of real drums and percussion, to create the drum sounds. Notable among these early models were the Roland CR-78 (one of the first programmable rhythm machines), and the more affordable Boss "Doctor Rhythm" DR-55.

Then in 1980 the Linn LM-1 drum machine was introduced. This was the first drum machine to use digital samples (i.e., real recordings) of drums. The LM-1 caused an immediate sensation and was used on numerous hit records from the 1980s, notably by Human League, Prince, Gary Numan, and many others.

Starting in the late 1980s, analog drum machines such as the Roland TR-808 and TR-909 became very popular within the hip-hop and electronic dance music community. These drum sounds have been sampled endlessly and have been used on a great many recordings up until the present time. Drum machines are also convenient as a practice, teaching and rehearsal tool.

Now we'll look at music example in a funk style, which uses a preset pattern from the vintage SR-16 drum machine (manufactured by Alesis). The featured instrument on this track is a "modeled" clavinet sound.

TRACK 43

Funk

Listen to the track, and you'll hear that the clavinet is on the right channel, and the rest of the band (including the SR-16 drum pattern) is on the left channel. The clavinet sound is created with physical modeling (see p. 141), using the Vintage Clav softsynth within Logic. The backing band on the left channel also includes some Native Instruments plug-ins: the 'Scarbee' Red Bass, and an organ pad from Vintage Organs.

Harmony/Theory Notes

Note that the above clavinet part is derived mainly from the roots and 5ths of the various chords, creating perfect 4th and 5th interval voicings. This technique is well-suited to the staccato sound of the clavinet, and is commonly used in R&B/funk comping grooves.

DX7

The **Yamaha DX7** is one of the most famous and best-selling synthesizers of all time. It uses frequency modulation (FM) synthesis (see p. 70), a method made possible by the advances in digital signal processing (DSP) technology in the 1980s. The DX7 was the first commercially successful digital synthesizer (see p. 41). Its clean, bright sound was a big contrast to the analog synthesizers available at the time. It was particularly good at creating electric pianos, bells, and other metallic sounds, and was heard on innumerable pop records throughout the 1980s. Although the DX7 has long since been discontinued, FM synthesis lives on in various forms, including softsynths such as the well-known FM8 from Native Instruments.

Now we'll look at a couple of music examples using DX7-type sounds. Our first uses a pop-rock style, featuring a lead synth sound typical of the DX7 and of FM-style synthesis:

TRACK 44

Pop/Rock

Listen to the track and you'll hear that the synth lead is on the right channel, and the rest of the band is on the left channel. The lead synth sound was produced using the FM8 softsynth from Native Instruments. This sound has a bright, metallic quality with high harmonics, and is reminiscent of the old DX7. Notice that some pitch bend (see p. 143) is being used in this lead synth part, indicated by the curved lines leading into some of the notes on the staff. Here the pitch bend wheel is pulled back before the note is played, then allowed to return to its center position, raising the pitch to the correct level. The exception is in measure 15, where the pitch is bent up a half-step (from G up to A♭) and then back again.

The backing band on the left channel also includes the Native Instruments Scarbee Red Bass virtual instrument, the BFD virtual drum instrument, the RealStrat virtual guitar instrument, and a Rhodes electric piano from the Vintage Electric Piano plug-in within Logic.

Harmony/Theory Notes

Note how this synth solo is organized around a "target note" approach—i.e., a specific target note (chord function) is used for each measure. For example, we go from the root of the Cm7 chord in measure 1 (C), to the 3rd of the B♭m7 chord in measure 2 (D♭), to the 3rd of the Cm7 chord in measure 3 (E♭), and so on. This gives the solo some structure, and we can then fill in between with appropriate chord and/or scale tones. In the busier section beginning in measure 9, note that we are using pentatonic scale runs to connect between the target notes. For example, the 16th notes in measure 9 are derived from the C minor pentatonic scale, the 16th notes in measure 10 are from the B♭ minor pentatonic scale, and so on. See p. 168 for more information on synth soloing.

TRACK 45

Our next example is in a New Age style, and features a bell sound typical of the DX7:

New Age

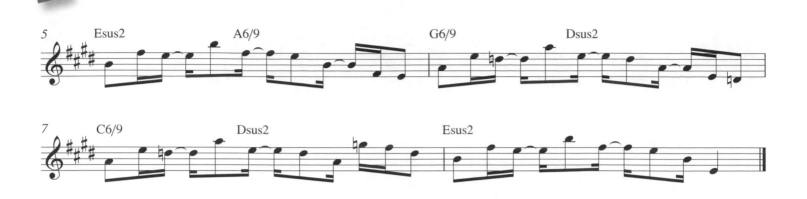

Listen to the track and you'll hear that the synth bells are on the right channel, and the other instruments are on the left channel. The bell sound was produced using the FM8 softsynth. On the left channel, we have the "Italian Grand" piano from the Ivory virtual instrument (see p. 93), as well as a soft string pad from the Absynth softsynth from Native Instruments.

Harmony/Theory Notes

Note how this synth bell line is created using inversions of double-4th shapes (using two consecutive 4th intervals). For example, the first measure takes the double-4th shape F#-B-E, and then inverts and re-arranges it to go over the Esus2 and A6/9 chords. We can say that the F#-B-E double-4th is "built from" the 9th of the Esus2 chord, and the 6th of the A6/9 chord. Similarly, the E-A-D double-4th is then "built from" the 6th of the G6/9 chord, and the 9th of the Dsus2 chord, and so on. Double-4th shapes and their inversions are an effective contemporary voicing technique.

Further Reading

For more information on keyboard voicing techniques including double-4ths, please check out a couple of my other books: *Smooth Jazz: The Complete Guide with Audio!* and *The Pop Piano Book*. Both books are published by Hal Leonard LLC.

EAR TRAINING

Ear training is a vital area of your musicianship, particularly if you are playing contemporary styles such as pop, rock, and jazz. Ear training has two very important benefits for today's keyboard players:

1) It helps you hear ahead in your playing and writing.

2) It helps you recognize and transcribe music that you hear.

My ear training books and classes use the solfège system.

In this case, DO (the tonic, or home base) is the note C; however DO could be assigned to any note (this is sometimes referred to as a moveable-DO concept).

The first step in our ear training is to recognize the movements between active tones and resting tones in the major scale. We hear these movements in relation to DO, the tonic of the scale.

TRACK 46

In all major keys, the following active tones like to move (or resolve) to their resting neighbors:

- The 2nd degree (RE) resolves down to the 1st degree (DO).
- The 4th degree (FA) resolves down to the 3rd degree (MI).
- The 6th degree (LA) resolves down to the 5th degree (SO).
- The 7th degree (TI) resolves up to the 1st degree (DO).

Simpler melodies (for example, folk and traditional songs) normally contain a lot of these resolutions. More sophisticated styles will not always resolve the active tones to their adjacent resting tones; however, an active tone will still sound active, whether or not the resolution to the adjacent resting tone actually occurs. Here is a vocal exercise that you can use to begin recognizing these resolutions in the major scale.

TRACK 47

When you can recognize these sounds by ear, you'll have completed an important first step in your ear training!

Further Reading

Ear training is a big subject, one I have written complete courses on! Please check out my *Contemporary Eartraining: Levels One* and *Two*, both published by Hal Leonard LLC.

EFFECTS

An **effect** is a treatment or manipulation applied to a sound that modifies its characteristics. Effects can be applied to keyboard synthesizers and softsynths, as well as other instruments such as guitar, bass, drums, and so on. Effects were first widely available with the use of effects pedals or "stomp boxes" for live performance, and larger rack-mounted units for recording applications. Then by the late 1980s, effects capability was added to the digital synthesizers of the time, notably including the Korg M1 workstation keyboard (see p. 113). Into the 21st century, there are many hardware and software products providing effects capability, such as:

- Modern-day effects pedals and stomp-boxes made by Roland/Boss, Korg, Zoom, et al.

- Rackmount studio units made by Lexicon, Eventide, TC Electronic, et al.

- Workstation keyboards made by Korg, Yamaha, Roland, et al.

- Digital Audio Workstations (software programs) including Cubase, Logic, Digital Performer, et al.

- Softsynths/virtual instruments including Omnisphere, Kontakt, Ivory, et al.

- Dedicated software effects plug-ins made by IK Multimedia, Sonnox, AudioEase, et al.

- Amplifier Simulators ("amp-sims") made by Native Instruments, IK Multimedia, Waves, et al.

Here is a brief summary of some commonly used audio effects:

- *Reverb* is the simulation of sound being produced in an enclosed space, reflecting off the surfaces and then blending together. This is perceived as adding space and depth to the sound.

- *Chorus* blends a slightly delayed and pitch-shifted signal with the original. This is perceived as adding warmth and "sweetening" the sound. The delay time is short, so that it is not perceived as echo.

- *Flanging* also blends a delayed signal with the original, this time using a continuously variable delay time. This is a DSP (digital signal processing) re-creation of how flanging used to be done, by using two synchronized tape players and pressing the "flange" of one of the players, so that it would fall out-of-phase with the other. Flanging can be an intense effect, sometimes perceived as having a jet plane or "whooshing" sonic characteristic.

- *Phasing* splits the signal into two parts and applies an "all-pass" filter to one of them that alters the phase. This is then re-combined with the original signal. Phasing is a similar effect to flanging and was also originally created using tape machines. Phasing produces a filter-sweep type effect, and is often perceived as giving an artificial or otherworldly character to the sound.

- *Delay* (or *echo*) adds one or more delayed signals to the original. To be perceived as delay rather than reverb, the delay time has to be around 50 milliseconds or more. Delay can be used to add a dense or ethereal quality to both acoustic and electronic instruments.

- *Overdrive* (or *distortion*) amplifies the signal past the limits of the amplifier, resulting in audio clipping. This is perceived as adding warmth or "fuzziness," particularly to electric guitar sounds.

Now we'll listen to an analog synthesizer repeating the same part through some of these effects:

TRACK 48

Listen to the track and you'll hear the same synth line repeated, as follows:

- 1st time: No effects
- 2nd time: With reverb
- 3rd time: With chorus
- 4th time: With flanging
- 5th time: With delay

The featured instrument is an analog synthesizer sound from the Absynth softsynth, from Native Instruments. The reverb effect is courtesy of IK Multimedia's Classik Studio Reverb plug-in, and the other effects (chorus, flanging, and delay) were internally applied within the DAW (in this case Logic). The delay was synced to the tempo of the track and was set to a 16th-note—i.e., the delayed signal comes in a 16th-note after the original signal.

EIGHTH NOTES AND RESTS

An **eighth note** lasts for a half a beat. This is also equivalent to an eighth of a measure in 4/4 time. Here is an example of some different ways that eighth notes can be written.

The rhythmic counting (1 & 2 & 3 & 4 &, etc.) is shown below the notes in this measure.

An eighth note is written with a black (or filled-in) notehead, with a stem attached, and either a flag if the note is by itself (like the first four notes in the above example) or a beam if the note is joined to other notes (as in the remaining notes in the example). Sometimes the beam may join two eighth notes together within one beat (as in the second half of the first measure), or the beam may join all the eighth notes within two successive beats (as in the second measure).

Next we'll see an example of an eighth rest, which also lasts for half a beat:

Here's a notation example that combines eighth notes and rests.

In the notation example, the eighth rests fall on beats 3 and 4 in measures 1 and 3. Note that the rhythmic sum of all the notes and rests in each measure agrees with the time signature (i.e., four beats for each 4/4 measure).

For information on other basic rhythmic values, see *Half Notes and Rests* (p. 83), *Quarter Notes and Rests* (p. 155), *Sixteenth Notes and Rests* (p. 167), and *Whole Notes and Rests* (p. 196).

EIGHT-NOTE SCALES

Eight-note (or **octatonic**) **scales** are the result of dividing an octave into four equal parts, and then further subdividing into half steps and whole steps. For example, if we take an octave from middle C up to the C an octave higher, and divide it into four equal parts, we get C-E♭-F#-A-C (which actually spells a C diminished seventh chord). Each of the internal intervals is a minor 3rd (three half steps). If we then further divide each of these minor 3rds into a half-step/whole-step pair, we get an eight-note dominant scale.

As this scale starts with a half step, and alternates between half steps and whole steps throughout, it is sometimes referred to as a "half-step/whole-step scale." The name "dominant scale" is applied because the scale can be used over a dominant chord.

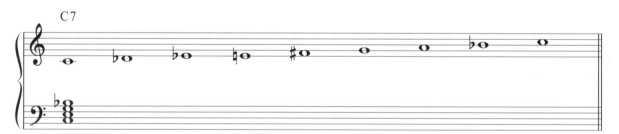

In addition to the basic chord tones of the C7 chord, this scale also adds the following extensions and alterations: ♭9, #9, #11, and 13.

Alternatively, if we divide each internal minor 3rd (C-E♭-F#-A-C) into a whole-step/half-step pair (instead of half-step/whole-step), we get an eight-note diminished scale.

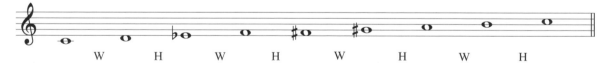

As this scale starts with a whole step, and alternates between whole steps and half steps throughout, it is sometimes referred to as a "whole-step/half-step scale." The name "diminished scale" is applied because the scale can be used over a diminished chord.

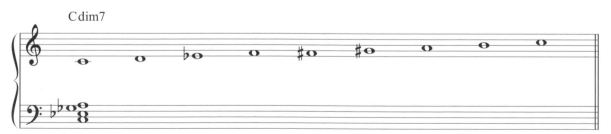

In addition to the basic chord tones of the Cdim7 chord, this scale also adds the following extensions and alterations: 9, 11, ♭13, and 14 (a major 7th above the root).

Further Reading

For more information on eight-note scales and their uses over different chords, please check out my *Contemporary Music Theory: Level Three*, published by Hal Leonard LLC.

ELECTRONIC MUSIC

Electronic music is an umbrella term for music styles based on electronic instruments and technology (synthesizers, drum machines, loops/samples, computers, etc.). Although in the 21st century almost all recordings and live performances rely on electronics, the term electronic music is generally reserved for those styles that use electronics as their main focal point or inspiration.

Here is a summary of some of the more popular electronic music styles:

- *Drum and Bass* (see p. 48), also known as jungle, emerged in the early 1990s and uses "broken beat" drums at fast tempos, usually 155–180 beats per minute. Bass lines are normally sampled or synthesized and can be quite complex.

- *Dubstep* is an electronic dance music style that emerged in London in the late 1990s, blending Jamaican influences with other electronic styles such as techno and jungle. Tempos are normally 135–145 beats per minute, and the bass lines often contain prominent sub-bass frequencies.

- *Electro* is short for electro funk, sometimes referred to as robot hip hop. This is an electronic style of hip hop, influenced by bands such as Kraftwerk. Vocals are often mechanical-sounding and electronically processed.

- *Hip hop* (see p. 85), also known as rap, is an urban, mid-tempo music style that first emerged in the late 1970s, using a rhythmic style of spoken-word vocals (rapping) over backing beats. Modern hip hop makes extensive use of samples and sequenced loops.

- *House* (see p. 87) is an electronic dance music style, usually using medium-to-fast tempos (120–135 beats per minute). House music has considerable soul, funk, and disco influences, and a more "live" or organic feel compared to other electronic styles such as techno and trance.

- *Industrial music* is intensely mechanical, using unconventional samples, noise elements, and provocative lyrics. This genre reached a peak in the 1990s, also influencing the rock and metal styles of the period.

- *Synth-pop* (see p. 175) is a genre that makes extensive use of synthesizers and drum machines, within mostly conventional pop song structures and arrangements. This style's heyday was the early-to-mid 1980s, although it remains popular today.

- *Techno* (see p. 178) is an electronic dance music style that emerged in the late 1980s. Techno uses synthesized sounds and drum loops at fast tempos (135–155 beats per minute). Techno tracks often have little or no harmonic structure when compared to other electronic styles like trance.

- *Trance* (see p. 181) is another electronic dance music style that emerged in the late 1980s. This style uses repetitive synthesizer phrases and melodies at fast tempos (130–165 beats per minute) and often has more of a musical form (i.e., a recognizable chord progression and arrangement) than other styles such as techno or hip hop.

- *Trip hop*, which emerged in the UK during the 1990s, is a variation of hip hop that uses a laid-back, slower beat, with a moody and "spacey" feel. Trip hop tracks often use samples taken from old vinyl jazz records.

Also, progressive rock (see p. 149), while not an electronic music style per se, makes extensive use of synthesizers alongside more traditional instruments such as guitar, bass, and drums.

ENVELOPE

An **envelope**, also referred to as an **envelope generator** or **ADSR envelope**, is a component of many synthesizers and electronic musical instruments. Its purpose is to modify some aspect of the instrument's sound, usually either the tone color (timbre) or the volume (amplitude). In the earlier analog synthesizers, the envelope was a separate circuit or physical module. With the advent of digital synthesizers, envelopes are implemented in the software of the unit (or softsynth).

When you listen to an acoustic instrument, the volume and/or timbre of each note will change over time. For example, when a note is played on a cello, it normally takes a moment for the note to reach full volume, and the note will then sustain as long as the bowing continues. By contrast, when a note is played on a guitar, the maximum volume occurs immediately after the string is plucked, and the sound then fades afterward. These volume (amplitude) characteristics can be imitated in a synthesizer by applying an envelope to the amplifier stage.

Also, when a note is played on a brass instrument, it normally takes a moment for the upper harmonics to emerge—sometimes referred to as the "splat" of a trumpet or trombone, for example. These timbral characteristics can be imitated in a synthesizer by applying an envelope to the filter stage (see p. 67).

The typical ADSR envelope has the following components or stages:

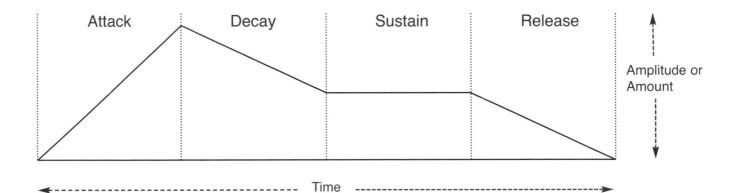

- The first stage is the *attack time* (see p. 19). This is the time taken for the envelope to reach its peak. The attack peak corresponds to the maximum volume if the envelope is applied to the amplifier, or to the maximium brightness if the envelope is applied to the filter.

- The second stage is the *decay time* (see p. 36). This is the time taken for the envelope to move from the peak to the sustain level. During this period the sound will become either quieter or darker, again depending on how the envelope is being applied.

- The third stage is the *sustain* (see p. 173). It's important to realize that this parameter is not a time period like the other stages of the envelope, but rather a level that applies as long as the note is sustained (i.e., held down on the keyboard). This value will govern the overall volume or timbre of the sound, once the attack and decay times have passed.

- The fourth stage is the *release time* (see p. 158). This is the time taken for the envelope to close, once the note has been released. This value will control how quickly the note fades away, or how quickly the brightness will change back to the level specified in the filter.

Here are a few more tips from the trenches to bear in mind when you're next programming the envelopes in your favorite keyboard or softsynth:

- For many sounds, you'll want to apply envelopes to both the filter and amplifier stages. Most modern-day synths allow you to do this. Don't forget that there's an interaction between these two envelopes—for example, if you're not hearing the effect of your filter envelope, it could be because your amplifier envelope is not letting the sound through (i.e., if the sustain level is too low).

- You'll also want to control the degree to which your envelope will modify the filter. This is variously referred to as "envelope intensity," "envelope amount," etc. on different synths. So again, if you're not hearing the effect of your filter envelope, you may need to adjust this intensity parameter.

- When an envelope is modifying the filter, the "baseline" frequency, equivalent to the bottom horizontal line on our diagram, is set by the filter cutoff parameter (see p. 67). So to get the best results from your filter envelope, you may need to adjust the cutoff. In general, the lower the filter cutoff, the more room the filter envelope has to work with, meaning that you will hear a greater timbral difference as the envelope is applied.

Now we'll hear two examples of envelopes being applied to synthesizer sounds, both using a simple series of whole notes:

TRACK 49

Listen to Track 49 to hear a filter envelope applied to a synth brass sound. The filter opens to a peak brightness (during an attack time of 870 milliseconds) before reducing brightness (during a decay time of 440 ms) down to the sustain level.

TRACK 50

Listen to Track 50 to hear an amplifier envelope applied to a synth string sound. The amplifier builds to the peak loudness (during an attack time of 1400 ms) before reducing volume (during a decay time of 1200 ms) down to the sustain level.

Both of these synth brass and string sounds were produced from the ES2 softsynth within Logic. ES2 is a great softsynth to use for practicing your envelope programming, as the GUI (graphical user interface) is very well laid out and easy to use.

EQUIPMENT

Equipment is a big topic for today's keyboard player! In this brief summary, we'll discuss acoustic pianos and electronic pianos/keyboards—which hopefully will help when you make your next equipment purchase.

When you strike a key on an acoustic piano, a felt-covered hammer strikes the strings to produce the sound—a purely physical process. By contrast, when you strike a key on an electronic keyboard, the sound is generated digitally, and the signal needs to be fed to an amplifier and speakers (either in the instrument itself, or a separate system) for it to be heard.

Here is a quick summary of the pros and cons of acoustic and electronic instruments.

Acoustic

Pros: Unique sound (the "real thing"), with physical responsiveness and sensitivity that are not easy to duplicate with electronic instruments.

Cons: Higher cost; more maintenance required; take up more space; harder to move; harder to record.

Electronic

Pros: Lower cost; less maintenance required; smaller footprint; better portability; easier to record. Continually better approximations of that distinctive piano sound (the "real thing").

Cons: Keyboard often lacks the weight, responsiveness, and sensitivity of the real piano. Needs electricity and a speaker system.

There are two fundamental categories of acoustic pianos: vertical (upright) and horizontal (grand). Grand pianos have a louder and fuller tone than uprights, due to their longer strings and larger soundboards. However, upright pianos are less expensive and have a considerably smaller footprint.

Upright piano

Baby grand piano

There are three basic categories of electronic pianos and keyboard instruments (with many hybrids and variations): digital pianos, synthesizers and workstations, and software instruments.

Digital Piano

Synthesizer/Workstation

1) **Digital pianos** are often the most tempting option for people who want a sound close to the "real thing," and who don't want to deal with computers and MIDI technology. They have 88 weighted keys, and come with a selection of piano sounds as well as a handful of other sounds. They are designed to be used as stand-alone instruments, either in the home or in a school classroom. They normally have built-in speakers, and a headphone output so you can practice quietly.

2) **Synthesizers and workstations** constitute a vast category! Synthesizers are keyboard instruments capable of playing different sounds, which by the late 1980s typically included samples (digital recordings) of real instruments, including piano. When onboard sequencing (multi-channel recording) was added to these keyboards, workstations were born. Functionally today's workstations are similar, but with more features, memory, sounds, and polyphony (number of voices that can sound at once). These instruments normally don't have built-in speakers, so you need to run them through an external amplifier and speaker system (or combo amp) or listen to them on headphones.

3) **Software instruments** offer the greatest realism if you need to get as close as possible to the real sound of a piano. These instruments can run on a Mac or PC, either natively or within a software host. You then hook up your MIDI controller (a keyboard capable of generating MIDI data, which almost all modern keyboards do) to the computer. You may also need an audio interface to convert the digital signal back into audio, so as to feed it to your speaker system. Software instruments take advantage of the faster speed of today's computers (together with large hard drives and fast access times) to store huge sample libraries of instrument sounds, far larger than the memory available on workstation synths. For piano sounds, this means individual samples of multiple velocity levels per note, which all adds up to an unprecedented level of realism. You've already heard software pianos on many recordings (though you may not have realized that it wasn't the "real thing")!

EXERCISES

This section contains some **exercises** to use for warm-up purposes, and to help build your piano technique. First we'll look at an arpeggio exercise.

TRACK 51

Major-Triad Arpeggio Exercise

Try to articulate this exercise as evenly and cleanly as you can. Note that the first four measures outline a C major triad, and the next four measures outline a D♭ major triad. You should then continue these arpeggios in an ascending chromatic sequence (i.e., D, E♭, E♮, F, and so on). This is a great warm-up, and will also come in handy in various contemporary styles.

 Next up is a pentatonic scale exercise.

TRACK 52

Pentatonic Scale Exercise

Note that the first eight measures use a C pentatonic scale, and the next eight measures use a D♭ pentatonic scale. You should then continue the exercise in an ascending chromatic sequence (i.e., D, E♭, E♮, F, and so on). This exercise uses pentatonic-scale subgroups (contiguous groups of notes within the scale). For example, in measure 1 we start off with C-D-E-G in both hands, followed by D-E-G-A, E-G-A-C, and so on. Having these subgroups under your fingers is also very useful when improvising in contemporary styles. For example, see the country/rock improvisation in *Soloing* (p. 168).

To develop your technical facility further, please check out my *Piano Fitness* book/audio package, published by Hal Leonard LLC.

FAKING IT

A musician is **faking it** when he or she improvises a comping (accompaniment) or melody treatment of a song, working either from a chart or from memory. This requires an ability to voice chords in a stylistically appropriate manner, and a knowledge of the various rhythmic patterns used for each style. Here's a comping example in a pop/rock style.

Pop/Rock: Chord Chart

Pop/Rock Comping

In measures 1–8, the right hand is playing upper-structure triads, and the left hand is providing a steady eighth-note pulse, playing the root of each chord. In measures 9–16, the right hand switches to a series of 4ths, over a left-hand octave pattern on the root of each chord.

Chord Voicing Tips

In measures 1–8, this pop/rock example uses alternating triads in the right hand.

- Alternating between major triads built from the seventh and the third, on both the Dm7 and Gm7 chords.

- Alternating between major triads built from the fourth and the root, on the C chord. This interior IV-I triad movement is also known as "backcycling," which is also used on Track 22 (p. 24).

In measures 9–16, this example uses 4ths derived from the D minor pentatonic scale (equivalent to the F pentatonic scale) in the right hand. These intervals (G-C, A-D, C-F, and D-G) float over the different chords, which works because the whole progression is in the key of D minor. This is a signature rock music sound.

Next we'll look at a leadsheet that has melody and chord symbols. This time we need to play the melody, not just comp over the changes.

Jazz Swing: Lead Sheet

TRACK 54

Jazz Swing: Melody Treatment

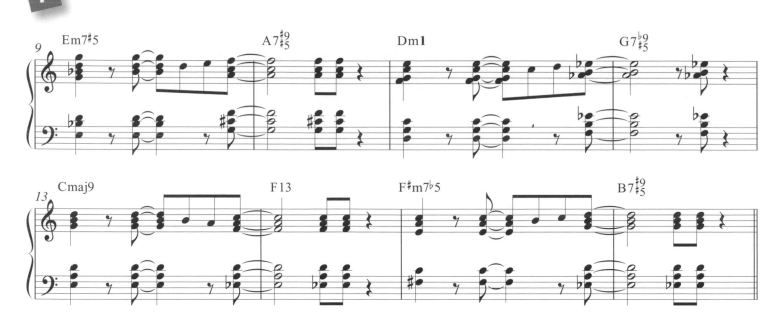

This jazz swing example uses "7-3" voicings (the sevenths and thirds of the chords) below the melody in measures 1–8. These voicings are a good solution in mainstream jazz styles. In this melody treatment, the upper fingers of the right hand are playing the melody, and the lower fingers of the right hand are playing the "7-3" voicings in between the melody, using typical jazz swing rhythmic figures and syncopation. The left hand is playing root-seventh intervals, with the root on beat 1 or anticipating beat 1, and the seventh "locking up" with the right-hand voicings. In measures 9–16, we switch to polychord voicings, with the left hand playing double-4th shapes (a stack of two 4ths) and the right hand playing triads.

Chord Voicing Tips

In measures 9–16, this jazz swing example uses double 4ths in the left hand, and triads in the right hand, as follows:

- The Em7♭5 and F♯m7♭5 chords are voiced by building minor triads from the third in the right hand, over a double-4th shape (root-flatted fifth-seventh) or a root-flatted fifth interval built from the root in the left hand.

- The Dm11 chord is voiced by building a major triad from the seventh in the right hand (and adding the third of the chord), over a double-4th shape (root-eleventh-seventh) built from the root in the left hand.

- The A7(♯5,♯9) chord is voiced by building a major triad from the sharped fifth in the right hand, over a double-4th shape (seventh-third-sharped fifth) built from the seventh in the left hand.

- The G7(♯5,♭9) chord is voiced by building a minor triad from the flatted ninth in the right hand, over a double-4th shape (seventh-third-sharped fifth) built from the seventh in the left hand.

- The F13 chord is voiced by building a major triad from the root in the right hand, over a double-4th shape (seventh-third-thirteenth) built from the seventh in the left hand.

- The B7(♯5,♯9) chord is voiced by building a major triad from the sharped fifth in the right hand, over a double-4th shape (third-seventh-sharped ninth) built from the third in the left hand.

- The Cmaj9 chord is voiced by building a major triad from the fifth in the right hand, over a double-4th shape (third-sixth-ninth) built from the third in the left hand.

FERMATA

A **fermata** is a sign over the music indicating a held note or chord, or a pause. This is often used at the end of a song to indicate that the last chord is held, as in the following pop ballad example.

TRACK 55

Note the **fermata** signs used on the last D major chord, in the treble and bass clefs.

This example uses basic triads derived from the chord symbols in the right hand, over open-triad arpeggios in the left hand. As in most ballad styles, make sure that you depress the sustain pedal for the duration of each chord.

FILTER

In the synthesizer world, the **filter** is the component that controls the timbre (tone color) of the sound. Filters are either low-pass (eliminating the higher frequencies above the filter cut-off point), high-pass (eliminating the higher frequencies below the filter cut-off point), or band-pass (eliminating the frequencies outside a specified band or range). Of these, the low-pass filter is by far the most commonly used.

Another important factor is the slope of the filter, which is the rate at which the frequencies are attenuated (reduced) after the cut-off point, expressed in "decibels per octave." Typical slopes for synthesizer filters are either 6, 12, or 24 dB per octave. (The higher the slope number, the more sharply the frequencies are reduced after the cut-off point).

The filter stage in a synthesizer can be controlled by two important modifiers: the envelope (see p. 58) and the low-frequency oscillator or LFO. When an envelope is applied to the filter stage, the tone color of each note changes over time according to how the envelope is programmed. For example, a synth brass sound might have a longer attack time (see p. 19) programmed in the filter envelope, so that the upper harmonics of the sound take a moment to build when the note is played.

When a low-frequency oscillator (or LFO) is applied to the filter stage in a synthesizer, a cyclical variation in timbre occurs over time, depending on the waveform and speed of the LFO, and the degree (intensity) to which this is then applied to the filter. A wah-wah effect is a typical application of this technique.

Now we'll listen to an analog synthesizer repeating the same line, with different filtering applied each time:

TRACK 56

Listen to the track and you'll hear the same synth line repeated, as follows:

- 1st time: No filtering applied. The (full) sawtooth waveform, with all frequencies present.

- 2nd time: Low-pass filtering applied. Note how the sound becomes darker, as the higher frequencies have been attenuated.

- 3rd time: High-pass filtering applied. Note how the sound becomes tinny and narrow, as the lower frequencies have been attenuated.

This analog synth sawtooth waveform was again produced from the ES2 softsynth within Logic.

FINDING A TEACHER

If you want to study in order to improve your musical skills, there are three basic paths you can take.

1) Self-study using instructional books/audio/video

2) Private lessons with a teacher in your area, or online

3) Group lessons or classes at a community college, music trade school, or other institution

Of all the people around the world who use my music instruction books and audio/video, the majority do so on a self-study basis. However, many people prefer to work with a teacher to get one-on-one guidance and to stay focused and motivated. Recently there has been a significant increase in online music instruction. Most of my own private students are in countries all around the world. Computer apps such as Skype and FaceTime have made this an easy and practical option for many musicians. Here are some ways to find a private teacher.

1) Fire up Google and research online instruction services, including ours at *harrisonmusic.com*!

2) Call or visit your local music store and ask for teacher referrals. Many stores will have an approved "teacher list," which will often include people working at the store. Some stores also offer lessons and classes on the premises.

3) Call your local college or university (or music school, if there is one in your area) for recommendations.

4) Check local newspapers, bulletin boards, etc.

Here are some other issues to bear in mind when evaluating private teachers and lessons.

1) Location (If meeting with the teacher in-person rather than online): Decide whether you need somebody to come to your house, or whether you are able to travel to the teacher. Most established/experienced teachers will require you to travel to their studios.

2) **Duration and frequency**: Decide how long a lesson you need (for example, a typical arrangement might be a single one-hour lesson per week). I teach only adult students, and I find it's hard to get anything worthwhile accomplished unless the lesson lasts at least an hour. Of course, for children a shorter lesson—perhaps half an hour—normally works better, due to attention span and other issues.

3) **Price**: Lesson rates start at around $40 per hour for a private instructor. However, this figure may rise substantially depending on the teacher's experience and reputation. Don't be coerced into paying for a whole series of lessons in advance, before you've had a chance to evaluate the teacher properly.

4) **References**: It is perfectly appropriate to inquire about other people whom the teacher has instructed (or schools/institutions where the teacher has worked), and to get references. I tend not to get this type of inquiry very much, as most of my students have either bought my music instruction books or seen our website or YouTube channel. However, most teachers out there won't have the profile that I'm lucky enough to have, so make sure you find out as much as you can about the teacher before committing yourself.

5) **Qualifications**: Make sure the teacher is qualified (and I don't just mean the certificates he or she may have on the wall!) to teach the style(s) you are interested in. For example, I specialize in contemporary pop and jazz styles, and I don't teach classical music—so when I get inquiries from people who want classical lessons, I refer them to someone else. Your teacher should be an expert in the areas you need!

FLASHCARDS

Obviously, it is very important for all piano players to know the notes in the treble and bass clefs (collectively referred to as the grand staff). Most music is notated within a two-octave span on either side of middle C, so you should make it a goal to learn and memorize all the notes in the following four-octave range:

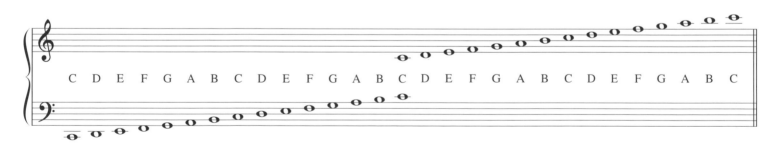

The best way to do this is to use **flashcards**, together with sightreading exercises appropriate for your level. A set of flashcards contains a card for each note in the treble and bass clefs, showing the notation (how the note is written) on the front, and the note name and keyboard location on the back. Work through the cards one at a time, and see how quickly you can name and/or find each note on the keyboard. If there are particular notes you have difficulty with (for example, many beginners are slower to learn the bass-clef notes), create a separate stack of these particular cards and work on them more frequently.

Sets of flashcards are available online and at most music stores, and may also include cards showing different rhythmic values and other aspects of notation and harmony—a simple, yet very effective, learning tool!

FREQUENCY MODULATION (FM)

Frequency Modulation (FM) is a method of synthesis where the tone color of a simple waveform (see p. 195) is frequency modulated by another oscillator in the audio range. This results in complex sounds with multiple harmonics present. In FM-speak, the oscillator being modulated is known as the carrier, while the oscillator doing the modulating is (not surprisingly!) known as the modulator.

Technical note: For synthesizing harmonic or "pitched" sounds, the modulator must have a harmonic relationship to the carrier (i.e., the frequency must be an integer multiple). However, FM is also particularly good at generating non-pitched sounds such as bells and percussion, and this is achieved by using modulator frequencies which are not integer multiples of the carrier frequency.

By the 1980s FM had been licensed to Yamaha, and was the basis of their hugely successful DX7 synthesizer (see p. 50). Modern-day keyboard synthesizers and softsynths often incorporate FM alongside other synthesis methods—such as subtractive, sample-based, and so on. In the 21st century, Native Instruments' FM8 is a notable softsynth using FM synthesis.

Now we'll hear some examples of FM synthesis, using the FM8 softsynth. First we have an example in a dramatic/film score style, featuring a very active, morphing "drone" sound typical of FM:

TRACK 57

Dramatic/Film Score

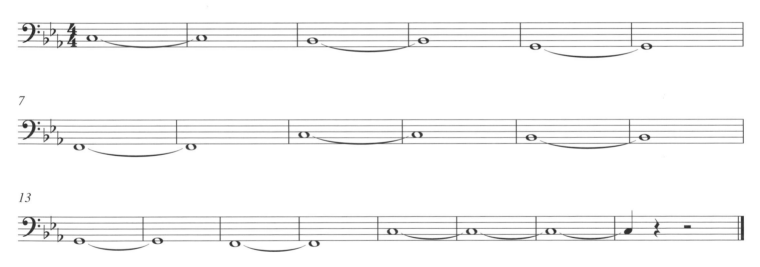

Listen to the track and you'll hear that the FM "drone" synth is on the right channel, with the other instruments on the left channel. Note that although the music part is very simple (tied whole notes), the sound imparts a lot of energy and motion to the track. On the left channel we also have an "evolving" synth texture from the Massive softsynth (again from Native Instruments), as well as some orchestral percussion courtesy of the Kontakt software sampler/synth.

Our next example is in a trance style, and features a bright, staccato comping synth that is perfect for the genre:

TRACK 58

Trance

Listen to the track and you'll hear that the FM8 trance synth is on the right channel, with the rest of the band (including an analog synth bass) on the left channel.

Harmony/Theory Notes

Note how this synth part uses interior movements (resolutions) within triads. For example, the E♭ within the C minor triad in measure 1 moves to the D within the Csus2 chord in measure 2. This same note movement (E♭ to D) occurs in measures 3-4, this time between the A♭ and A♭(♭5) chords. This adds a melodic element to this trance example and is a great way to spice up your synth parts!

FUNK

Funk is an American music style that emerged in the 1970s (within the overall family of R&B styles), and this style still has a large footprint in the 21st century. Funk music can be instrumental or vocal-based, and has a heavy emphasis on groove and syncopation. Most funk tunes use 16th-note rhythms, as does our first example.

TRACK 59

This type of keyboard part is typical of funk styles, and sounds best when played with an electric piano or clavinet sound. Note the rhythmic conversation between the hands, within the framework of the left hand landing on beat 1 and the right hand landing on beats 2 and 4 (the backbeats).

Chord Voicing Tips

This example mostly uses "7-3" voicings (the sevenths and thirds of the chords) in the right hand, alternating with a half-step leading tone into the lowest note. For example, on the Cm7 chord in measure 1, the "7-3" voicing has B♭ on the bottom, alternating with A (a half step below B♭). This is a signature funk sound.

The right hand is also using upper-structure and other devices as follows:

- On the Cm7 chords, the other 4th (C-F) is derived from the C minor pentatonic scale.

- On the B♭13sus4 chords, a major-seventh shape is built from the seventh (A♭maj7/B♭) and a minor triad is built from the fifth (Fm/B♭).

- On the final Cm7 chord, a major triad is built from the third (E♭/C).

Next up we have an example using a swing-16ths rhythmic feel—like the one on Track 12 (p. 15)—typical of funk shuffle styles.

TRACK 60

Funk Shuffle

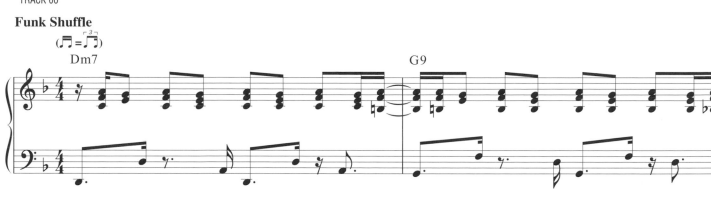

Again, note the rhythmic interplay between the hands, this time using a more consistent eighth-note rhythmic pattern in the right hand, apart from the anticipations of beat 1. The left hand is playing the roots of the chords on beats 1 and 3, and other chord tones (fifths and sevenths) in the rhythmic gaps between the right-hand figures.

Chord Voicing Tips

In this example the right hand is using upper structures, alternating triads, and modal harmony as follows:

- On the Dm7 chords, we are alternating between major triads built from the third (F/D) and seventh (C/D).

- On the B♭maj9 chord, we are alternating between major triads built from the fifth (F/B♭) and ninth (C/B♭).

- On the G9 and E♭9 chords, the voicings are based on four-part minor-seventh-flatted-fifth chord shapes built from the third (Bm7♭5/G and Gm7♭5/E♭), with additional passing tones from the G and E♭ Mixolydian modes.

- On the C13sus4 chords, the voicing is based on a four-part major-seventh chord shape built from the seventh (B♭maj7/C), with the additional passing tones coming from the C Mixolydian mode.

- On the Fmaj9 chords, the voicing is based on a four-part minor-seventh chord shape built from the third (Am7/F), with the additional passing tones coming from the F major scale.

- The A7alt symbol implies that all dominant chord alterations (♭5, #5, ♭9, #9) are available. The main root-flatted fifth-seventh voicing alternates with the third and sharped fifth of the chord, with the flatted ninth added during beat 4.

Further Reading

For more information on funk keyboard styles, please check out a couple of my other books: *R&B Keyboard: The Complete Guide with Audio!* and *The Pop Piano Book*, both published by Hal Leonard LLC.

GARAGEBAND

Garageband is a streamlined and basic digital audio workstation (DAW), used for music recording and production. It is manufactured by Apple and comes installed on all new and recent Mac computers. Garageband runs only on the Macintosh computer platform and can be viewed as a stripped-down version of Logic, Apple's professional-level DAW.

Garageband provides fun and enjoyment to a great many beginners and hobbyists who otherwise might not have dabbled in music sequencing and recording. It comes with a lot of pre-recorded loops in various styles, which the user can string together to make songs and arrangements. It also has some basic software instruments for recording.

Garageband can import MIDI files and has piano-roll and notation-style editing. It supports audio recording and playback, and has some basic effects capability. All in all, Garageband is a great entry-level program to get you started in music production if you have a recent Mac. When you outgrow it, as you probably will, I recommend upgrading to Logic Pro (see p. 111), which offers state-of-the-art features at a great price.

GIG PREPARATION

Preparation is key to the success of your next **gig**, whether you're performing pop, jazz, or classical music. Here are some tips "from the trenches" on how to be prepared, and how to get the best out of the gig.

1) **Be ready to play:** Make sure that you've gone over your parts, not just in rehearsal with the band, but during your own practice time. When preparing for a gig with my original jazz fusion band, I'll try to play through our whole set on the three or four consecutive days before the gig, either solo piano or with backing tracks/ sequences that I have prepared. As my band members are in-demand guys, sometimes we get only minimal rehearsal time, so everyone has to come to the gig prepared. If you're on a "chart gig" and you have the music ahead of time, scan through the tunes before the gig, making sure you know the road map and form of each song, and so on. If you're reading music at a classical recital, again, make sure you've had sufficient practice time with the music, and that all your page-turns are okay. One exception to all this, of course, is if you're just showing up to a jam session, in which case you're winging it using your playing skills and your ears!

2) **Make sure your equipment is ready:** If you're just showing up to a jazz gig or classical recital, and will be playing the piano that is already there, you can skip to the next section.... Otherwise, always make sure your equipment is in good working order and that you have all of the components you need. I have a checklist I run down for keyboards, amplifiers, speakers, pedals, cables, plugboards, extensions, and so on—*before* I leave for the gig. *Always* carry spare cables (audio, MIDI, a/c mains, mic cables, etc.). If one of your keyboards or some other equipment has a technical problem, *never* use it on the gig in the hope that it will "behave itself"— that's a disaster waiting to happen. Get it fixed, and use another piece of equipment (perhaps a rental or loaner) in the meantime.

3) **Be punctual:** This sounds simple and obvious, but it's extremely important. If you get to the gig in plenty of time, you're likely to be more relaxed when you set up, and you'll have more time to deal with any curve balls thrown at you during

the setup, soundcheck, and so on. Allow even more time to get to the gig if it's a venue you're playing for the first time, so that you can find the place, sort out the equipment load-in, parking, etc. When playing with my own jazz fusion band or with my Steely Dan tribute band in the Los Angeles area, I generally get to the gig two to three hours before showtime, depending on the particular setup and logistics involved. And I have to allow for the L.A. traffic!

4) **Be relaxed and have a pleasant attitude:** Less-experienced players sometimes suffer from nervousness or stage fright when performing in public. Well, players of all levels experience "nerves" from time to time; the trick is to get that nervous energy to stimulate you into giving a great performance, instead of holding you back. Especially if you're just starting out, get some family or friends to come to the gig and support you; then if an anxious moment strikes, you can look around and be comforted by familiar faces who want you to do well! We're always our own worst critics when it comes to our performance, but your audience will still most likely enjoy it and have a good time, provided you *keep going*. Always be courteous and have a pleasant attitude toward your bandmates, the engineer(s), the venue staff, and any audience members you come into contact with. If you project a relaxed and sunny attitude, it will influence those around you—to everybody's benefit.

GIG PROMOTION

So now that you've got that all-important gig for your band, how are you going to promote it so that people attend? Well, here are some **gig promotion** techniques you should know about.

1) **Internet:** Most bands I know have their own websites (i.e., www.yourband.com) and Facebook or ReverbNation pages. Make sure your upcoming shows are posted on your website. You can also set up separate Facebook events to publicize your gigs. If you're prepared to put in the time and effort to expand your Facebook friends network, send messages to people about your shows, and update your blog regularly with pictures, videos, and audio tracks, this can be an effective way to get people to your performances. If you haven't yet established your own band website, you can do so easily at sites such as hostbaby.com and brandzoogle.com. (Our Steely Dan tribute band website *doctorwuband.com* was created with Bandzoogle!)

2) **Email:** Most bands these days send out one or more emails to everyone on their email list to promote each gig. Make sure you collect email addresses whenever you can (i.e., with sign-up sheets at your gigs, when selling your CDs, etc.). These days everybody gets tons of email, so try to make your gig emails stand out—for example, by including pictures as well as text. You might also consider combining your email list with those of other bands you know, to reap the benefits of the combined list. (An email list manager for gig promotion is a cool feature of the Hostbaby site mentioned above.)

3) **Papers/magazines:** Check out the free papers in your area to see if there are listings of club gigs. For example, here in Los Angeles we have the *LA Weekly*, which has club listings by genre (rock, jazz, blues, etc.) for each night of the week. If the club is providing this information to the paper, make sure they have all the correct details about your band. If not, you can submit this information to the paper yourself. Depending on your budget, you might also consider paying for a display ad promoting your show. Make sure they run this in the same area of the paper as the gig listings, and if possible give them camera-ready artwork to use, as you will get more predictable results (and possibly a cheaper price).

4) **Flyers in the club:** Normally around two weeks before a club gig with my own band, I go into the club and put up posters promoting our show. This can be useful, as they will be seen by people who already go to the club. The flyers should show the band name and photo, the gig date and time, the cover charge (if applicable), and band website and/or FaceBook page. You can also post flyers in the surrounding area if there are any suitable locations.

Good luck promoting your gigs!

GLIDE

Glide, also known as **portamento**, is a continuous slide between successive pitches, and has been heard on synthesizers since the progressive rock era of the 1970s, associated with Keith Emerson's playing style in particular. Of course, the ability to continuously vary the pitch between notes is not limited to the synthesizer. Unfretted stringed instruments (such as the violin), wind instruments without valves (such as the trombone), and the human voice, are all instruments which have this capability.

Many keyboard synthesizers and softsynths have glide parameters, specifying how much glide (portamento) is required between successive notes. This effect is still used in today's electronic music and progressive styles. Here's an example of glide being used on a synth lead sound, in a classic rock style:

TRACK 61
Classic Rock

Listen to the track and you'll hear the lead synth on the right channel, accompanied by an organ on the left channel. Notice that on the larger intervals (for example, the octave at the beginning of the first measure) the glide takes a little longer to reach the destination pitch. Experiment with different glide amounts applied to your lead synth sounds!

The lead synth on the right channel was produced from the ES2 softsynth within Logic, using an analog synth square wave (see p. 170). The organ sound on the left channel is from the Native Instruments Vintage Organs virtual instrument. These are typical sounds from the progressive and classic rock eras.

GOSPEL

Gospel music originated in southern African-American churches in the early 20th century as a combination of hymns, spiritual songs, and Southern folk music, bound together with religious lyrics of joy and celebration. Gospel styles have also blended with other styles, notably creating country gospel and blues gospel. Blues, country, and gospel collectively created the foundation for rock 'n' roll to emerge in the 1950s.

Traditional gospel frequently uses either an eighth-note triplet subdivision at a slow-to-medium tempo (think "Amazing Grace"), or 16th-note rhythms and syncopations at a faster tempo (as in the Paul Simon gospel standard "Gone at Last"). Here is our first example, in a slow gospel 3/4 style:

TRACK 62

This example uses an eighth-note triplet subdivision within a 3/4 time signature. (In fact, you may sometimes see the alternate time signature of 9/8—nine eighth notes per measure—used to notate this type of music.) Normally, both hands "lock up" on beat 1, with rhythmic variations (the hands either together or alternating) in the remainder of the measure.

Chord Voicing Tips

In this example, the right hand is using upper structures and modal harmony as follows:

- On the G7 chords in measures 1 and 8, the four-part right-hand voicing is a combination of a major triad built from the root (G/G: top three notes) and a diminished triad built from the third (Bdim/G: bottom three notes).

- Elsewhere, on the first G7 chord, we are using Bdim, C, and Dm triads in the right hand (all from the G Mixolydian mode), and a four-part minor-seventh-flatted-fifth chord shape built from the third (Bm7♭5/G).

- The C7 chord is voiced by building a diminished triad from the third (Edim/C), and the passing F major triad on the last 16th note of beat 4 also comes from the C Mixolydian mode.

- The C♯dim7 chord is voiced with different inversions of the basic four-part chord (a common gospel sound).

- The first and last triads used over the D7 chord are Bm and Am (both coming from the D Mixolydian mode), and the chromatic passing triad in between is a B♭m triad (another signature gospel device).

- On the G/D chord, the movement between the upper G and C major triads is another example of backcycling (IV-I triad movements within the chord), as encountered on Track 22 (p. 24).

The next example is in a fast gospel style, using 16th-note rhythms and anticipations.

TRACK 63

Fast Gospel (4/4 time)

Note the exciting cross-rhythms created between the hands in this example. The left hand provides a steady eighth-note pulse using octaves, except during beat 2 of each measure where the left hand plays on the first two 16th notes in the beat, leading into the right-hand voicing halfway through beat 2 (the "and" of 2). Also, the right-hand voicings on the last 16th of beat 1 and the second 16th of beat 4 are very effective syncopations that land in between the left-hand octaves.

Chord Voicing Tips

In this example, the right hand is using upper structures and modal harmony as follows:

- On the A7 and G7 chords, the first voicing is the same as the first G7 voicing in the previous example (a combination of major and diminished triads, resulting in the seventh-third-fifth-root of the chord from bottom to top).

- Elsewhere, all the upper triads come from the Mixolydian modes, built from the root of each chord. For example, on the A7 chord the C♯dim, D, and Em triads all come from A Mixolydian; on the G7 chord the Bdim, C, and Dm triads all come from G Mixolydian, and so on.

Further Reading

For more information on gospel piano techniques, please check out my *Gospel Keyboard Styles*, published by Hal Leonard LLC.

GRACE NOTES

A **grace note** is a note of very short duration that is "squeezed in" before another note. This type of right-hand ornamentation is useful across a range of contemporary styles. Here's an example using grace notes, in a Nashville-era country style.

TRACK 64

You can see that the grace notes are much smaller than the "real" notes on the staff (for example, in measure 1 of the right hand, the E right before beat 2). Also the grace notes have no rhythmic value in the notation (i.e., if the grace note were removed from measure 1, the remaining notes and rests would still add up to four beats).

This traditional country pattern is a variation on the pentatonic scale techniques we saw in Track 29 (p. 34). On the D major chord in measure 1, we are using a D pentatonic scale, moving between E and F♯ below an upper drone on A. The 4ths at the end of the measure (B-E and A-D) also come from this scale. Similarly, on the G major chord in measure 2, a G pentatonic scale is being used, and so on.

Note that the right hand is anticipating the D major triad leading into measures 3 and 8, and is also moving between E and F# during beat 4 of measures 2 and 7. This can be understood as ninth-third movement within the D major chord. (These two notes are also found in a D pentatonic scale.) The left hand is mostly playing a root-fifth pattern on each chord, typical of mainstream country styles.

GRANULAR SYNTHESIS

Granular synthesis is a method of synthesis where waveforms or samples are split into very short pieces of up to 50 milliseconds in length. These small pieces (called "grains") can then be arranged and layered and played back at different tempos and volume levels. The grains can be further modified by changing their duration, density, spatial position, and so on. The result is a "soundscape," sometimes referred to as a "cloud," usable for both music and sound effects. Granular synthesis can produce unique, dynamic textures that morph over time, and sound different to most other synthesis methods.

There are a number of interesting softsynths that offer granular synthesis, including Sound Guru's The Mangle, Steinberg's Pad Shop, and New Sonic Arts' Granite. Also, the popular digital audio workstation software Reason includes a softsynth called Malstrom, which the manufacturers Propellerhead call a "graintable" synth, as it combines granular and wavetable synthesis methods.

Now we'll hear two music examples in an ambient electronic style, created in Reason and using the Malstrom "graintable" softsynth. Our first example features a Malstrom synth preset called "Graindrops":

TRACK 65

Ambient Electronic

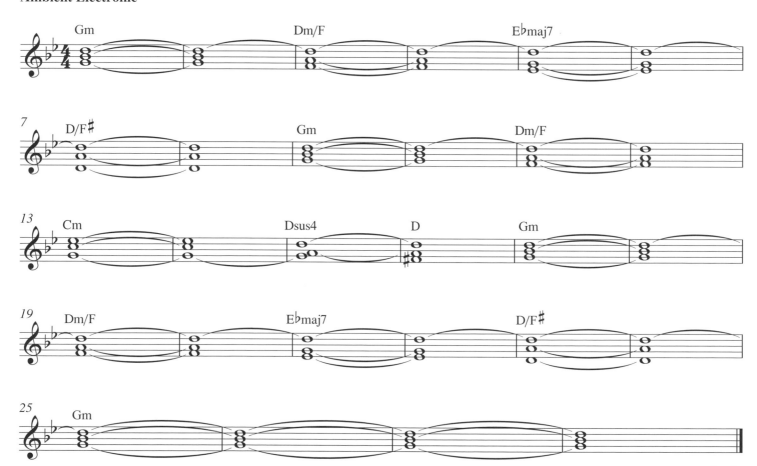

Listen to the track and you'll hear that the evolving synth pad is on the right channel, with the other instruments on the left channel, including an analog synth bass and lead synth from Thor, another great Reason softsynth.

Note that although the music part is very simple (many whole notes!), the sound imparts a lot of motion to the track. Our next example features another evolving synth sound from Reason, similar to the sound on the previous track, but with more upper harmonics present:

TRACK 66

Ambient Electronic

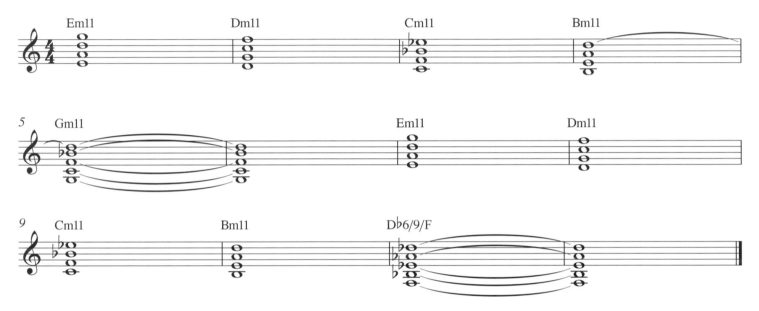

Listen to the track and you'll hear that the evolving string synth is on the right channel with the rest of the band, again including an analog synth bass from the Thor softsynth, on the left channel.

Harmony/Theory Notes

Note how this synth part uses voicings creating by stacking a series of perfect 4th intervals (or double-4th shapes that we have seen in earlier examples), creating a modern, transparent sound. These voicings are ideally suited for this particular synth texture. Also, we see that no key signature has been written, as the piece moves rapidly between different key centers due to the chords being used.

Further Reading

For more information on all types of chord voicings, including double-4th shapes, please check out my book, *Contemporary Music Theory, Level Three*, published by Hal Leonard LLC.

HALF NOTES AND RESTS

A **half note** lasts for two beats. This is equivalent to half a measure in 4/4 time. Here is an example of how half notes are written.

The rhythmic counting (1 2 3 4) is shown below the notes in this measure.

The half note is written as a white (or empty) notehead, with a stem attached.

Next we see an example of a **half rest**, which also lasts for two beats.

Here's a notation example that uses some half notes and rests.

Note that the rhythmic sum of all the notes and rests in each measure agrees with the time signature (i.e., four beats in each 4/4 measure).

For information on other basic rhythmic values, see *Eighth Notes and Rests* (p. 55), *Quarter Notes and Rests* (p. 155), *Sixteenth Notes and Rests* (p. 167), and *Whole Notes and Rests* (p. 196).

HALF STEP

The **half step** is the smallest unit of interval measurement in conventional Western music. If we move from any note on the keyboard to the nearest key to the right or left, this movement is a half step. Here are some examples of half steps.

Half steps may occur between white keys and/or black keys as follows:

- The half step C-D♭ is between a white key and a black key.

- The half step E-F is between two white keys that do not have a black key in between.

- The half step G♯-A is between a black key and a white key.

- The half step B-C is again between two white keys that do not have a black key in between.

Half steps and whole steps are the most common building blocks used when creating scales. Another important relationship to know is that there are 12 half steps per octave.

HAND POSITION

Hand position (not surprisingly!) refers to the position of the hands on the keyboard. When playing simple songs, one or both hands might remain in the same position throughout. However, once you are playing songs beyond the beginner level, you will often need to move your hands to different positions on the keyboard. Here are some basics concerning finger numbers and hand positions. (Go ahead and skip this section if you're beyond the beginner level!) First, here are the finger numbers for both hands.

The fingering numbers for both hands are:

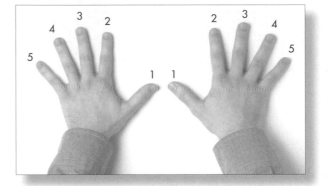

- 1 thumb
- 2 index finger
- 3 middle finger
- 4 ring finger
- 5 pinkie, or little finger

The following illustration shows a basic right-hand C-position, with the right thumb on middle C, and the pinkie on the G above.

Here's a simple folk song you can play entirely within this hand position. The finger numbers are shown above the staff.

"Go Tell Aunt Rhody" (Traditional)

Further Reading

For more information on hand positions, fingerings, and other beginner-level piano techniques, please check out my book/audio *All About Piano: A Fun and Simple Guide to Playing Keyboard*, published by Hal Leonard LLC.

HARMONIC

Harmonic is a term used to describe a component frequency of a sound signal. A musical sound (for example, when a guitar string is plucked) normally consists of a fundamental frequency and harmonics (overtones) that are an integer multiple of the fundamental frequency. To take a mathematical example: If x is the fundamental frequency of a sound, then the harmonics would have the frequencies 2x, 3x, 4x, and so on, in gradually decreasing proportions relative to the fundamental frequency. Relating this to musical pitches, if x in this example is the note C three octaves below middle C (sometimes referred to as C1), then the other harmonics will have the following pitches:

- 2x: one octave above (the C two octaves below middle C, or C2)

- 3x: one octave and a fifth above (the G one-and-a-half octaves below middle C, or G2)

- 4x: two octaves above (the C one octave below middle C, or C3)

- 5x: two octaves and a third above (the E nearly two octaves below middle C, or E3)

- 6x: two octaves and a fifth above (the G below middle C, or G3)

… and so on.

The presence of harmonics in addition to the fundamental, and the proportions in which they are present, determine the timbre (tone color) of the sound. Human ears have the tendency to combine harmonically related frequencies into an overall tonal impression, rather than hearing these frequencies individually.

In sounds without a specific pitch (e.g., bells, percussion), the harmonics are not exact integer multiples of the fundamental frequency. These are often referred to as inharmonics. Synthesis methods such as additive and frequency modulation (see p. 70) are good at creating these types of inharmonic sounds. When multiple harmonics are present with no discernable fundamental frequency, the human ear perceives this as noise (see p. 129).

HIP HOP

Hip hop, also referred to as **rap**, is a type of music that uses a rhythmic style of speaking (rapping) over backing beats. This genre originally emerged in the 1970s, and has continued to grow and develop until the present day. Modern hip hop production makes extensive use of samplers, sequencers, synthesizers, and drum machines. The main unifying element of this style is the drum groove (loop), which is then accompanied by a bass line and other sampled or sequenced instrumental parts.

Hip hop tracks are often structurally basic, for example taking a simple two-measure phrase and repeating it for the duration of the song. However, modern hip hop sometimes features melodic, "song form" elements. Most hip hop tracks use medium tempos, typically around 90–100 beats per minute. Samples are frequently taken from old vinyl records and used in hip hop songs, which can be controversial and involve various "sample clearance" and legal issues. Hip hop production values have also blended with other styles, notably with soul and R&B to create neo-soul in the 21st century.

Now we'll look at a couple of hip hop instrumental examples, and spotlight the synth bass part on each. Our first is in a jazzy hip hop style (think Black Eyed Peas) and was created in Logic (see p. 111), using its internal sounds and plug-ins:

TRACK 67

Jazzy Hip Hop

Listen to the track and you'll hear that the synth bass is on the right channel, with the other instruments on the left channel. This example has a 16th-note subdivision; in other words, the smallest rhythmic subdivision used is a 16th-note. The synth bass has a pronounced low end (typical of hip hop styles), and a short, punchy attack. Filling out the sound on the left channel is a "modeled" electric piano with some phasing, tremolo, and a little distortion added.

The next example is in an abstract hip hop style and was created in Reason using its internal sounds and plug-ins:

TRACK 68

Abstract Hip Hop

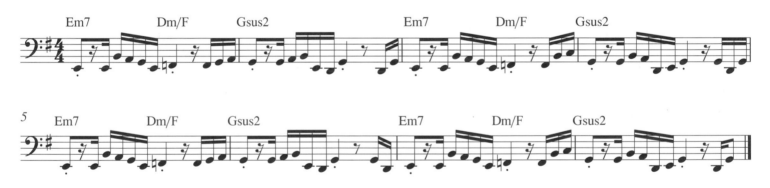

Listen to the track and you'll again hear that the synth bass is on the right channel, with the other instruments on the left channel. This time the synth bass is produced by Subtractor (an analog softsynth within Reason), using a sawtooth wave and a fairly low filter cut-off. The synth figure on the left channel is courtesy of the Thor softsynth, with a tempo-synced delay effect (see p. 54) added. Like the previous example, this one uses a 16th-note subdivision, but with a swing-16ths feel quite common in hip hop styles.

HOUSE

House is an electronic dance music style that emerged in the 1980s, with significant soul, funk, and disco influences. House music is normally at medium to fast tempos (120–135 beats per minute) and borrows disco's use of a prominent kick drum on every beat (called "four-on-the-floor"), and open hi-hat cymbals on the eighth-note offbeats. This is then accompanied by a heavy synthesized or sampled bass line. Other drums, instruments (real and/or sampled), and effects can then be added. Although house music shares some structural elements with styles such as trance and techno, it generally has a "live" music, organic feel when compared with the synthetic sound of other electronic styles.

Let's look at a couple of instrumental house examples. Our first is in a funky, "classic house" style and was created in Logic (see p. 111), with some third-party softsynth sounds. Here we'll spotlight the synth comping part:

TRACK 69
House

Listen to the track and you'll hear that the synth comping part is on the right channel, with the other instruments on the left channel. This big, bright comping synth comes from Massive, another great Native Instruments softsynth that combines a "wavetable engine" with analog-style filtering. This is a fun track to play along with; fire up your favorite "bright polysynth" and give it a shot! On the left channel is a synth bass (also from Massive) using an analog synth square wave, and a couple of digital synth comping parts (one coming in for the last eight measures) courtesy of the FM8 frequency-modulation softsynth.

The next example is in a deeper house style and was created in Reason, using its internal sounds and plug-ins. Here we'll spotlight the synthesized piano comping part.

House

Listen to the track and you'll again hear that the synth piano is on the right channel, with the other instruments on the left channel. This was created using the Thor softsynth within Reason, using a combination of analog and wavetable oscillators. The synth bass on the left channel is from Malstrom, another softsynth within Reason, using layered sine and sawtooth waveforms. Finally, the percussive organ part that begins in measure 9 uses the "House Organ" patch within the Subtractor softsynth.

Harmony/Theory Notes

The above synth piano part makes use of upper structure triads. For example, the right-hand notes on the Cm7 chord form an E♭ major triad (E♭ G B♭). These are the 3rd, 5th, and 7th of the Cm7 chord, and can be thought of as a major triad (E♭ major in this case) built from the 3rd of the chord (Cm7 in this case). Other upper structure triads are also used in this example, as follows:

- the right hand notes on the Gm7 chord form a B♭ major triad (built from the 3rd of the chord)

- the right hand notes on the Fm7 chord form an A♭ major triad (built from the 3rd of the chord)

- the right hand notes on the Dm7 chord form an F major triad (built from the 3rd of the chord)

- the right hand notes on the G11 chord form an F major triad (built from the 7th of the chord)

IMPROVISATION

Improvisation occurs when a musician creates a part spontaneously (that is, without reading or having memorized it in advance). In contemporary styles, there are normally two general contexts in which this term is used.

1) If a keyboardist is spontaneously creating a complete part—whether comping or playing the melody together with the harmonization—the process can be referred to as improvisation, or playing by ear, or faking it.

2) If a keyboardist is extemporizing a single-note right-hand melodic line over a chord progression, this is also referred to as improvising, or *soloing*. In this case, the chord voicings might be played by the keyboardist's left hand and/or the rest of the band.

Both of these types of improvisation occur within contemporary pop and jazz styles. Here are some further observations on how improvisation might apply in different musical genres.

Classical: Except in certain experimental or "fringe" situations, you are expected to play the notes on the page, either by reading the sheet music or by memorizing it beforehand. Improvisation (adding your own notes, or changing what is written) is not appropriate, which is ironic given that many classical composers were also noted improvisers. Classical pianists do, however, have major interpretive responsibilities in areas such as dynamics, articulation, phrasing, and tempo. Through this interpretation process, the performer's musical personality emerges.

Jazz and Latin: The majority of jazz compositions are written with just a melody and chord symbols. With the exception of some of the more "highly arranged" contemporary jazz styles, the chord voicings and melody phrasings are normally improvised by the players. Solos, in particular, are improvised on the spot, and true jazz performers never play a solo the same way twice, though they might have favorite phrases or "licks" that recur often in their solos. Latin styles such as bossa nova and samba also come under this general heading, as they typically use the full range of jazz melody and harmony options, and have a similar approach in terms of improvisation.

Pop/rock/R&B: The majority of contemporary pop, rock, and R&B songs are performed within a specific structure or form (intro, verse, chorus, etc.). Most bands playing these styles are performing from memory, although some may be reading from leadsheets or fakebooks. There is not normally much improvisation, except for instrumental solos—and even then the solo may be a recognizable signature played the same way each time. Yet, some rock bands do incorporate more extended improvisational jams—notably the Grateful Dead and the Dave Matthews Band.

INTERPRETING CHORD PROGRESSIONS

In *Comping* (p. 30) and *Faking It* (p.64), we saw various examples of how chord symbols could be interpreted in contemporary styles. Now we'll look at how a single chord progression might be realized in different styles.

Here's the progression we'll be using for this section:

Chord Chart

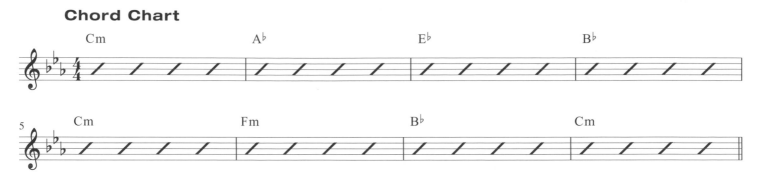

The chart consists of just chord symbols and slashes without a melody, which tells you to comp in the appropriate style. Our first interpretation is in a driving eighth-note pop/rock style.

TRACK 71

Pop/Rock

The right hand is using a mix of 4ths, alternating triads, and inverted double-4th shapes, with some rhythmic anticipations. The left hand is playing the chord roots in octaves, with eighth-note pickups into beat 3.

Chord Voicing Tips

In measures 2, 4, and 6, this example uses alternating triads in the right hand.

- Alternating between major triads built from the fifth and the root, on the A♭ chord (adding the seventh and ninth).

- Alternating between major triads built from the seventh and the third, on the Fm chord (adding the seventh, ninth, and eleventh).

- Alternating between major triads built from the fourth and the root, on the B♭ chords. This interior IV-I triad movement is also known as backcycling, first introduced on Track 22 (p. 24).

In measures 1, 3, and 5, this example uses 4ths derived from the C minor pentatonic scale (equivalent to the E♭ pentatonic scale) in the right hand. Also, at the start of measures 2 and 6, an inverted double-4th shape (B♭-E♭-A♭) has been built from the ninth of the A♭ chord and the eleventh of the Fm chord, respectively. This is a very useful sound in more advanced rock styles.

Next, we'll interpret the same progression in a New Age style. Here we want to create a dreamy or floating effect, with sustained right-hand voicings and light left-hand arpeggio patterns.

TRACK 72

The right hand is playing a mix of root-and-fifth voicings, basic triads derived from the chord symbols, and inverted double-4th shapes. The left hand is using open-triad arpeggio patterns, here adding the ninth of each chord (a signature New Age sound) on beat 2 of each measure.

Finally, we'll interpret the same progression in a 16th-note R&B/funk style.

TRACK 73

The right hand is playing a mix of upper triads and pentatonic 4ths, landing on beat 1, halfway through beat 3, and on the second 16th note of beat 4—a signature funk rhythmic figure. The left hand is playing the root and fifth of each chord, landing on all the downbeats, and with 16th-note pickups leading into beats 1, 3, and 4 of each measure. Note how the two hands land together on beat 1, and then "interleave" rhythmically during the remainder of each measure.

INTERVALS

An **interval** is the distance between two notes. First of all, we'll take a look at the intervals created between the note C and the other notes in the C major scale (over a range of two octaves).

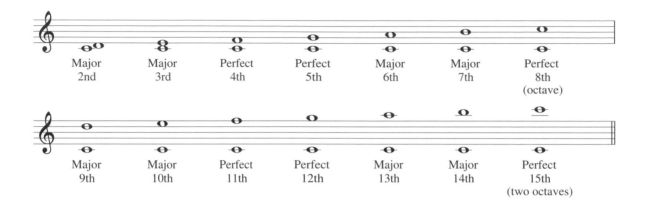

Note that each interval name contains a description (major, perfect) and a number (2nd, 3rd, 4th, etc.). The number part is easy to figure out: simply count up from the bottom note on the staff (starting at 1) until you reach the top note. For instance, looking at the major 3rd from the example above: the bottom note is C (1), the next note up on the staff would be D (2), and the next note up is E (3), which is the top note of the interval. The description will always be major or perfect if the top note of the interval is contained within the major scale built from the bottom note. As a quick rule of thumb, the 4ths, 5ths, and octaves (and these intervals plus one octave: i.e., 11th, 12th, etc.) are perfect, and the remaining intervals are major. Note that if we add or subtract the number 7 to/from an interval, we increase or reduce it by one octave (i.e., a 3rd plus an octave is a 10th: 3 + 7 = 10).

Some other descriptions apply when the above intervals are increased or reduced by a half step. Here is a summary of the rules you need to know.

- A major interval reduced by a half step becomes a minor interval.
  Example: C up to B is a major 7th, so C up to B♭ is a minor 7th.

- A minor interval reduced by a further half step becomes a diminished interval.
  Example: C up to B♭ is a minor 7th, so C up to B♭♭ is a diminished 7th.

- A major interval increased by a half step becomes an augmented interval.
  Example: C up to A is a major 6th, so C up to A♯ is an augmented 6th.

- A perfect interval reduced by a half step becomes a diminished interval.
  Example: C up to G is a perfect 5th, so C up to G♭ is a diminished 5th.

- A perfect interval increased by a half step becomes an augmented interval.
  Example: C up to F is a perfect 4th, so C up to F♯ is an augmented 4th.

Note that some of the above intervals are equivalent—i.e., the minor 7th (C-B♭) is equivalent to the augmented 6th (C-A♯). These intervals look the same on the keyboard (and sound the same, of course), but are written differently. Knowing all these intervals makes spelling your triads and seventh chords a snap! Also note that the half step is equivalent to a minor 2nd, and the whole step is equivalent to a major 2nd.

IVORY

Ivory is a software piano manufactured by Synthogy. It works as a plug-in within all major Digital Audio Workstations (DAWs, see p. 39) or as a stand-alone application or your desktop or laptop computer. Ivory includes sampled versions of world-class grand pianos such as the Steinway D, Bosendorfer Imperial 290, Yamaha C7, and Fazioli 308. Each piano has individual samples for each note (at multiple velocity levels), and sophisticated controls for soundboard and sustain resonance.

In the late 2010s the software piano market has become more crowded, and Ivory now has a number of serious competitors. However, Ivory is still the software piano of choice for many players and writers, due to its great sound and ease of use.

Now we'll look at a music example using Ivory. This is in a New Age style and uses the Fazioli 308 grand piano sample:

TRACK 74

New Age

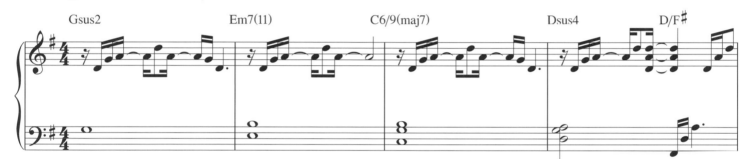

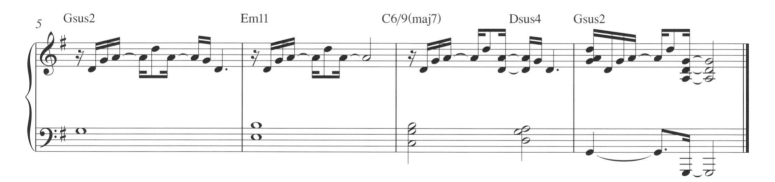

Listen to the track and you'll hear that the piano right hand (treble clef) part is on the right channel, and the left hand (bass clef) part is on the left channel.

Harmony/Theory Notes

Note how this piano part uses inversions of double-4th shapes (using two consective 4th intervals). The right hand plays the double-4th shape A-D-G, in different inversions, and then arpeggiates these over the all the chords. Double-4th voicings are a particularly effective New Age technique.

Further Reading

For much more information on New Age styles and double-4th voicings, please check out my keyboard method *The Pop Piano Book*, published by Hal Leonard LLC.

JAZZ

Jazz music has similar historical origins to the blues, in that it emerged in the late 19th century and then flourished and developed in the 20th century. The main jazz styles and eras to develop are New Orleans and Dixieland (1910s–1920s), swing (1930s), bebop (1940s), cool jazz and post-bop (1950s), fusion (late 1960s–1970s), and contemporary jazz (1980s onward). Jazz styles are noted for their improvisation and sophisticated harmony.

Our first jazz example is from the swing era, with four-part block voicings in the style of George Shearing.

TRACK 75

The right-hand voicings are mostly four-part upper structures on the various chords, and in this style the left hand is doubling the top note of the right-hand voicings, one octave lower. This means the root of the chord is often not played in the piano part (that is, rootless voicings are being used). This example features typical jazz swing rhythms: i.e., anticipating beat 3 (measure 1), anticipating beat 1 (measures 4 and 8), and so on.

Chord Voicing Tips

This jazz swing example uses upper-structure four-part chord shapes as follows:

- The Em9 chords are voiced by building a major-seventh shape from the third (Gmaj7/E) and a minor-seventh shape from the root (Em7/E).

- The A13 chord is voiced by building a major-seventh-flatted-fifth shape from the seventh (Gmaj7♭5/A) and a minor-seventh-flatted-fifth shape from the third (C♯m7♭5/A).

- The A13♭9 chord is voiced with two different upper structures:

  - a hybrid four-part shape (G-B♭-C♯-F♯) that is a combination of a diminished triad (Gdim: bottom three notes) built from the seventh, and a major triad (F♯: top three notes) built from the thirteenth

  - a diminished-seventh four-part shape built from the third (C♯dim7/A)

- The Dmaj9 chords are voiced by building a minor-seventh shape from the third (F♯m7/D), a minor-seventh shape from the sixth (Bm7/D), and a major-seventh shape from the root (Dmaj7/D).

Most jazz styles up to the 1950s used a swing-eighths rhythmic subdivision (as in the previous swing example). However, with the advent of fusion, straight-eighths rhythms began to appear. Our next example uses modal harmony in a straight-eighths rhythm, in the style of Herbie Hancock. This is typical of the jazz/rock fusion that was emerging by the late 1960s.

TRACK 76

Jazz/Rock Fusion

These voicings are all derived from Dorian modes. In measures 1–4 and 9–12 on the Dm7 chord, the right hand is playing a repeated top note (or drone) of D above the moving triads Dm, Em, and F, which all come from D Dorian. The left hand is sustaining the root below a moving line that doubles the top note of each triad an octave lower. Similarly, on the E♭m7 chord, the right hand is playing E♭ as a drone above the moving triads E♭m, Fm, and G♭, which all come from E♭ Dorian. At the end of measure 12, we're using Cmaj7 and Dm7 four-part block shapes (again from D Dorian), in a style similar to that of the previous example.

Further Reading

This tip gives you a brief glimpse into the vast world of jazz piano!

For more information on the history and development of jazz styles, as well as keyboard techniques for contemporary and smooth jazz, please check out my *Smooth Jazz Piano: The Complete Guide with Audio!*; and for a comprehensive reference guide to the chords, voicings, and shapes used in jazz piano, see my *Contemporary Music Theory: Level Three*. Both of these books are published by Hal Leonard LLC.

JAZZ/BLUES

The paths of jazz and blues have been significantly intertwined, from the swing-band era of the 1930s to the fusion music of the 1970s and beyond. The term **jazz-blues** describes music combining jazz elements (rhythms, advanced harmonies, and improvisation) with blues elements (song form, melodic phrasing, blues scales).

Our first jazz-blues example has a 12-measure blues form, but uses more sophisticated chords commonly found in mainstream jazz styles. This example is reminiscent of jazz/blues icons from the swing era, such as Count Basie and Duke Elllington.

TRACK 77

Jazz-Blues Swing

This example uses polychord (chord-over-chord) voicings, with typical jazz swing rhythms and anticipations.

Chord Voicing Tips

This jazz/blues swing example uses filled-in octave voicings, triads, four-part chords, and double-4th shapes between the hands. Double 4ths here include shapes with a diminished 4th (equal to a major 3rd) on top.

- The C9 chords are voiced by playing one of the following in the right hand: the root in octaves (filled in with the fifth), a major triad built from the root, or a minor triad built from the fifth. These are all placed over a double-4th shape (third-seventh-ninth) built from the third in the left hand.

- The F13 chords are voiced by playing either the fifth in octaves (filled in with the ninth) or a double-4th shape (third-thirteenth-ninth) built from the third in the right hand, over a double-4th shape (seventh-third-thirteenth) built from the seventh in the left hand.

- The Gm7 chord is voiced by building a major triad from the third in the right hand, over a double-4th shape (root-eleventh-seventh) built from the root in the left hand.

- The C13 chords are voiced by building either a minor triad or a double-4th shape (thirteenth-ninth-fifth) from the thirteenth in the right hand, over a double-4th shape (third-seventh-ninth) built from the third in the left hand.

- The B♭13 chord is voiced by building a double-4th shape (seventh-third-thirteenth) from the seventh in the right hand, over a double-4th shape (third-seventh-ninth) built from the third in the left hand.

- The A7(♯5,♯9) chord is voiced by building a major triad from the sharped fifth in the right hand, over a double-4th shape (seventh-third-sharped fifth) built from the seventh in the left hand.

- The Dm11 chord is voiced by building a major triad from the seventh in the right hand, over a four-part major-seventh shape built from the third in the left hand.

- The G7(♯5,♯9) chord is voiced by building a four-part major-seventh-sharped-fifth chord shape from the third in the right hand, over a double-4th shape (seventh-third-sharped fifth) built from the seventh in the left hand.

- The G7(♭5,♭9) chord is voiced by building a four-part dominant-seventh shape from the flatted fifth in the right hand, over a double-4th shape (seventh-third-sharped fifth) built from the seventh in the left hand.

- The Dm9 chord is voiced by building a four-part major-seventh shape from the third in the right hand, over another four-part major-seventh shape built from the third in the left hand.

- The G7(♯5,♭9) chord is voiced by building a minor triad from the flatted ninth in the right hand, over a double-4th shape (seventh-third-sharped fifth) built from the seventh in the left hand.

The next example is typical of the driving soul/jazz style pioneered by Gene Harris in the 1960s. This was an exciting blend of jazz, blues, soul, and gospel influences.

TRACK 78

In this example, the right hand is playing triads from Mixolydian modes in measures 1–6. For instance, on the G7 chord in measure 1, the upper triads Dm, C, Bdim, and Am all come from the G Mixolydian mode. From measure 7, the right hand is playing basic upper shapes derived from the chord symbols, leading to a pair of seventh-third-thirteenth double-4th voicings on the A♭13 and G13 chords in measure 8. The left-hand octave pattern follows the root of each chord (on beat 1) with a scalewise or half-step line leading to the next chord.

Further Reading

For more information on jazz/blues piano styles, please check out my *Jazz-Blues Piano: The Complete Guide with Audio!*, published by Hal Leonard LLC.

JAZZ STANDARD

A **jazz standard** is a well-established tune in the jazz repertoire, played frequently by successive generations of performers. Standards have strong and enduring melodies, and offer jazz musicians considerable potential for improvisation. Most jazzers play standards either from memory or from a chart in a fake book. Try playing through this arrangement similar to a classic jazz standard.

TRACK 79

This example uses "7-3" voicings (the sevenths and thirds of the chords) below the melody, similar to the first half of Track 54 (p. 65). Note the rhythmic phrasing and syncopations used (i.e., landing on the upbeats in measures 2, 4, and 6), all very typical of jazz swing styles.

The left hand is playing either the root of the chord, or a root-seventh interval. The root-seventh is a common left-hand voicing in jazz styles, giving good support to the right hand. Don't play these intervals too low on the piano or they will sound muddy. Let your ears be the judge!

JUPITER-8

The **Roland Jupiter-8** is one of the most famous analog synthesizers to emerge in the early 1980s. It was an eight-voice polyphonic synth (i.e., it had the ability to sound up to eight notes at one time), and its characteristically "fat" sound was heard on many classic 1980s recordings by artists such as Duran Duran, Michael Jackson, Howard Jones, and David Bowie.

The Jupiter-8 had some advanced performance features for its time, including adjustable glide (portamento, see p. 77), a versatile arpeggiator, and performance splits (the ability to split the keyboard into two zones, with different sounds assigned to each). The Jupiter-8 sounds are still in demand into the 21st century, notably for electronic dance music styles such as house and trance. In 2007 the software manufacturer Arturia introduced their Jupiter-8V softsynth, considered to be a good emulation of this classic synth. Also, the noted softsynth Omnisphere (see p. 133) includes samples of the Roland Jupiter-8, enabling it to re-create these sounds with convincing realism.

Now we'll look at a couple of music examples using Jupiter-8 sounds, derived using the Omnisphere softsynth. Our first is in a progressive rock style, featuring a lead/melody synth sound typical of the Jupiter-8:

TRACK 80

Progressive Rock

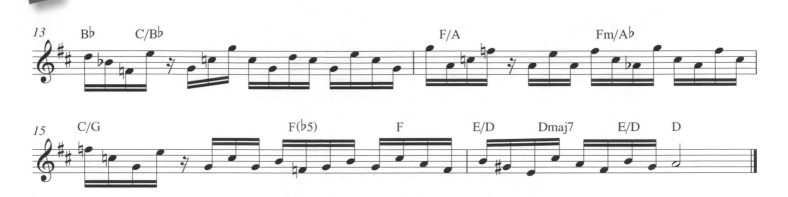

Listen to the track and you'll hear that the synth lead is on the right channel, and the rest of the band is on the left channel. The backing band on the left channel includes the Native Instruments Scarbee Red Bass virtual instrument, the BFD virtual drum instrument, the Ivory virtual piano (see p. 93), and an analog synth pad from the Massive softsynth (from Native Instruments).

Harmony/Theory Notes

Note that, during the first eight measures, this synth melody/solo again uses a "target note" approach, with arpeggios in between. For example, we go from the 3rd of the D chord to the 3rd of the E chord (over D in the bass) in measures 1–4, and this leads to the root of the A chord in measure 2 (over D in the bass) and measure 4 (over C♯ in the bass). A similar motif occurs over the C, D/C, G/C, and G/B chords in measures 5–8. From measure 9 onward, the synth part gets busier with 16th-note arpeggios, based on the upper triads within the chord symbols.

Our next example is in a pop/rock shuffle style, this time featuring a typical Jupiter-8 brass synth sound, derived from Omnisphere:

TRACK 81

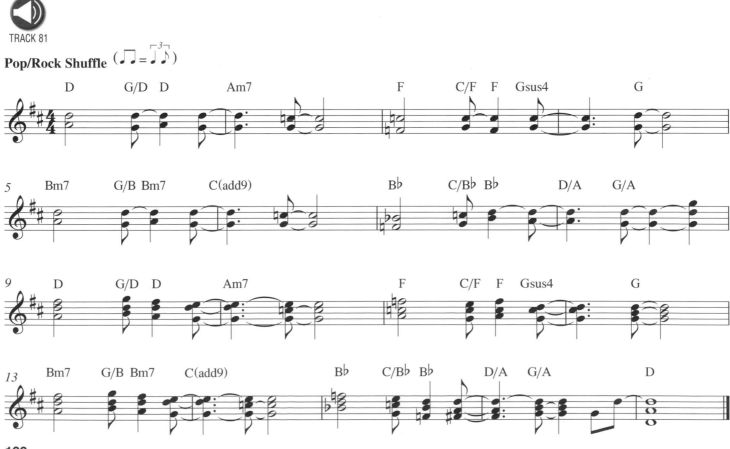

Listen to the track, and you'll hear that the brass synth comping is on the right channel, with the rest of the band on the left channel. This example uses a swing-eighths feel in which each pair of eighth notes sounds like a quarter-note/eighth-note triplet.

The backing band on the left channel again includes the Native Instruments Scarbee bass, the BFD drums, and the Ivory piano.

Harmony/Theory Notes

Note how this synth part uses two-note voicings with some resolutions or interior movements within the chords, during measures 1–8. Then starting in measure 9, we build up to three-note triad voicings, using an alternating triad voicing concept. For example, during measure 9 we are alternating between the D and G major triads (over D in the bass). This is a signature pop/rock keyboard sound.

Further Reading

For much more information on pop/rock keyboard styles and the use of alternating triads, please check out my keyboard method *The Pop Piano Book*, published by Hal Leonard LLC.

KEEP GOING!

Keep going, no matter what happens. This applies to all performance situations and musical styles! Whether you're in the middle of Beethoven's "Moonlight Sonata," Coltrane's "Giant Steps," or the Beatles' "Lady Madonna," you should never stop if you fumble in mid-performance. Instead, you should keep going at all costs, striving to maintain the rhythm as consistently as you can. As musicians we always tend to be our own worst critics, but I guarantee you that the great majority of your audience will not notice those imperfections—provided that you keep going, and are "in the pocket" rhythmically. As I sometimes say in my classes: "If you keep going, maybe two percent of your audience will notice that you made a mistake. If you stop, then 100 percent of them will know!"

If you're on a pop or jazz gig and you lose your place in the form of the song, use your ears and try to figure out where the rest of the band is (i.e., are they on a I chord, the V chord, or somewhere else). At worst, if you're playing a tune with a repetitive form (like a jazz standard or a blues), try to catch up when the band returns to the top of the form again!

Refer also to the comments on "practicing the performance" in *Practice Habits* (p. 148).

KEY SIGNATURES AND KEYS

A **key signature** is a group of sharps or flats at the beginning of the music that lets you know which **key** you are in (and which major scale to use). When we play the C major scale, we can hear that the note C sounds like the "home base" or *tonic* of the scale. If a song uses the C major scale, it is most likely to be in the key of C. As the C major scale contains only white keys, the key signature for C major contains no sharps and no flats.

When we build the F major scale, we need B♭ as the 4th degree of the scale. So the key signature of F major reminds you to play B♭ (instead of B♮) when playing in the key of F. That way we don't need to keep writing flat signs for every B♭ that comes up in the music.

Similarly, as the G major scale requires F♯ as its 7th degree, the key signature of G major reminds you to play F♯ (instead of F♮) when playing in the key of G.

Each of these key signatures also works for a minor key that is relative to the major key. If we re-position the C major scale to start on A (i.e., A-B-C-D-E-F-G-A), we get an A natural minor scale. This scale is used in the key of A minor, and the key signature would again have no sharps and no flats. The relative minor always begins on the 6th degree of the corresponding major scale: in our example, A is the 6th degree of the C major scale. So if you see a key signature with no sharps and no flats, how do you know if you're in the key of C major or A minor? Well, you have to make a contextual judgement in the music: for example, if the tonic were C, you would most likely be in C major; whereas if the tonic were A, you would be in A minor. Many tunes also move back and forth between the major and relative minor keys (several Beatles' songs—including "Yesterday"—do this).

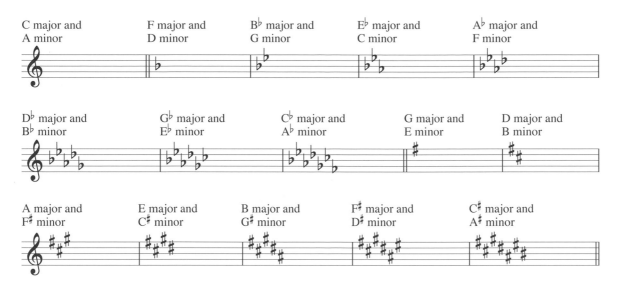

Here, for reference, are all the major and minor key signatures:

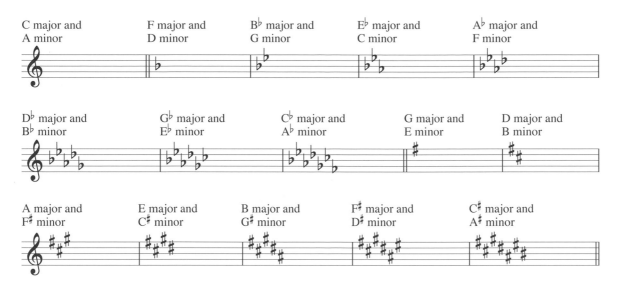

KONTAKT

Kontakt is a software synthesizer and sampler manufactured by Native Instruments. It works as a plug-in within all major digital audio workstations (DAWs, see p. 39), or as a stand-alone application. Kontakt has a straightforward user interface, and yet it also has deep editing and scripting features. As a result, its playback engine, known as Kontakt Player, is often licensed by different manufacturers for use with their software instruments and sample libraries. These third-party virtual instruments are normally bundled with a version of Kontakt Player, so you can use them "right out of the box" even if you don't own Kontakt.

If you do purchase Kontakt, you basically get the Kontakt Player plus their sound content (samples). The content covers most typical sound categories: guitars, synths, basses, drums, keyboards, orchestral sounds, and so on. In this respect, Kontakt is in competition with other all-in-one softsynth samplers/workstations such as MOTU's Mach Five and Steinberg's Halion.

Now we'll look at some music examples using the sounds included in Kontakt. First up is an example in a rock style, and on this one we're spotlighting the synth comping/ arpeggio part:

TRACK 82

Rock

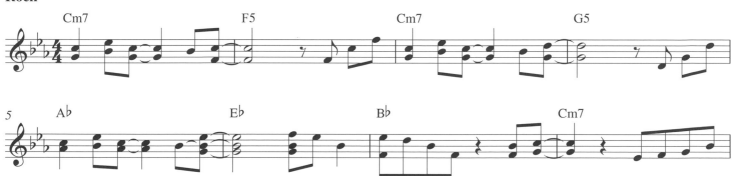

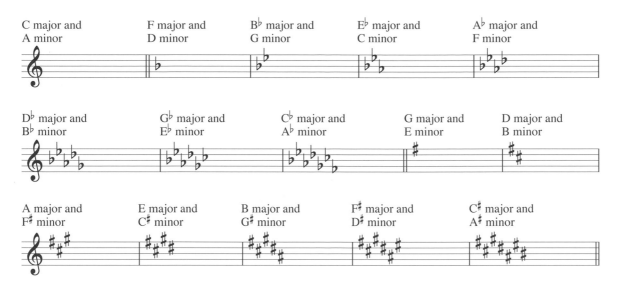

103

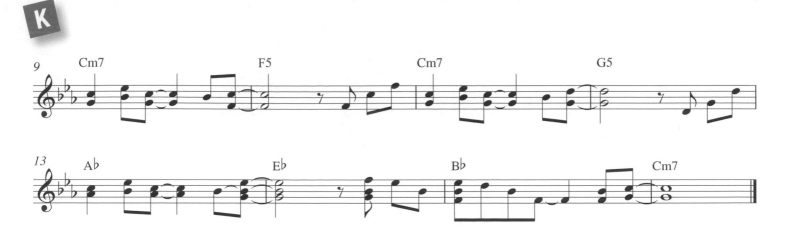

Listen to the track, and you'll hear that the synth comping/arpeggio part is on the right channel, with the rest of the band on the left channel. The synth used is an FM-style staccato synth within Kontakt. In the backing band on the left channel, we have more Kontakt instruments: a Wurlitzer A200 electric piano sample, a funk-style electric bass, and a rock drum kit.

Harmony/Theory Notes

Note that the synth part over the Cm7 chords is using 4th intervals from the C minor pentatonic scale (C Eb F G Bb). Then on the F5 and G5 chords the synth is playing just the roots and 5ths of the chords, and on the Ab, Eb and Bb chords the synth is playing the basic triads, with some arpeggios and resolutions. These are all typical voicing solutions in pop/rock styles.

Our next example is in a dramatic/film score style, and uses some of the orchestral sounds available within Kontakt. This time we're spotlighting the cello ensemble part:

Dramatic/Film Score

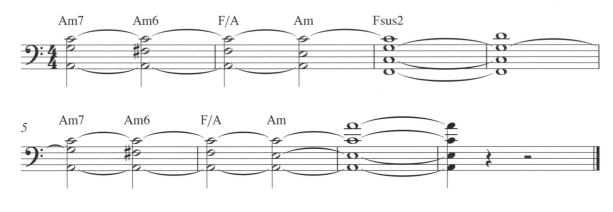

Listen to the track and you'll hear that the cello ensemble part is on the right channel, with the other instruments on the left channel. On the left channel, we have a bass ensemble drone, some timpani, a flute, and some light synth bells. Everything here is derived from Kontakt.

Harmony/Theory Notes

Note that the cello part uses three- and four-note "open" voicings, which have an overall span greater than an octave, and contain larger (4th, 5th, and 6th) intervals. Also, we're using common tones (e.g., the middle C that is held on top in measures 1–3) and close voice-leading (e.g., the half-step movements G-F#-F-E in measures 1–2). All this adds authenticity to orchestral string parts recorded with samples.

LEAD

A **synth lead** is an instrumental solo or improvisation performed on a synthesizer. In vocal music styles, a synth solo might be used to "break up" the vocal sections in a song, and to add interest and excitement (think Tina Turner's "Nutbush City Limits" or Emerson, Lake and Palmer's "Lucky Man"). Synth solos are used in many styles, from progressive rock and pop/rock through to synth-pop and contemporary jazz (including smooth jazz). Synth solo timbres can range from fat analog textures (a perennial favorite), to cutting FM-style synths (common in 1980s pop), to morphing wavetable synths, and so on.

Our first synth lead example is in a synth-pop style, and features a bright FM-style lead synth courtesy of the Absynth softsynth (from Native Instruments):

TRACK 84

Synth-Pop

Listen to the track and you'll hear that the synth lead is on the right channel, with the other instruments on the left channel. The lead synth has a bright, cutting quality with some inbuilt vibrato, and is typical of 1980s synth-pop. On the left channel, the bass and comping synths (including the tempo-synced comping part) are all produced from the ES2 softsynth within Logic.

Harmony/Theory Notes

A "target note" approach is used in this synth solo. For example, we move from the root of the Em chord (E) in measure 1, to the root of the D chord (D) in measure 2, to the 5th of the Em chord (B) in measure 3, to the root of the A chord (A) in measure 4, and so on.

The connecting tones in between are from the E minor pentatonic scale (E G A B D). Then the busier section starting in measure 9 is based on arpeggios of the chord symbols, with some scale-wise connecting tones added. This is varied in measure 12 with the use of an E blues scale (E G A B♭ B D) over the A major chord.

Our next synth lead example is in a pop/rock style, and features a Minimoog-style lead from the Omnisphere softstynth (see p. 133):

TRACK 85

Pop/Rock

Listen to the track and you'll again hear that the synth lead is on the right channel, with the other instruments on the left channel. This time the synth lead has a characteristically warm, analog quality, with a small amount of glide (see p. 77) added between the notes. The backing band on the left channel features an all-star virtual instrument line-up: BFD virtual drums, Native Instruments Scarbee virtual bass, RealStrat virtual guitar, Ivory virtual piano, and an analog synth comp from the Massive softsynth.

Harmony/Theory Notes

Again, we see a "target note" approach being used in this synth solo as we move from the 3rd of the Dm chord, to the root of the G chord (inverted over B in the bass), to the 3rd of the C chord, and so on. The busier section starting in measure 9 is based on arpeggios of the chords, with pentatonic scale tones added.

LEDGER LINES

Ledger lines are small staff lines placed above or below the staff in order to write notes that are too high or too low to be placed on the staff. Here is a grand staff showing all the Cs two octaves either side of middle C.

Middle C is a little above the bass clef, and a little below the treble clef. So we need to extend each clef (by adding a ledger line) to accommodate middle C. The Cs one octave above and below middle C are comfortably within each staff, but the Cs two octaves above and below middle C each need two ledger lines (above the treble staff, and below the bass staff).

As explained in *Flashcards* (p. 69), most piano music is written within this four-octave range—so the notes in this range are the most important ones to learn to recognize.

LEFT-HAND PATTERNS

In most contemporary piano styles, the left hand needs to provide a consistent rhythmic foundation. This is especially true in blues styles, as the left hand propels the rhythm while also defining the harmonic progression. Our first **left-hand pattern** can be used across a range of blues, blues/rock, and shuffle styles.

TRACK 86

This example is based on dominant seventh chords within a basic 12-measure blues form. The left-hand pattern uses root-fifth, root-sixth, and root-seventh intervals within each chord. You should play this with a steady, driving feel, and with a little extra emphasis on the downbeats. It's a good idea to learn this blues staple in as many keys as possible!

Next up we have a classic pop/rock groove, using the root of each chord in an octave pattern.

TRACK 87

Pop/Rock

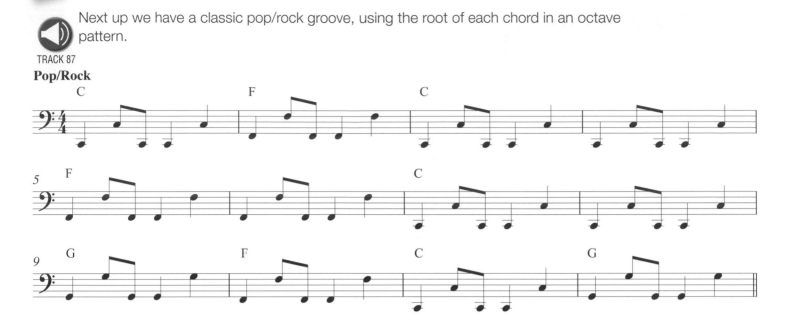

Note that this example uses the same 12-measure form, this time with basic triad chord symbols. The left-hand pattern is imitating a pop-rock rhythm section, with the low root landing on beats 1 and 3 (where the kick drum and bass would typically lock up), and the high root landing on beats 2 and 4 (the backbeats where the snare drum would normally be played).

Our final left-hand pattern is in a quarter-note walking-bass style, suitable for jazz and jazz/blues tunes.

TRACK 88

Jazz-Blues Swing

Again, we are using the same form, this time with quarter notes on each downbeat (varied with eighth notes in measures 5 and 9). There are many ways to construct this type of walking bass line over chord changes. These general guidelines will get you started.

1) The root of the chord is almost always played on beat 1 of each measure, except when a chord continues into a second measure. In this case, other basic chord tones (i.e., third, fifth, or seventh) can be used on beat 1 of the second measure.

2) Once you know how high or low you want to play the root of the next chord, you can then design an ascending or descending line during the preceding measure, so as to lead into that root. These lines often have scalewise movement using

Mixolydian modes (i.e., measure 4 descends using C Mixolydian), or chordal arpeggios (i.e., measure 2 ascends using the root, third, fifth, and thirteenth of the F7 chord).

3) Successive ascending or descending half steps are often used—for example in measures 3, 7, and 12 (ascending), and in measures 8, 10, and 11 (descending).

4) A half step is often used between beat 4 of a measure and the root of the next chord on the following beat 1 (for example, leading into measures 2, 9, 11, and 12). This kind of half-step approach is a signature sound in jazz styles.

LEGATO PLAYING

To play **legato** means to play in a smooth and connected style (as opposed to *staccato*). This is normally indicated in the music by a slur, which is a curved line drawn across the musical phrase, from the first to the last note. **Legato playing** is commonly needed in ballad and New Age styles, as in the following example of a **legato** piano melody accompanied by strings.

TRACK 89

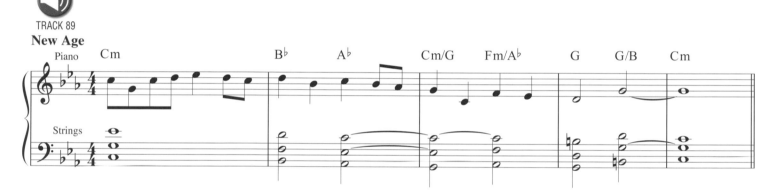

A couple of other interesting points to note about this example:

1) The string part uses open triads (the middle note of the triad has been transposed up an octave). This is an effective string arranging technique, and will help your synth strings to sound more realistic (as opposed to simply playing closed-position triads).

2) Note the slash chord symbols (i.e., Cm/G and Fm/A♭). This type of chord symbol is often used when a note other than the root (i.e., the third or fifth) is the lowest voice. In this case the Cm chord has its fifth (G) on the bottom, and the Fm chord has its third (A♭) on the bottom. This technique enables the lowest string voice to move by half steps, creating a smooth melodic effect.

LIVE PERFORMANCES

As musicians, there are two types of **live performances** we are concerned with: either we are going to see someone else play, or we are performing ourselves. If you are seeing another band perform, you might be showing up to support some friends in the band (always appreciated!), and/or you may be seeing a top act that will inspire and motivate you in your own musical endeavors. Always try to make time to get out to live shows as often as you can. Here in Los Angeles I regularly interact with a lot of pro jazz players, and because there are great musicians playing club gigs here every night of the week, we bemoan the fact that the public is often apathetic and that it can be tough to get people out to shows! So, no matter where you live, check out your local gig listings and/or internet postings, and support live music. It's in everybody's best interest!

If you are performing yourself, you'll of course want to promote your show as effectively as you can; some suggestions for this are given in *Gig Promotion* (p. 76). If you are looking for live performance opportunities, the following guidelines should get you started.

SOLO GIGS

If you are new to playing solo gigs, an open-mic session at a local club or coffeehouse is a good place to get started—particularly if they already have a piano set up. The musicians at these events are mostly singer/songwriters, and you normally get to do one to three songs, depending on the time available.

A lot of clubs, bars, and restaurants have solo piano players, and most of them are also singers. The style of music varies, depending on the establishment. Check out the venues in your area, the musical styles they feature, and the nights of the week when they have music. You can inquire directly with the management at the club or through their agent. For a solo artist or band to be considered by a venue, you'll normally need to submit an EPK (Electronic Press Kit) with an up-to-date bio, pictures, audio tracks, and links to your website and/or YouTube videos if available.

At a higher level of solo work, there is the hotel circuit. Some of my students have played at the Beverly Hills Hotel Polo Lounge, which is perhaps the best hotel gig in the Los Angeles area. These high-end gigs are normally found either by personal recommendation or referral, or through the hotel management or an agent. To have a shot at this type of gig, you need to be very personable and presentable, and have a good repertoire of pop and jazz standards, show tunes, and popular classical music.

BAND GIGS

If your band plays original rock, you need to hit the clubs that cater to that world. (In Los Angeles, that would be the rock clubs along the Sunset Strip, such as the Whisky and the Roxy.) If you play pop/rock/R&B covers, this opens up a wider range of possibilities to play at clubs, bars, and restaurants, particularly on the weekends. Acoustic straight-ahead jazz normally finds a home in coffeehouses, bookstores, hotels, restaurants, and jazz clubs, while contemporary electric jazz is usually performed in clubs specifically dedicated to that style.

Tribute bands can also find work at rock clubs, which will sometimes have a "tribute-band night" (often on a weekend) featuring several groups on one bill. Outdoor events such as festivals, seasonal concerts, and arts-and-crafts shows are also options for cover bands, tribute bands, and jazz bands. These events are often coordinated by city offices or corporate sponsors. Also, some bands specialize in playing at private parties, weddings, and functions; to compete for this type of work, your repertoire, stylistic versatility, and appearance all have to be top-notch!

LOGIC PRO X

Logic Pro is one of the leading DAW (digital audio workstation, see p. 39) software programs currently available. It runs only on the Macintosh computer platform. Logic Pro is a capable all-in-one production suite, and features some great softsynths, including ES2 (an analog and wavetable synthesizer), Sculpture (a physical modeling synth), and Ultrabeat (a drum synthesizer and step sequencer).

Now we'll listen to a couple of musical examples that were created in Logic Pro, and use only the included softsynths (i.e., no third-party instruments). Our first example is in an R&B/funk style, and here we'll spotlight the staccato synth part:

TRACK 90
R&B/Funk

Listen to the track and you'll hear that the synth sound is on the right channel, with the remaining instruments on the left channel. This is a metallic-sounding staccato synth from the ES2 softsynth within Logic. The backing band on the left channel is also all Logic virtual instruments: the electric piano is a "modeled" Rhodes piano from the Vintage Electric Piano instrument, the synth bass is from the EXS24 software sampler, and the drum groove is from the Ultrabeat drum softsynth.

Harmony/Theory Notes

This synth part is created from minor pentatonic scales, built from the root of each chord. For example, the figure in measures 1–2 is derived from the E minor pentatonic scale (E G A B D) built from the root of the E7sus4 chord. Similarly, the figure in measures 3–4 is derived from the F minor pentatonic scale (F A♭ B♭ C E♭) and so on. In measures 1–8 the figure alternates between 4th intervals (i.e., the A-D and B-E intervals in measures 1–2) and single notes, most often the root of the chord. Then in measures 9–16 the single-note figure continues with a lot of 16th-note upbeats or anticipations. This is common in busier funk and fusion styles.

Our next example is in a pop/rock style and features a synth brass comping part:

TRACK 91

Pop/Rock

Listen to the track and you'll hear that the synth brass sound is on the right channel, with the remaining instruments on the left channel. The brass synth sound is produced by the ES2 softsynth, and the backing band includes a clavinet from the Vintage Clav instrument, and the "Fingered Bass" sample from the EXS24 software sampler.

Harmony/Theory Notes

This synth part is mostly created from triads, with some interior resolutions within chords. For example, in measure 3 on the C(add9) chord, the 9th (D) moves to the 3rd (E). Similarly, in measure 4 on the D chord, the 4th (G) moves to the 3rd (F♯). This type of motion adds interest to the part, and is typical of the more "evolved" pop/rock that emerged in the 1980s.

M1

The **Korg M1** is the best-selling digital keyboard of all time, and the best-known workstation keyboard, combining sound generation and sequencing capabilities. From its release in 1988 until it was discontinued six years later, more than 250,000 units were sold. The M1 was a 16-voice polyphonic synthesizer, and it set new standards for other synthesizer manufacturers and models to follow.

The big news about the M1 was that it included samples of real acoustic instruments (piano, bass, guitar, etc.). These were typically used for the attack part of the sound, with the sustain part coming from synthesized waveforms. These were then passed through filter and amplifier sections, and an independent effects section including reverb, delay, flanger and chorus. The sampled waveforms (although basic by today's standards), together with the onboard effects, gave the M1 a depth and realism that was revolutionary at the time.

The M1 also had a Combi (Combination) mode enabling up to eight different sounds (programs) to play simultaneously, up to the unit's polyphony limitations. This structural hierarchy has been used on subsequent generations of Korg workstation keyboards.

Its acoustic piano was perhaps the most famous sound from the M1. This was very compressed, and not at all realistic-sounding by today's standards. However, it became a classic sound in its own right, and was used on many recordings. Here's an example in a "half-time" rock style, using the classic M1 piano sound:

TRACK 92

Half-time Rock

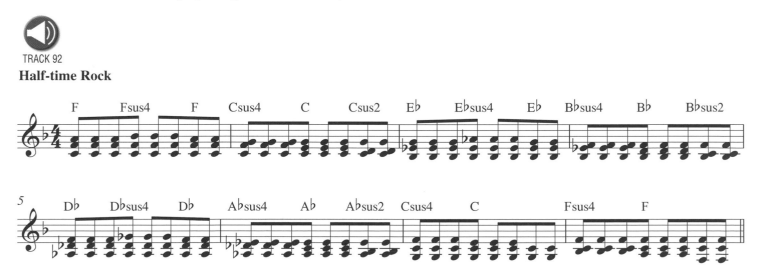

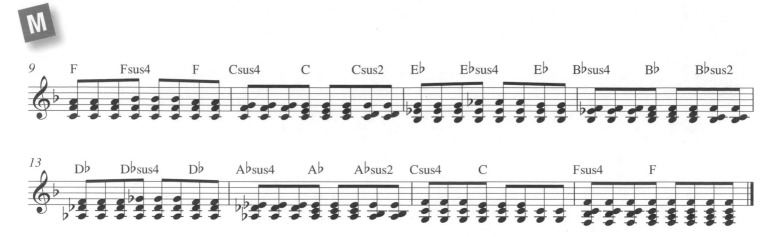

Listen to the track and you'll hear that the M1 piano is on the right channel, and the rest of the band is on the left channel. This piano was recorded using the Korg N364 keyboard (one of the successor generations of Korg workstations), which has the M1 piano as a "legacy sound" on the unit. The backing band on the left channel includes the "Fingered Bass" sample from the EXS24 software sampler within Logic, and, from measure 9 onward, an electric guitar courtesy of the RealStrat virtual instrument.

Harmony/Theory Notes

Note that this piano part consists of eighth-note chords throughout, using interior movements or resolutions. For example, in measure 1 within the F major chord, the note A moves to B♭ and back again: this results in the chord symbols of F, Fsus4, and back to F in this measure. Similarly, in measure 2 within the C major chord, the note F moves to E and then to D: this results in the chord symbols of Csus4, C, and Csus2 in this measure.

The "half-time rock" description refers to the drum groove, with the snare drum landing only on beat 4 of each measure, instead of the more typical 2 and 4. Strictly speaking, the term half-time more correctly refers to the snare drum landing on beat 3; however, the term is also (more informally) used to describe this particular type of situation.

MAJOR SCALE

The **major scale** is the most commonly used scale in Western music. Most famous melodies that you know are constructed from major scales. Like all scales, the major scale is a sequence of notes created using a specific set of intervals. Most scales (including the major scale) are created using half steps and whole steps, although some scales contain larger intervals. Here is a C major scale, showing the specific sequence of whole steps and half steps:

When we construct this pattern of intervals starting on the note C, we use all the remaining white keys on the keyboard. If we start this pattern of intervals from any other note, we'll end up with a mixture of white and black keys. The major scale is a seven-note scale (i.e., there are seven different pitches) that uses all the letter names in the musical alphabet consecutively (with no letter name being used more than once). Now we'll build this pattern of whole steps and half steps from F, to create the F major scale:

Notice that we now have the note B♭ as the 4th degree of this scale. This is because we need a half step between the 3rd and 4th degrees: we already have A as the 3rd degree, and we need to use the next consecutive letter name (B) for the next note, so we flat the B (to B♭) to get the required half step above A. Next, we'll use the same method to build a G major scale:

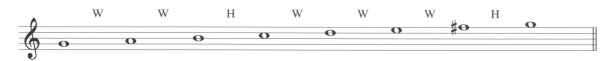

Notice that we now have the note F♯ as the 7th degree of this scale. This is because we need a whole step between the 6th and 7th degrees: we already have E as the 6th degree, and we need to use the next consecutive letter name (F) for the next note, so we sharp the F (to F♯) to get the required whole step above E.

Key Signatures and Keys (p. 102) gives the key signatures for these (and all other) major scales. I would recommend, however, that you learn to build your major scales by using the whole steps and half steps shown above (rather than using key signatures to figure them out), as this more closely parallels how your ear relates to the scale. In other words, your ear will recognize the pattern of whole steps and half steps from any starting note, but it doesn't care how many sharps or flats there are! Thus, I think it is better to build your scales in a way that your ear understands.

MEMORIZING SONGS

In my classes I am sometimes asked about techniques for **memorizing songs**. Memorization is important if you are building up a repertoire, and in particular if you are playing function or casual gigs, where your stylistic versatility and fast transitions between tunes will mean they'll hire you rather than the next guy (or girl)! Also, musical style is a factor when deciding whether the music should be memorized. For example, on jazz gigs it is generally acceptable for musicians to read charts, but on rock gigs the musicians normally play from memory (having charts onstage is not compatible with the energy and vibe of rock music, and in any case most rock musicians play by ear). When I perform with my contemporary jazz quintet here in L.A., I'll take charts for any cover tunes we're doing, but when I perform with my Steely Dan tribute band (which is a rock gig, albeit more sophisticated than the typical rock gig), I have everything memorized.

In contemporary styles, the key to memorizing songs is not to memorize the whole keyboard arrangement (with the exception of any signature parts essential to the song), but rather to memorize the melody, chord changes, and form (i.e., the different sections of the tune, how many measures in each section, etc.). In other words, memorize the information that would be on a chart or leadsheet. Then you can play the voicings and rhythms in a more spontaneous way when you perform the song, as discussed in *Faking It* (p. 64). That way you'll be memorizing less data per song, which should enable you to memorize more songs more quickly! The musical style will influence the degree to which your performance will vary from one gig to the next, as you recall this basic information for each song. For example, on a jazz gig you are more likely to interpret the same song differently each time, whereas in pop or rock styles you're more likely to perform the song in a similar way from one gig to the next.

MIDI

MIDI stands for **musical instrument digital interface**, and is a protocol that keyboards, computers, and other pieces of equipment use to communicate with each other. You can think of MIDI data as a "digital piano roll," containing information regarding which notes are played, their duration, volume, and so on. When MIDI technology first appeared back in the 1980s, there was great excitement at being able to play one keyboard and hear the sounds from another, having connected them with a MIDI cable. This is all very routine today, of course, but back then it was pretty revolutionary.

MIDI technology has several uses. Here are some of the more common ones if you are a performing musician and/or recording music in a home studio environment:

1. Connecting the "MIDI Out" from a controller keyboard to the "MIDI In" of another sound source: either another MIDI keyboard as described above, or a MIDI rack module (a synthesizer and/or sample playback device without a physical keyboard attached), or a MIDI rack computer device (such as the Muse Receptor) that enables you to play back softsynths and plug-ins. You play the controller keyboard and hear the sound(s) of the attached keyboard or module. If your controller keyboard also has onboard sounds, you can then layer and blend the sounds between the different sources.

2. Connecting the "MIDI Out" from a controller keyboard to the "MIDI In" of a MIDI interface connected to a Mac or PC (or, in some cases, directly to the computer). This will then enable you to get MIDI data into and out of your computer, which is useful in various ways including the following:

    a. If you are recording with digital audio workstation (DAW) software (see p. 39), the MIDI data recorded from your controller can then be used to trigger softsynths installed in your computer, and/or external MIDI devices in your system. The MIDI data can be edited and manipulated as needed in your DAW, and this process can then be repeated for each track/instrument in your song.

    b. If you are creating a chart or score with music notation software such as Finale or Sibelius, the MIDI data can be read by the software to produce the score. You'll still probably need to edit and further refine the score somewhat, but this is still much faster than creating the score from scratch. Most DAWs also have notation printing capabilities that are getting better all the time. However, for professional "publishing quality" notation I still prefer to use dedicated music notation software.

    c. If you have acquired MIDI files that you wish to play back and you don't want to use a standard MIDI file player program or your softsynths, you can route the MIDI data to any external MIDI device in your setup, to hear the MIDI files play back on that particular device.

MINIMOOG

The **Minimoog**, manufactured by Moog Music, is perhaps the most famous and revered analog synthesizer of all time. It was a monophonic (one note at once) synthesizer, first released in 1970. Up to that point in time, analog synths were large, modular machines, so the groundbreaking all-in-one design of the Minimoog was largely responsible for synthesizers moving out of the studio and into the world of live performance.

The Minimoog has three voltage-controlled oscillators (VCOs), which then pass through a voltage-controlled filter (VCF) and a voltage-controlled amplifier (VCA). The units have separate envelopes (see p. 58) assigned to the filter and amplifier stages, called ADSD envelopes instead of the more typical ADSR, because both the decay and release times are controlled by a single knob.

The Minimoog's filters use "transistor ladder" technology, a design patented by Moog Music. The Moog filter design is credited with imparting a uniquely warm, vibrant quality to the sound. In the 1970s the Minimoog was popularized by the progressive rock keyboardists Keith Emerson and Rick Wakeman. Emerson is credited with first developing pitch-bending techniques on the instrument, while Wakeman is famously quoted as saying that with a Minimoog, he could "for the first time, go out onstage and give the guitarist a run for his money."

Now we'll look at a couple of music examples using Minimoog-type sounds. Our first example is in a progressive rock style, featuring a lead synth sound with a little glide or portamento (see p. 77) added:

TRACK 93
Progressive Rock

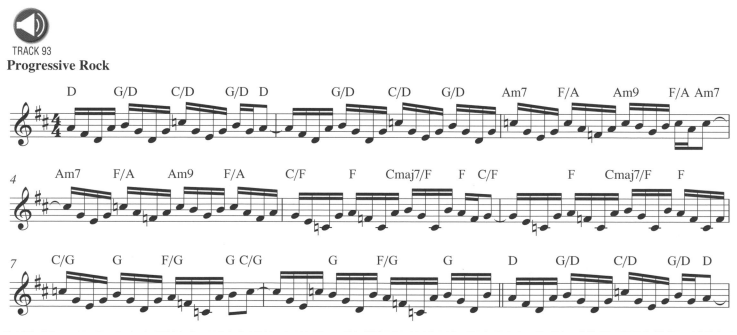

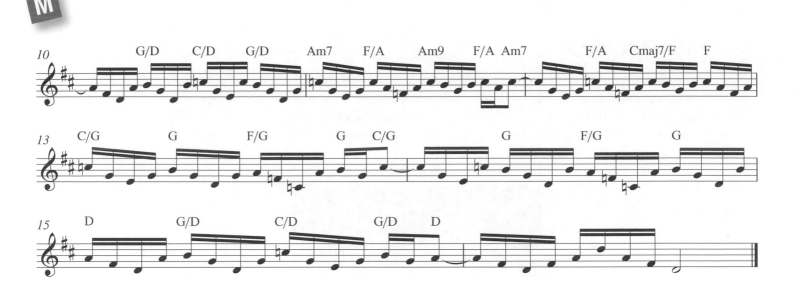

Listen to the track and you'll hear that the synth lead is on the right channel, and the rest of the band is on the left channel. The lead synth sound is a Minimoog emulation from the ES2 softsynth within Logic. The backing band on the left channel includes a bass sound from the EXS24 software sampler (again within Logic), and an organ sound from the Vintage Organs virtual organ instrument (by Native Instruments).

Harmony/Theory Notes

Note that the synth solo part is arpeggiating the upper triads and/or extensions of the chords, using a 16th-note rhythmic subdivision. The drum groove is also placing the snare drum on beat 3 (instead of beat 4) in the odd-numbered measures (i.e., measures 1, 3, 5, etc.). All this is typical of 1970s progressive rock—the band Yes, in particular.

Our next example is in a funk shuffle style, this time featuring a Minimoog-style bass synth sound:

TRACK 94

Funk Shuffle

Listen to the track and you'll hear that the bass synth is on the right channel, with the rest of the band on the left channel. This example uses a swing-16ths feel, in which each pair of 16th notes sounds like a eighth-note/16th-note triplet. This time the Minimoog-style bass is from the Omnisphere softsynth (see p. 133). On the left channel, the backing band includes an electric piano courtesy of the Vintage Electric Piano instrument within Logic.

MINOR SCALES

There are three **minor scales** in common usage: melodic, harmonic, and natural. Here we'll take a look at the intervals present in each, how we can alter a major scale to create each one, and how we might use them in minor-key situations.

First, we'll look at the C melodic minor scale, noting the whole steps and half steps used.

The melodic minor scale is widely used in jazz styles. If we were to take a C major scale and alter it to create a C melodic minor scale, we would lower the 3rd degree by half step (E becomes E♭). If we were to use the C melodic minor scale within a C minor key signature, we would contradict the key signature by raising the 6th and 7th degrees by half step (A♭ becomes A♮, and B♭ becomes B♮). Depending on the musical style, all minor scales may potentially be used in a minor key, which may then require accidentals (sharps or flats contradicting the key signature).

Next up is the C harmonic minor scale.

Note the unusual interval toward the top of this scale: a minor 3rd (equivalent to three half steps, or one-and-a-half steps). Melodically, this gives the scale a somewhat angular sound, which is exploited in various ethnic and Middle Eastern music. Harmonically, the scale is useful for deriving chords in jazz, in part due to the two half steps in the upper part of the scale. If we were to take a C major scale and alter it to create a C harmonic minor scale, we would lower the 3rd and 6th degrees by half step (E becomes E♭, and A becomes A♭). If we were to use the C harmonic minor scale within a C minor key signature, we would contradict the key signature by raising the 7th degree by half step (B♭ becomes B♮).

Our last scale is the C natural minor scale:

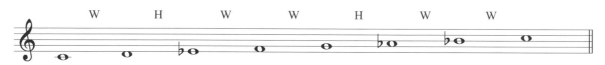

The natural minor scale is widely used in pop and rock styles, and is equivalent to an Aeolian mode (a major scale—E♭ major, in this case—re-positioned to start on its 6th degree). If we were to take a C major scale and alter it to create a C natural minor scale, we would lower the 3rd, 6th, and 7th degrees by half step (E becomes E♭, A becomes A♭, and B becomes B♭). If we were to use the C natural minor scale within a C minor key signature, no adjustments would be needed, as everything conforms to the key signature.

Further Reading

For more information on the harmonic implications of the different minor scales, as well as their uses in minor keys, please check out my *Contemporary Music Theory: Level Two*, published by Hal Leonard LLC.

MIXOLYDIAN MODE

A mode (or modal scale) is created when we take a major scale and displace it to start on another scale degree. An example of this is the **Mixolydian mode**, created when the major scale is displaced to start on the 5th degree. The following example shows a C major scale displaced to create a G Mixolydian mode.

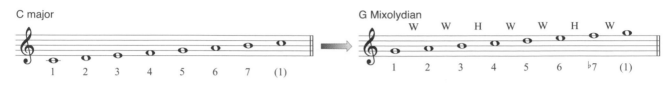

If you compare these two scales, you'll see that the notes are the same; they just begin and end in a different place. Thus each has a different tonic and a different pattern of whole and half steps. You can also think of the Mixolydian mode as a major scale with a flatted 7th degree (1-2-3-4-5-6-♭7). This mode has a dominant sound and is a basic scale source for a dominant seventh chord. We could say that C major is the relative major scale of G Mixolydian, as C major was the scale originally displaced to create the mode.

To use a Mixolydian mode harmonically, we would simply put the tonic of the mode (G in the above example) in the bass, and then place notes and/or chords from the mode (or from its relative major) above this bass note. A common tactic is to use diatonic triads from the relative major. For example, the diatonic triads in C major are C, Dm, Em, F, G, Am, and Bdim. Placing any of these above the tonic G is an effective way to create Mixolydian harmony.

Our first example is in a swing-sixteenths funk or hip-hop style, and uses triads from the C, B♭, A♭, and F Mixolydian modes. For example, on the C7 chords we are using a mix of Edim, F, Gm, Am, and B♭ upper triads, all of which are diatonic to the F major scale (the relative major of C Mixolydian). Similarly, on the B♭7 chords we are using triads (Ddim, E♭, and F) from the B♭ Mixolydian mode (relative of the E♭ major scale), and so on.

TRACK 95

Hip-Hop Funk

Note the alternating 16th-note rhythms between the hands, typical of contemporary funk styles.

Next up we have a blues shuffle using Mixolydian modes and triads.

TRACK 96

This 12-measure blues example uses D Mixolydian triads (F♯dim, G, Am, Bm) over the D7 chord, then uses G Mixolydian triads (Am, G, F) over the G7 chord, and so on. Note the left-hand pattern that moves from the flatted third to the third of each chord during beats 2 and 4 of each measure. This is a signature sound in Chicago-style blues.

Also notice that both of these Mixolydian examples use a lot of inverted triads in the right-hand parts. Modal triads tend to sound better when inverted. Second-inversion triads are used the most, due to their strong and powerful sound.

For another important mode, see *Dorian Mode* (p. 44).

MODAL SCALES

A **mode** (or **modal scale**) is created when we take a major scale and displace it to start on another scale degree. We'll use the C major scale as the basis for these examples. The mode name given to an undisplaced major scale (i.e., a major scale starting on its regular tonic) is Ionian.

C major (or C Ionian)

This scale can then be displaced to start on other scale degrees, creating the following modes.

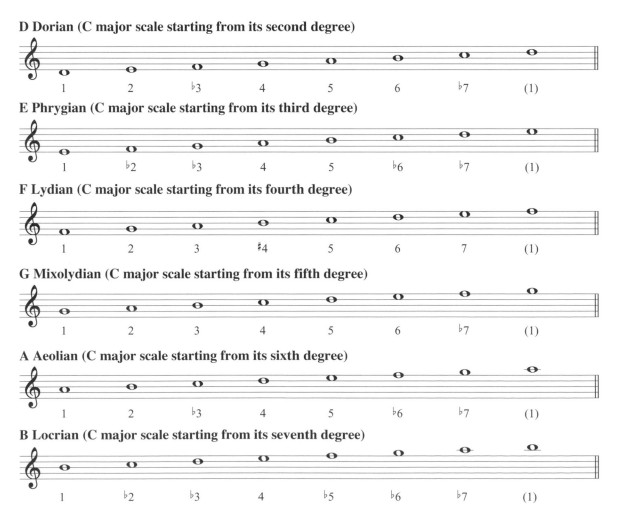

D Dorian (C major scale starting from its second degree)

E Phrygian (C major scale starting from its third degree)

F Lydian (C major scale starting from its fourth degree)

G Mixolydian (C major scale starting from its fifth degree)

A Aeolian (C major scale starting from its sixth degree)

B Locrian (C major scale starting from its seventh degree)

Modal scales (especially the Dorian and Mixolydian) are widely used in contemporary music. The more angular sounds of the Phrygian and Locrian modes (which both start with a half step) are generally reserved for jazz and other more sophisticated styles.

MODULATION

In the synthesizer world, **modulation** is the process of continuously varying a component of the sound, creating a particular effect or sonic characteristic. Some of the more commonly used types of modulation are listed as follows:

- *Amplitude Modulation* occurs when the amplifier stage is modulated, for example, by a low-frequency oscillator to produce a tremolo effect. [Note that we are not talking here about amplitude modulation (or AM) as the term applies to radio waves or communication technology.]

- *Filter Modulation* occurs when the filter stage is modulated, for example, by an LFO to produce a wah-wah or filter-sweep effect.

- *Frequency Modulation* (see p. 70) is a synthesis method that modulates a simple waveform with another waveform in the audio range, creating complex sounds.

- *Pitch Modulation* occurs when the pitch of a sound is modulated, for example, by a low-frequency oscillator to produce a vibrato effect (see p. 189).

- *Ring Modulation* is the product of taking two different waveforms and then outputting the sum and difference of the frequencies present in each waveform. This resulting signal is rich in overtones, and useful for metallic and bell-like sounds. This feature was commonly implemented on early modular synthesizers, but was less common on all-in-one analog synthesizers and workstation keyboards. However, with the advent of physical modeling (see p. 141) and softsynths, ring modulation has had something of a resurgence in popularity.

MODULATION WHEEL

On a synthesizer, the **modulation wheel** (or **mod wheel**) is a controller in the shape of a wheel, normally to the immediate left of the lowest note on the keyboard. The wheel is imbedded in the surface of the unit, so that only the top part is visible. Movement of the wheel is then used to add expression or to modulate some aspect of the sound. This is normally a programmable function, meaning that the mod wheel's effect can be programmed within a particular sound (or program) on the synthesizer. Typical uses of the mod wheel include the following:

- adding vibrato (repetitive variation in pitch, see p. 189).

- changing the timbre of the sound by altering the filter cut-off frequency (see p. 67).

- adding or altering effects (see p. 54): for example, increasing the reverb, or changing the speed of rotary speaker emulation.

- detuning (or increasing the "out-of-tuneness") between two oscillators.

The following example contains two single notes, and demonstrates two of these mod wheel usages: the timbre change (on the first note), and the detuning between two oscillators (on the second note). The simple analog synth sound used is from the ES2 softsynth within Logic.

First note:

For this synth program, the mod wheel is routed to the filter cutoff point. The note starts off fairly dark, due to the filter's low cutoff frequency. Then as the mod wheel is moved, the note gets brighter as the cutoff is raised, which then "opens" the filter.

Second note:

For this synth program, the mod wheel is routed to the detuning between the oscillators. The note starts off "in tune." Then as the mod wheel is moved, the note gets progressively more "out-of-tune" as the oscillators are slightly detuned from one another. Then as the mod wheel is moved back, the note becomes "in tune" again.

MONOPHONIC SYNTHESIZER

A **monophonic synthesizer** can sound only one note at a time. The first analog synthesizers were almost always monophonic, although some early units, notably the ARP Odyssey and the Moog Sonic Six, offered duophonic (two-note) capability. By the late 1970s polyphonic synthesizers, with the ability to sound multiple notes at once, began to emerge.

Although the arrival of polyphonic synthesizers was very significant, this did not mean that monophonic synthesizers were no longer used. For example, musicians playing synth bass or lead parts (two of the most common uses for classic analog synths) need only one note at a time. So, monophonic and polyphonic synths are often found side-by-side in today's professional keyboard rigs.

It is desirable for modern keyboard synthesizers (and softsynths) to be able to emulate a monophonic playing mode (mono mode) to prevent multiple notes from "overlapping." Some synthesizers also offer a *legato* option within the monophonic mode, which prevents the note being "re-triggered" as long as a key is being held down on the keyboard. We'll now demonstrate these playing options with the following music example:

TRACK 98

Note that this example contains multiple parts on the same staff. For instance, in measure 1 the first A (whole note) lasts for four beats, and this is held while the remaining notes are played during the measure.

This track uses an analog lead synth sound from the ES2 softsynth within Logic, and is played three times with exactly the same playing technique each time: the low A is played and held down by the thumb at the beginning of each measure, while the other notes are played with the upper fingers of the right hand. However, the sound is very different each time, depending on the playing mode setting on the synthesizer:

Poly (polyphonic) mode   For the initial performance of this example, the synth is in **poly mode**. This is the normal (default) mode for most synths. Each part in the example is played, and all notes "trigger" their respective envelopes, which for this sound results in a short, pronounced attack for each note.

Mono (monophonic) mode

The second time, the synth is in **mono mode**. This allows only one note to be played at one time (which is always the most recent note played on the keyboard, if more than one note is being held down). So in this music example, the low A "cuts out" when the high A is played, halfway through beat 1. Then at the start of beat 2, the low A is "re-triggered" when the high A is released on the keyboard. This is again "cut out" by the G which follows, and so on.

Legato mode

The third time, the synth is in **legato mode**. This is a type of mono mode where the envelopes are not re-triggered as long as a note is being held down on the keyboard. As soon as all notes are released, the very next note will re-trigger, and so on. In this example, we hear only the short attack of the first A in each measure; the other notes sound smooth and legato, as their envelopes are not re-triggering. Then because all the notes are released right before the second measure, the envelopes are re-triggered for the first A in that measure, and so on.

NEIGHBOR TONES

Neighbor tones are embellishments added to a melody or solo line, which lead into another note by a whole step or half step. First of all, we'll see how to add neighbor tones to a melody in a basic country/pop style.

TRACK 99

Country/Pop

The first eight measures show the melody without neighbor tones. In the last eight measures the same melody is repeated, this time with neighbor tones added. In this simple country style, the neighbor tones are *grace notes*, most a whole step away from the main note. The melody is derived from pentatonic scales (i.e., G pentatonic over the G chord, C pentatonic over the C chord, etc.), and the neighbor tones can also be derived from these scales. In this style, neighbor tones (sometimes referred to as "hammers") are typically of short duration.

The next example applies neighbor tones when improvising in a jazz swing style. When soloing over chord changes, one of the various techniques available is to use arpeggios. We can then add neighbor tones to these arpeggios for further variation and interest. This example uses a II-V-I progression (four-part chords built from the 2nd, 5th, and 1st degrees of the key), which is a staple sound in mainstream jazz styles. The first eight measures show just the arpeggiated chord tones, which we will use as our *target notes*, a framework for embellishment. The last eight measures then show upper and lower neighbors built around these chord tones. In this jazz swing style, the upper neighbors are normally diatonic to the key (in this case C major), but the lower neighbors can always move by half step. For example, in measure 10 the A (fifth of the Dm7 chord) is preceded by the upper neighbor B and lower neighbor G# during beat 4 of the previous measure. B is a diatonic upper neighbor, while G# is a chromatic lower neighbor (i.e., it is not contained within a C major scale). The extra "leading" quality of these half steps is a signature jazz improv sound.

TRACK 100

Jazz/Swing

There are, of course, many rhythmic re-phrasing possibilities here. Try applying some eighth-note anticipations, and don't forget to swing the eighth notes!

NEW AGE

New Age is an American instrumental music style that emerged in the 1980s, with an emphasis on calming sounds and the avoidance of harsh textures. Most piano-based New Age music uses arpeggios in the left and/or right hands at slow-to-medium tempos, and often borrows from classical and smooth jazz styles. Our first New Age example uses two-handed arpeggios within an eighth-note rhythmic subdivision.

TRACK 101

New Age (Eighths)

This example uses gently flowing arpeggios that begin in the left hand and continue with the right hand, anticipating beats 3 and 4 in each measure. Almost all New Age styles require you to depress the sustain pedal for each chord (make sure you release the pedal at the point of chord change). Note the very open, transparent sound that results from using the various double-4th voicings in the right hand.

Chord Voicing Tips

This example uses the root and fifth of each chord in the left hand, with various double-4th (two consecutive 4ths) shapes and their inversions in the right hand, as follows:

- The G⁶/₉ and F⁶/₉ chords are voiced by building a double 4th from the sixth (E-A-D and D-G-C, respectively).

- The Csus2, Dsus2, and Gsus2 chords are all voiced by building double 4ths from the ninth (D-G-C, E-A-D and A-D-G, respectively) with some inversions and octave doubling.

- The B♭⁶/₉ chord is voiced by building a double 4th from the third (D-G-C).

The next New Age example uses a 16th-note rhythmic subdivision, and is again played in a very legato and flowing style. This time the right hand alternates between 5ths and 6ths intervals within the various upper-structure triads. For example, in the right hand of measure 1 on the Dmaj9 chord, we have an A major triad (bottom to top: E-A-C♯-E) split so that the A and the top E land on beat 1, and the C♯ and the bottom E land on the last 16th of beat 1. Splitting a triad (with the top note doubled an octave lower) into intervals this way is a common technique in ballad and New Age styles.

TRACK 102

New Age (16ths)

The left hand is playing open arpeggio patterns on each chord, similar to the open triads on Track 109 (p. 135), but with some extensions added to the chords.

Chord Voicing Tips

In this example, the right hand is using upper-structure triads (split into 5ths and 6ths) as follows:

- The Dmaj9, Cmaj9, and B♭maj9 chords are all voiced by building major triads from the fifth: A/D, G/C, and F/B♭.

- The B11 and A11 chords are voiced by building major triads from the seventh: A/B and G/A.

Also, the Dsus2 chord is voiced by building a double 4th from the ninth (E-A-D), with the D doubled an octave below.

The left hand is playing the following open arpeggio patterns:

- The Dmaj9, Cmaj9, and B♭maj9 chords all use a "1-5-7" pattern (D-A-C♯, C-G-B, and B♭-F-A).

- The B11 and A11 chords use a "1-5-9" pattern (B-F♯-C♯ and A-E-B).

- The G/B and A/C♯ chords use a "3-1-3" pattern (B-G-B and C♯-A-C♯).

NOISE GENERATOR

In a synthesizer, a **noise generator** is an oscillator that produces noise instead of a pitched waveform. Noise is an important component of many synthesized sounds, including "breathy" synth pads, seashore and wind sound effects, and electronic percussion sounds, to name just a few.

Different types of noise have different combinations of frequencies, and are described with colors (white noise, pink noise, etc.). This is an analogy to the appearance of colors with a similar frequency makeup. For example, white noise has all frequencies equally represented, and is called "white" because white light contains all optical frequencies. White noise has a very bright sound, and is used to synthesize electronic drum sounds such as snare drums, hi-hats, and crash cymbals.

Pink noise is also commonly used, and sounds darker than white noise. In pink noise, every octave (successive doubling of the frequency) contains the same energy and volume, which is why this type of noise is used as a reference signal by engineers. Pink noise can be derived by applying a low-pass filter (see p. 67) to white noise, progressively attenuating the higher frquencies. Pink noise is very useful as a component in warm-sounding synth pads, and in generating ocean wave effects.

Here are examples of white noise and pink noise, produced using the Atmosphere softsynth:

TRACK 103

The first noise segment on this track is a *white noise* example.

The second noise segment on this track is a *pink noise* example.

Here are some more noise types you may encounter:

- *Red noise* is darker than pink noise, with more filtering of the upper frequencies (a "steeper slope" applied to the low-pass filter).

- *Blue noise* is equivalent to white noise passed through a high-pass filter, leaving minimal low frequencies and a lot of high frequencies.

- *Grey noise* boosts the lowest and highest frequencies, giving a perception of being equally loud at all frequencies, due to the natural bias of the human ear.

Many classic synthesizers (including the Minimoog, see p. 117) include a noise generator as one of their sound sources. This trend continues in the 21st century, in softsynths such as Logic's ES2 and Native Instruments' Reaktor.

OCTAVES

An **octave** is the interval between a note and the next-occurring note of the same name, either higher or lower on the keyboard. Many contemporary styles make use of octave patterns in the left- and/or right-hand parts. Our first example using octaves is in a boogie-woogie style.

TRACK 104

Boogie-Woogie

This example uses octaves throughout the right-hand part, giving a strong and powerful sound. The chord progression is a basic 12-bar blues in C, and the right-hand motifs are derived mostly from the C and A blues scales. A minor is the relative minor scale of C major, and it is common to use phrases from both the blues scales built from the tonic and the one built from the relative minor (i.e., the C blues scale and the A blues scale in the key of C). For example, in measures 1–2 the right-hand notes all come from the A blues scale, but in measures 3–4 the right-hand notes all come from the C blues scale. Meanwhile, the left hand is playing the root of each chord in octaves, before connecting the third to the fifth by half steps (E-F-F#-G on the C7 chord). This is all very typical of boogie-woogie and early blues styles.

Our next example is in a driving hard rock style, using octaves in both hands.

Hard Rock

Note that this example doesn't use any chords at all, just single lines in octaves. The chord symbols, however, are implied by the melody notes in conjunction with the bass line. The steady eighth-note pulse in the left hand is a common ingredient in pop/rock and hard rock styles.

Our last example is in a fast gospel style, using octaves within a straight-16th-note rhythmic subdivision.

Fast Gospel

Note that while the C7 chord is implied throughout this example, there is considerable movement within the chord—which is typical of more sophisticated gospel music. The I-IV-I (C major-F major-C major) right-hand movement over beats 1–2 in measures 1, 3, 5, and 7 is an example of backcycling, a technique first encountered on Track 29 (p. 34). Otherwise, the single-note lines in octaves are again derived from a mix of C and A blues scales. The left-hand octave pattern lands on the root of the chord (C) on beat 1 of each measure, and then either walks back up to the root in half steps (A-B♭-B♮-C) or up to the third in half steps (D-E♭-E♮). Make sure to catch the 16th-note anticipations in the right hand, as this is important to the style!

OMNISPHERE

Omnisphere is a softsynth or virtual instrument created by Spectrasonics, whose founder Eric Persing is one of the leading synthesists and sound designers in the world. Omnisphere runs as a plug-in within a digital audio workstation host (see p. 39), such as Digital Performer, Logic, Cubase, et al.

In a crowded softsynth market, Omnisphere stands out as a powerful and evocative creator of lush synth textures and dynamically morphing sounds. It has become a staple in studios and post-production facilities worldwide, and is constantly heard on movie soundtracks and trailers, TV scores, and commercial recordings.

Omnisphere synth sounds normally consist of two layers, each of which can be extensively edited to give an almost unlimited number of sounds. Our first music example is in an electronic/trance style, and features an Omnisphere sound created from layered samples of Roland Juno and Yamaha CS-80 synthesizers:

TRACK 107
Electronic/Trance

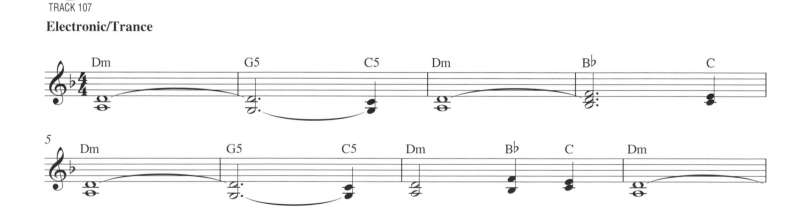

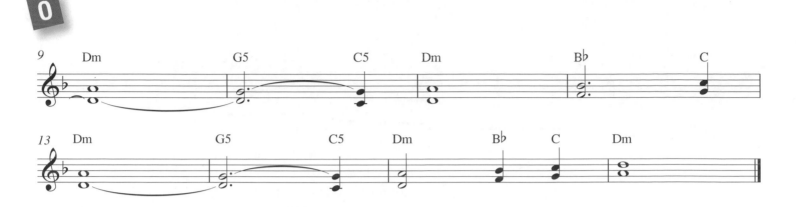

Listen to the track and you'll hear that the Omnisphere synth pad is on the right channel, and the rest of the band is on the left channel. The sweeping effect on the synth pad is caused by an envelope (see p. 58), which causes the filter (see p. 67) to open during the attack time (see p. 19) for each note. In the backing band, the ES2 synth plug-in within Logic (see p. 111) is providing a characteristic trance-style analog synth bass sound.

Harmony/Theory Notes

Note that the synth part consists mainly of roots and 5ths of the various chords. (The chord symbol suffix 5 means "the root and 5th of the chord only," i.e., omitting the 3rd.) This creates a simple, transparent voicing sound, and is used in many contemporary styles—from hard rock through to electronic dance music.

Our next Omnisphere example is in a dramatic/film score style, and features an evolving sound that handily demonstrates this softsynth's sound morphing capabilities. This sound was created by layering samples of granular and additive synthesizers:

TRACK 108

Dramatic/Film Score

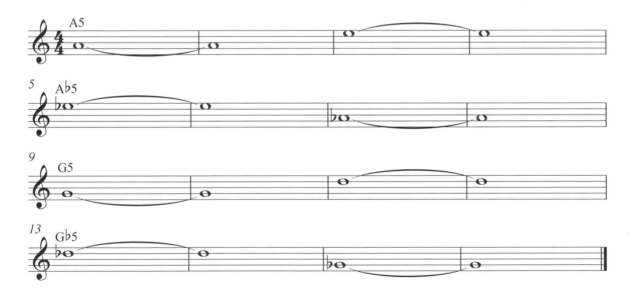

Notice how large and intricate the Omnisphere synth sounds on the right channel, even though only one note is being played! The remaining instruments on the left channel consist of a bass ensemble, timpani hits and rolls, and orchestral snare drums, all from the Kontakt software sampler and synthesizer (see p. 103).

OPEN TRIADS

An **open triad** is created when the middle note of a triad (whether in root position or inverted) is moved up or down by one octave. This creates an overall span, from the lowest to highest note, greater than one octave. We saw this technique used in *Legato Playing* (p. 109) to harmonize a melody with a string pad. In this section we will use open-triad arpeggios as a left-hand pattern in both eighth-note and 16th-note ballad styles. We'll apply these arpeggios to the same progression used on Tracks 17 and 18 (p. 20), beginning with this eighth-note pop ballad example.

TRACK 109

This example includes several chord symbols designating inverted harmonies in which a major or minor triad is placed over its third or fifth in the bass. Common open-triad left-hand patterns are: root-fifth-third when the chord symbol is not inverted (i.e., the Em chord); third-root-fifth when the triad is placed over its third in the bass (i.e., the D/F♯ chord); and fifth-third-root when the triad is placed over its fifth in the bass (i.e., the B/F♯ chord). The right-hand part is mostly a mix of triads, suspended chords, and add9 chords (note how the ninth resolves to the root in measures 2 and 6). Next, we'll see the same chord progression used with a 16th-note R&B ballad comping pattern.

TRACK 110

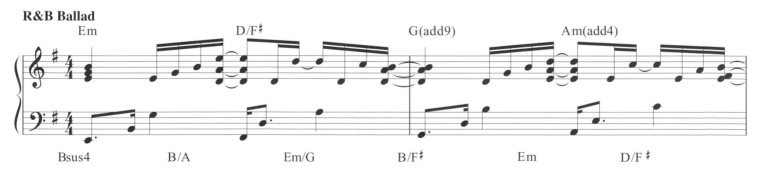

O

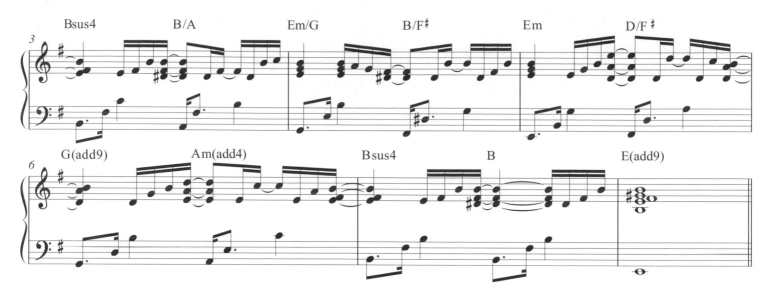

Here we see the voicings in the right hand anticipate beat 3 by a 16th-note in most measures, which is typical of R&B ballads. The right hand is playing triads, suspensions, and added ninths similar to those in the previous example, now with some 16th-note arpeggios during beats 2 and 4. The left hand is playing the same open-triad arpeggios as in the previous example, now rhythmically re-phrased for the 16th-note style (the middle note of the arpeggio is placed on either the second or fourth 16th-note of the beat).

OSTINATO

An **ostinato** is a musical figure that is repeated throughout a section of a song (or sometimes throughout the *whole* song). In contemporary piano styles, ostinatos are often repeated against changing chords, and can occur in the left or right hands. Our first example uses an ostinato in the left hand, in an R&B dance/pop style.

TRACK 111

The left-hand ostinato is a repeating two-measure phrase derived from an A minor pentatonic scale (A-C-D-E-G), placing the root of the Am7 chord on beat 1 and the root of the Dm7 chord on the last sixteenth note of beat 4 (anticipating the following downbeat) in measures 1, 3, 5, and 7.

Chord Voicing Tips

In this example the right hand is using upper-structure triads as follows:

- The Am7 and Dm7 chords are voiced by building major triads from the third: C/A and F/D.

The next example uses a two-measure ostinato in the right hand, in a pop/rock style. This right-hand part uses a double-4th shape (G-C-F) in a combination of first and second inversions (C-F-G and F-G-C), creating a right-hand shape of C-F-G-C from bottom to top. Although this might just look like a Csus4 chord (which is indeed the result when placed over C in the bass, as in the first measure), this same shape creates some very interesting chord qualities when placed over different roots.

TRACK 112

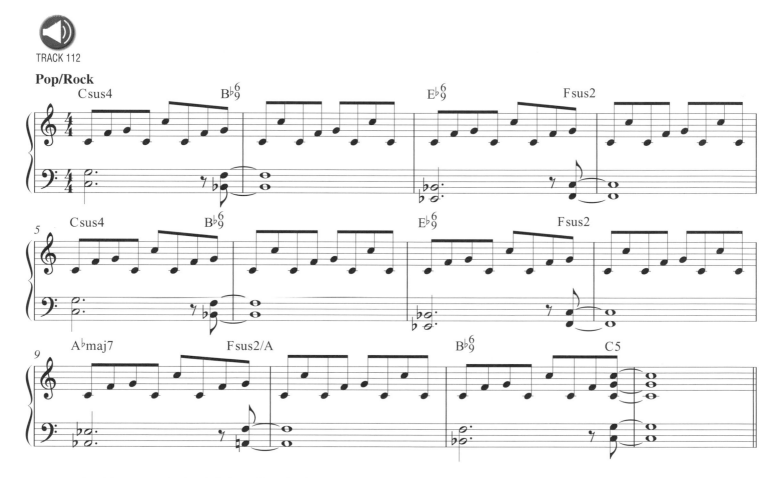

In this example the left hand is playing root-fifth intervals throughout (except for the third-root interval on the Fsus2/A chord), landing on beat 1 of the odd-numbered measures and anticipating beat 1 of all the even-numbered measures.

Chord Voicing Tips

In this example the right hand's double-4th shape G-C-F (inverted and doubled to create the C-F-G-C right-hand voicing) has been built from the following chord tones:

- The fifth of the Csus4 chord
- The sixth of the B♭6/9 chord
- The third of the E♭6/9 chord
- The ninth of the Fsus2 (and Fsus2/A) chords
- The seventh of the A♭maj7 chord

PAD

The term **pad** or **synth pad** is used in two different ways—as a music arrangement term, and as a sound description:

- In a music arrangement context, a synth pad is a sustained musical part played on a synthesizer. Normally a synth pad will use two or more notes at once, although the term is sometimes used to refer to single-note sustained lines.

- In a sound description context, a synth pad is a sustained, mellow sound suitable for background harmony and texture. Pad sounds often have slow attacks (see p. 19) and have string- or vocal-like characteristics that help them "blend in" with the track. Many of today's keyboard synthesizers and softsynths have one or more preset banks of pads for you to use.

Some synthesizers are particularly noted for the quality of their pads. That's the main reason the Omnisphere softsynth (see p. 133) has been so successful: the quality and depth of its pad sounds, even though it also includes a great selection of other types of sounds.

Now we'll check out a music example in a neo-soul style, which uses a synth pad in its arrangement:

TRACK 113

Neo-Soul

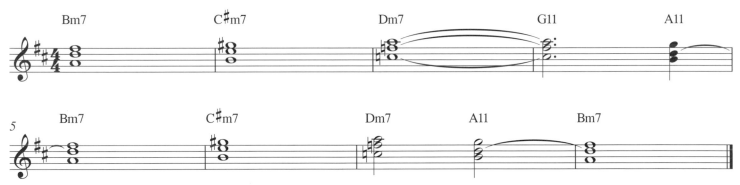

Listen to the track and you'll hear that the synth pad is on the right channel, with the rest of the band on the left channel. Try listening to the track both with and without the pad (i.e., by turning down the right channel), and you can also experiment with the level of the pad you think is appropriate. Most mixing engineers I know, prefer not to mix the synth pads at too high a level—the pads are a subtle glue that can hold the track together, and would be missed if they weren't there.

The pad in this case is produced from Native Instruments' Massive softsynth, using a blend of sawtooth and square waveforms, plus some noise to add breathiness to the sound. The backing band includes a Moog-style synth bass from the Omnisphere softsynth, and a Rhodes electric piano from Vintage Electric Piano within Logic.

Harmony/Theory Notes

The above synth pad part makes use of upper structure triads. For example, the right-hand notes on the Bm7 chord form a D major triad (D F♯ A). These are the 3rd, 5th and 7th of the Bm7 chord, and can be thought of as a major triad (D major in this case) built from the 3rd of the chord (Bm7 in this case). Other upper structure triads are also used in this example, as follows:

- the right-hand notes on the C♯m7 chord form an E major triad (built from the 3rd of the chord)

- the right-hand notes on the Dm7 chord form an F major triad (built from the 3rd of the chord)

- the right-hand notes on the G11 chord form an F major triad (built from the 7th of the chord)

- the right-hand notes on the A11 chord form a G major triad (built from the 7th of the chord)

PENTATONIC SCALE

The **pentatonic scale** (sometimes referred to as "major pentatonic") is a five-note scale that is widely used in rock, country, and gospel styles. Here is an example of a G pentatonic scale.

TRACK 114
Part 1

The G pentatonic scale contains the following notes (with intervals above the tonic G in parentheses): G, A (major 2nd), B (major 3rd), D (perfect 5th), and E (major 6th). This scale is equivalent to a major scale with the 4th and 7th degrees removed.

Here is an example, in a traditional 3/4 slow gospel style, that uses the pentatonic scale to create a fill.

TRACK 114
Part 2

In measure 2, the G pentatonic scale (G-A-B-D-E) is used in ascending octaves to connect between the G and C major chords. This is a very effective way to build energy and to change registers (the right-hand voicing on beat 1 of measure 3 is an octave higher than that on beat 1 of measure 2). Otherwise the right hand is playing triads (with octave doubling), and the left hand is playing a mix of intervals (root-fifth and root-sixth), octaves, and single notes.

Chord Voicing Tips

In this example, the right hand is using backcycling and upper-structure triads as follows:

- On the G chord, the right hand is backcycling (alternating between I and IV triads).
- On the C chord, the right hand is alternating between a major triad built from the root (C), and a minor triad built from the sixth (Am).
- The D11 chord is voiced by building different inversions of a major triad from the seventh: C/D.

PERSONAL DIGITAL STUDIO

A **personal digital studio** is a self-contained, portable hard-disk multitrack recorder, and can be thought of as the twenty-first-century successor to the tape-based Portastudio machines introduced in the 1980s. You can record parts from your favorite keyboard or synthesizer directly into the machine (by connecting the audio outputs from your keyboard to the audio inputs on the recorder). You can then record the piano part on track 1, bass on track 2, and so on. You can also record other non-keyboard instruments (guitar, sax, voice, etc.) with a microphone connected to the mic inputs. When you're done recording, you can then combine all the elements into a final mix and burn a CD. Some units will also have built-in drum loops and bass sounds to give you a head start with your rhythm section tracks.

Popular examples of personal digital studios (manufacturers in parentheses) are:

Budget:

DP-008EX (Tascam)

Micro-BR-80 (Boss)

Mid-range:

DP-24SD (Tascam)

R24 (Zoom)

High-end:

DP-32SD (Tascam)

Compared to stand-alone workstation keyboards and digital audio workstation software, the pros and cons of using a personal digital studio are:

> **Pros**: Self-contained and portable. Can go from start to finish (including burning an audio CD). Ability to record non-keyboard sounds (i.e., vocals, horns, etc.) using a microphone. Faders to control the volume levels of each track, which helps when mixing. Learning curve typically faster than for computer-based systems.

> **Cons**: Limited to number of tracks available in the machine. Limited editing, mixing, and effects functions compared to computer-based recording systems.

PHYSICAL MODELING

Physical modeling is a synthesis technology that uses algorithms and equations to digitally duplicate the physical characteristics of a particular instrument. Parameter values are entered which then affect the "modeled" sound which is produced. For example, in a modeled violin instrument, values might be entered to describe the width of the bow, the resonance of the strings, the soundboard response and so on. Similarly, in a modeled guitar instrument you might see parameters for string thickness, pick characteristics (how hard or soft), distance from the bridge where the string is plucked, and so on. Modeling can also create unique instruments, by using parameter values that have no real-world equivalent: for example, a piano with a 30-foot soundboard, or a guitar with strings one inch thick.

Physical modeling is often compared to sampling, as both synthesis methods are used to emulate the sound of an existing instrument. As you might expect, both approaches have their pros and cons. When you play a note using a trumpet sound on a sample-playback synth, what you hear is an exact digital recording of the trumpet. However, it is often difficult to impart expressiveness to a musical phrase (like a real trumpet player would) when you're simply playing back samples. By contrast, when playing a trumpet sound using a modeling instrument, you might be able to vary parameters such as lip tension, blowing pressure, valve positions and so on. This should all lead to a more expressive and authentic performance. How realistic it sounds will depend in part on how good the modeled instrument or softsynth is. Not surprisingly, this will be a matter of opinion (and debate!) among musicians.

The necessary processing power and storage/memory is another important difference between physical modeling and sampling. Sample playback needs less processing power, but more memory and/or disk drive capacity. Conversely, physical modeling can be very processor-intensive, but doesn't need the storage capacity since samples are not being used.

In the 21st century, increasingly sophisticated softsynths using physical modeling are possible, due to the increase in computer power now available. An interesting example is Modartt's Pianoteq, a modeled virtual piano instrument. The Pianoteq piano has a very clean sound, with good velocity response and many adjustable parameters including the tuning.

Now we'll look at a couple of physical modeling synthesis examples using Sculpture, a modeled synth plug-in included with Logic. The first example is in an instrumental New Age style and features a solo acoustic guitar playing arpeggio patterns. Note that this is not a sample of an acoustic guitar; this sound has been synthesized using the physical modeling capabilities within Sculpture:

TRACK 115

New Age

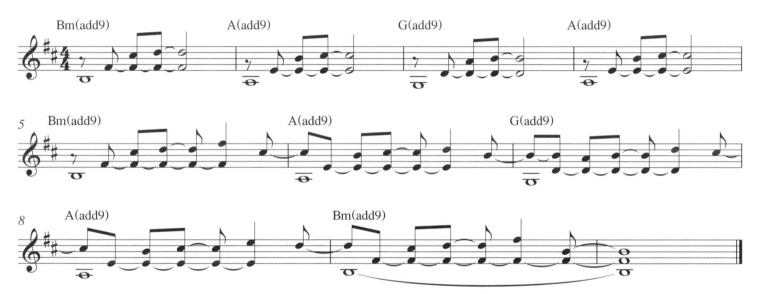

Harmony/Theory Notes

Note this part sounds an octave lower than written, for consistency with normal (or non-synthesized) guitar writing. The guitar is a transposing instrument, and a guitarist will play one octave lower than written on the guitar part. The guitar arpeggios use the root, 5th, 9th, and 3rd of each chord, resulting in a spacious, open sound.

Our next example is in a pop/funk style, featuring a modeled marimba sound from Sculpture:

TRACK 116

Pop/Funk

Listen to the track and you'll hear the modeled marimba sound on the right channel, and the rest of the band (including the Native Instruments Scarbee slap bass, and a chorused Rhodes piano from the Applied Acoustic Systems' Lounge Lizard virtual instrument) on the left channel.

Harmony/Theory Notes

This marimba part is derived from minor pentatonic scales. In the first two measures, the line over the Am11 chord is derived from the A minor pentatonic scale (A C D E G). Similarly, in the next two measures, the line over the Gm711 chord is derived from the G minor pentatonic scale (G B♭ C D F). These lines are then repeated over the following Fmaj9 and E♭maj9 chords, and so on. Also, no key signature has been written, as the keys are changing frequently in this example.

Other notable softsynths using physical modeling are Applied Acoustics Systems' String Studio (for guitars, basses, harps, and bowed instruments), and Arturia's Brass (for trumpets, trombones, and saxophones).

PITCH BEND

On a synthesizer, **pitch bend** occurs as a result of moving the **pitch bend wheel**, which is normally located to the left of the lowest note on the keyboard. When the wheel is moved up from its center position, the pitch is sharped; when the wheel is moved down from its center position, the pitch is flatted. The amount of pitch bend (i.e., the degree to which the pitch is sharped or flatted) is a programmable function on modern-day synthesizers.

Most sound programs (or patches) have a default pitch bend setting of a whole step. If you play the note C on a synth with this pitch bend setting, and then move the wheel all the way up, the pitch of the note will slide up to a D. If you wanted the pitch to bend up only by a half-step (C#), you will have to use your ears to determine when the wheel has been moved far enough. This is an important skill for synth lead and bass players to acquire.

Although the whole-step bend range is the most common, this range can be adjusted (e.g., to the interval of a 5th or to an octave) depending on the player's style and preference. Most modern synths have a spring-loaded mechanism to return the pitch bend wheel to the center position, and a "deadband" right around this center position, in which no pitch change occurs.

Our first music example is in a funk shuffle style, and applies pitch bend techniques to a synth bass. Here the pitch bend setting is the normal default of a whole-step, so I'm using my ears to make sure the half-step bends are correct in the bass part:

TRACK 117

Funk Shuffle

Listen to this track and you'll hear that the synth bass sound is on the right channel, and the rest of the band is on the left channel. This example uses a swing-16ths feel, in which each pair of 16th notes sounds like an eighth-note/16th-note triplet. Fire up a bass patch (with whole-step pitch bend) on your favorite synth and try playing along! Don't forget to listen to your pitch bends, to check that you are playing the half-step intervals correctly.

This Moog-style bass sound was produced by the Applied Acoustic Systems' Ultra Analog modeling synth. On the left channel, the backing band includes an organ pad from the Native Instruments Vintage Organs plug-in, a staccato comping synth from their FM8 softsynth, and acoustic drums courtesy of the BFD virtual drum instrument.

Harmony/Theory Notes

Like most funk bass lines, this bass part covers the roots of the chord at the "points of chord change," with some 16th-note rhythmic embellishments in between. The bass phrases can also be thought of in terms of scale sources. For example, the first two measures (including the F♯-G bend in measure 1) come from the E natural minor (a.k.a. E Aeolian) scale, and the next two measures (including the A-B♭ bend in measure 3) come from the E blues scale, hence the bluesy quality of the bass line in measure 3.

Our next example is in an R&B ballad style, and uses pitch bend on a lead synth sound. This time the part requires whole-step bends, so I'm moving the pitch bend wheel all the way up and back again. As before, the wheel has the default setting of a whole-step range.

TRACK 118

R&B Ballad

Listen to the track and you'll hear that the lead synth is on the right channel, with the rest of the band on the left channel. The lead synth is a "digital mono lead" from the FM8 softsynth, designed to emulate the characteristics of an EWI (electronic wind instrument, a synth controller for woodwind players). On the left channel, the backing band includes a synth bass from the Omnisphere softsynth, and a synth pad from Native Instruments' Massive softsynth.

Harmony/Theory Notes

This synth part is created mostly from pentatonic scales, built from the root or 5th of the major chords, and from the 7th of the suspended dominant chords. For example, the figure in measure 1 is derived from the C pentatonic scale (C D E G A), built from the root of the Cmaj9 and the 5th of the Fmaj9 chords respectively. Similarly, the figure in measure 2 is derived from the F pentatonic scale (F G A C D), built from the 5th of the B♭maj9 and the 7th of the G11 chords respectively.

Further Reading

For more information on using pentatonic and blues scales over different chords, please check out my book *Contemporary Music Theory, Level Two*, published by Hal Leonard LCC.

POP/ROCK

Pop/rock is a contemporary music style that uses medium-to-fast tempos, and combines the melodic hooks of pop with the driving energy of rock. Most pop/rock tunes have either a straight-eighths or swing-eighths (shuffle) rhythmic feel. Our first example uses right-hand alternating triads with a straight-eighths rhythmic subdivision, typical of 1980s pop/rock.

TRACK 119

The right-hand triads frequently anticipate beat 1 and then land on the "and" of 1 (leading into beat 2). Meanwhile, the left hand imparts a steady driving feel, with the low root landing on beats 1 and 3, and the root an octave higher landing on beats 2 and 4—the same pattern demonstrated on Track 87 (p. 108).

Chord Voicing Tips

This example uses alternating triads and upper structures in the right hand as follows:

- Alternating between major triads built from the fifth and the root, on the D chord (adding the seventh and ninth).

- Alternating between major triads built from the seventh and the third, on the Bm7 and Em7 chords (adding the ninth and eleventh).

- Alternating between major triads built from the seventh and the root, on the A11 chords.

- Alternating between major triads built from the fifth, ninth, and root, on the Gmaj7 chord (adding the ninth, sharped eleventh, and thirteenth).

- Alternating between major triads built from the 4th and the root, on the last D chord, and leading into the A chord. (This interior IV-I triad movement is also known as backcycling.)

- The B11 chord is voiced by building a major triad from the seventh: A/B.

The next example is in a swing-eighths (or *shuffle*) rhythmic style, and uses a mixture of different triads over a repeated bass note (sometimes referred to as a *pedal point*).

TRACK 120

Pop/Rock Shuffle

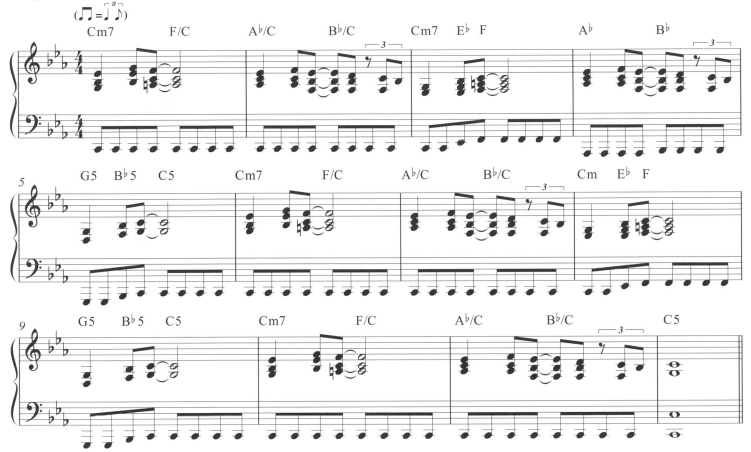

As well as the different triads placed over the same bass note in measures 1–2, 6–7, and 10–11, we have some root-fifth voicings in measures 5, 9, and 12, and some resolving suspensions (fourth moving to third) inside the B♭ triads. The left hand is providing a solid rhythmic pulse, mostly playing the tonic of C, and sometimes moving to other notes in the C minor pentatonic scale (E♭, F, G, B♭). The phrase-lengths are a little unusual here: five, then four, then three measures; see if you can hear this!

Chord Voicing Tips

The different right-hand triads placed over C in the left hand are derived as follows:

- The Cm7 chord is voiced by building a major triad from the third: E♭/C.

- The F/C chord is the result of placing the F chord over its fifth (C) in the bass.

- The A♭/C chord is the result of placing the A♭ chord over its third (C) in the bass. This is embellished with an Fm triad on beat 2 of these measures.

- The B♭/C chord is equivalent to a C11 (major triad built from the seventh). The upper B♭ triad has an interior 4-3 resolution (i.e., E♭ moving to D).

The G5, B♭5, and C5 chords are all voiced with root-fifth intervals in the right hand.

147

POSTURE AND POSITION

The key to having good **posture** is to be comfortable, but not to be hunched over or slumped in front of the keyboard. Your back should be fairly straight, and your hands, arms, wrists, and shoulder and back muscles should all be relaxed. You should resist any tendency to lean too far forward, and your feet should be resting on the floor. If you are sitting at the correct height, your hands and forearms should be parallel to the floor, with the fingers touching the keys, as shown:

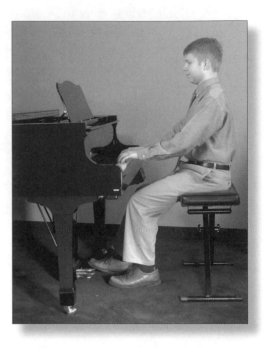

If you have bad posture (slumped or slouched back, forearms not parallel to floor, too much tension in wrists and/or fingers, etc.), a number of bad things can happen: backache, cramped hands, even carpal tunnel syndrome. So good posture is essential, and will enable you to enjoy playing a whole lot more!

The **position** of the hands and fingers while playing deserves special mention here. You should try to keep your fingers curved and your hands arched as much as you can. You'll build better stamina and technique this way, and have better access to all the keys on the keyboard.

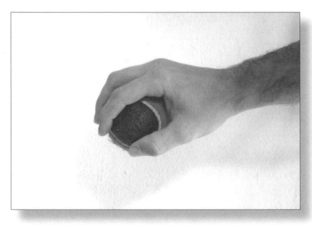

One way to learn this position is to hold a tennis ball in each hand. This way you will naturally arch the hand and curve the fingers, as shown here:

Do not tense up when learning this position; keep the wrist, hand, and fingers as relaxed as possible.

PRACTICE HABITS

Here are some good tips to help you get the most out of your valuable practice time.

1) **Set goals and priorities for each practice session**. For example, in a half-hour session, you might work for five or more minutes on technique (say, some scales and/or technique exercises), five or more minutes on sightreading (playing some music without having seen it before), and then the remaining time on the tune(s) you are currently learning.

2) **Aim to play the pieces you're working on as smoothly and clearly as possible**. Isolate any rough spots and work on these until you can play them without pausing. For beginners, this will often require finding the correct hand position and fingering.

3) **Play in tempo and slow the piece down as needed**. I sometimes hear beginning-level students rush through pieces too fast, stumble over some notes, then resume playing (too fast again), and so on. This is exactly the WRONG way to go about it (and is also irritating to listen to...)! You should find the tempo at which you are

comfortable playing (with no stumbles)—even if the tempo is really slow, it doesn't matter. This will help you play more evenly, as well as help to get the piece into your muscle memory so that your hands begin to learn it; then you can gradually increase the tempo as your facility improves.

4) **Practice pieces with hands separately as needed**. This is very important. Separating the two hands allows you to focus on each hand's part individually. Then, when you re-combine the hands, you'll have a head start, as you'll already be familiar with the individual parts. Actually, in contemporary styles such as blues and rock 'n' roll, the left-hand pattern is often rather repetitive, so practicing this part separately will help you put the left hand on "autopilot."

5) **Practice with a metronome as needed**. A metronome is a machine (either mechanical or electronic) that emits a steady ticking sound, reminding you of the tempo. Listen hard when playing along, to make sure you are not slowing down or speeding up. Beginning players should use a metronome for at least half of each practice session.

6) **Always try to keep going when practicing a performance**. When you see a tune for the first time (unless you're an experienced player!), it's normal to be a little uncertain and make mistakes as you learn it. But once you're familiar with the piece, then the next stage is to practice *performing* it. Do your best to convey the emotion and expressiveness of the music, and above all keep going even if you make a mistake. If there is still some work to do on certain sections of the piece, then isolate and work on them afterward.

7) **Make sure you are relaxed while practicing**. Maintain proper *posture* and *position*. Don't tense up; make sure your arms, wrists, and fingers are all relaxed. Take a short break every so often to relax, then start up again when you feel refreshed.

8) **Find the right practice environment**. Ideally you should practice in a quiet place, free from interruptions, phones ringing, etc. If your piano or keyboard is in a room where you can close the door, so much the better. Also try to find a time of day when you have some energy and are not too tired.

Good luck with your practicing!

PROGRESSIVE ROCK

Progressive rock, also known as **prog rock**, or simply **prog**, is a style of rock music that emerged in the late 1960s and early 1970s. This style went beyond the standard song structures of the time, creating complex arrangements and incorporating significant classical and jazz influences. Progressive rock songs sometimes have lengthy instrumental sections and abstract or conceptual lyrics. Rhythmically, this style often uses complex time signatures ("odd-time") as well as tempo changes in the middle of songs. Most progressive rock makes extensive use of synthesizers, alongside more traditional instruments such as guitar, bass, and drums. Although many people associate this genre with classic 1970s bands—such as Yes, Genesis, and ELP—progressive rock is alive and well in the 21st century, with groups like Spock's Beard, and the progressive metal band Dream Theater.

Our first progressive rock example is in a style reminiscent of the band Yes, and features an analog synth comping part courtesy of the ES2 softsynth (within Logic):

TRACK 121

Progressive Rock

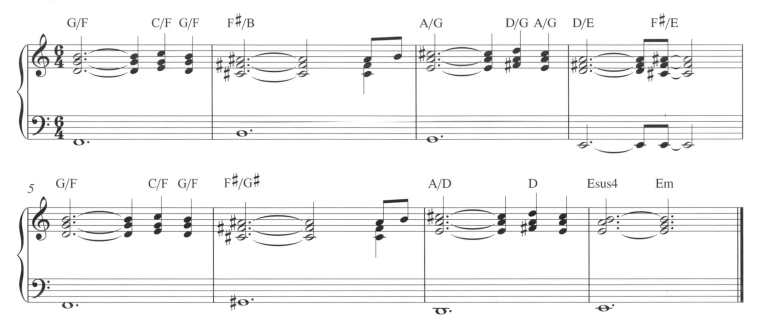

Listen to the track and you'll hear that the synth comping is on the right channel, with the other instruments on the left channel. Note that this example uses a 6/4 time signature and has a polyrhythmic feel, combining two different rhythmic subdivisions. You can tap your foot on the quarter notes (six per measure), and the above synth part is landing on some of these beats; you can also tap you foot on each dotted-quarter note (four per measure), which has more of a shuffle or 12/8 feel. Go ahead and try it! You'll also notice that there is no written key signature. The keys are changing frequently in this example, so any key signature written would have been arbitrary and not particularly helpful. These types of key changes are common in more advanced progressive rock styles.

On the left channel, the backing band includes an organ arpeggio part from Native Instruments' Vintage organs, a Moog-style synth bass from Applied Acoustic Systems' Ultra Analog, and acoustic drums from FXpansion's BFD virtual drum instrument.

Harmony/Theory Notes

This is a two-handed synth comping part, with the left hand playing the roots of the chords, and the right hand using upper structure triads and alternating triads. For example, in measure 1 in the treble clef we are alternating between G and C major triads, which are built from the 9th and 5th respectively of the implied F major chord, whose root is in the bass clef. Similar alternating triad movements are used in measures 3, 5, and 7, again all implying major harmony. In measure 4, the D major triad bult from the 7th (with respect to the root E) implies a suspended dominant chord, which moves to the F♯ major triad built from the 9th (implying a major chord with upper extensions—9th, ♯11th, and 13th). In measures 2 and 6, the F♯ major triad is built from the 5th of a B major chord, and the 7th of a G♯ suspended dominant chord, respectively.

150

Further Reading

For more information on the use of alternating triads in rock styles, please check out my keyboard method *The Pop Piano Book*, published by Hal Leonard LLC.

Our next progressive rock example is in a style reminiscent of the band Genesis, and features a soft analog lead synth sound from Applied Acoustic Systems' Ultra Analog softsynth:

TRACK 122

Progressive Rock

Listen to the track and you'll hear that the arpeggiated synth lead is on the right channel, with the rest of the band on the left channel. This type of synth part, together with the syncopated rhythm section and the 12-string acoustic guitar comping, is all typical of 1970s prog-rock. Again, no key signature is shown, as there are a number of key changes throughout the example.

On the left channel, the backing band includes Native Instruments' Scarbee Red Bass, MusicLab's RealGuitar (playing the acoustic 12-string), FXpansion's BFD virtual drums, and an organ sound from Native Instruments' Vintage Organs.

Harmony/Theory Notes

This solo part is based on chordal arpeggios and scale tones, with some resolutions within the chords. For example, in measure 1 the 3rd of the Dm chord (F) moves to the 9th or 2nd (E) of the Dsus2 chord; in measure 2 the 4th of the Asus4 chord (D) moves to the 3rd of the A chord (C♯), and so on. This resolution technique adds interest and sophistication to the synth line, and is commonly used in progressive rock and other styles.

PROPHET-5

The **Sequential Circuits Prophet-5** is a famous analog synthesizer, in production from 1978 until 1984. This unit was polyphonic (up to five notes at once) and was one of the first synthesizers featuring patch memory, for instant storage and recall of sounds. This, together with its extensive modulation capabilities and great sound, made the Prophet-5 an instant classic. This synth has been used on countless recordings, by artists such as the Doobie Brothers, Phil Collins, Level 42, Eurhythmics and INXS. As well as having a characteristically warm analog quality, the Prophet-5 was particularly noted for its bass sounds and sound effects.

The legendary sound of the Prophet-5 lives on in the 21st century, recreated by softsynths such as Native Instruments' Pro-53 (now discontinued, although available on the used market) and Arturia's Prophet V. Next up we have a music example in a funk style, featuring a synth comping part created in the Pro-53 softsynth:

TRACK 123

Funk

Listen to the track and you'll hear that the synth comping is on the right channel, and the rest of the band is on the left channel. This synth sound is a classic Prophet-style patch, with both oscillators producing pulse waves (see p. 153) set to different widths, and slightly detuned for a "fatter" sound. The funky rhythm section on the left channel is courtesy of Native Instruments' Scarbee Red Bass (using the slap bass samples) and FXpansion's BFD virtual drum instrument.

Harmony/Theory Notes

The musical form of this example is a 12-bar minor blues, in the key of A minor. The synth part uses some upper structure triads—for example, at the beginning of measure 1 the C major triad is built from the 3rd of the Am7 chord (the bass part is playing the low A, on the left channel). Similarly, on the Dm7 chord in measure 2, the F major triad is built from the 3rd of the chord. In measure 9 we are alternating between G and C major triads, which are built from the 9th and 5th respectively of the implied F major chord (whose root is again in the bass part). We are also using some interior resolutions within the chords—for example, in measure 1 the 7th of the Am7 chord (G) moves to the 6th of the Am6 chord (F♯). Similarly, in measure 2 the 7th of the Dm7 chord (C) moves to the 6th of the Dm6 chord (B), and so on. Most of the time, the synth part does not include the roots of the chords (the roots are being played in the bass part). This is a common contemporary voicing technique when the chord symbols are bigger than simple triads (i.e., four-part chords and larger).

Further Reading

For more information on the 12-bar blues form and blues keyboard stylings, please check out my book *Blues Piano: The Complete Guide with Audio!*, published by Hal Leonard LLC.

PULSE WAVE

A **pulse wave** is a basic type of waveform (see p. 195) available on many synthesizers. It has similar properties to a square wave (see p. 170), except that it does not have the perfectly symmetrical shape of a square wave:

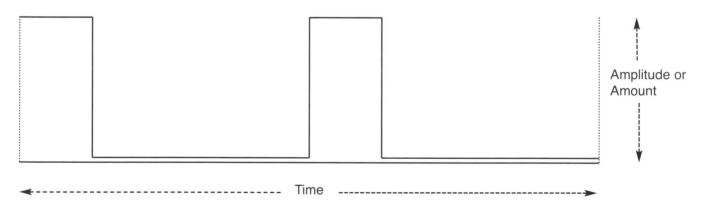

Pulse and square waves are either "all the way on" or "all the way off," and the ratio of how much time the waveform spends on and off is known at the duty cycle. (As the square wave is a symmetrical shape, its duty cycle is always 50 percent.) In the above pulse wave example, the duty cycle is 25 percent, as the wave is in the "on" position 25 percent of the time. Square waveforms in general have a hollow-sounding characteristic. The pulse wave is a thinner, narrower-sounding version of the square wave and re-introduces some even harmonics, compared to the square wave, which has odd harmonics only. Due to their thinner sound, pulse waves are often used as the basis for programming clavinet sounds on analog synthesizers.

The width of a pulse wave may also be cyclically modified over time, normally by a low-frequency oscillator. This is known as pulse width modulation, and imparts a detuning or chorus-like effect to the sound. This technique is often used when programming strings or bass drone sounds, to add more motion and realism. Technical note: Pulse width modulation is actually equivalent to the difference between two sawtooth waves (see p. 165).

On the audio track, we start out with a square wave (from the ES2 softsynth within Logic), and then modify the duty cycle to create two different pulse waves, so the following example is played three times in total:

TRACK 124

- The first performance of this phrase uses a pulse wave with a 50 percent duty cycle (i.e., a square wave), which has a rounded, hollow sound.

- The second uses a pulse wave with a 25 percent duty cycle, which results in an edgier, narrower sound.

- The third uses a pulse wave with a 10 percent duty cycle, resulting in a thinner, more nasal sound quality.

QUARTER NOTES AND RESTS

A **quarter note** lasts for one beat. This is equivalent to a quarter of a measure in 4/4 time. Here is an example of how quarter notes are written.

The rhythmic counting (1 2 3 4) is shown below the notes in this measure.

The quarter note is written as a black (or filled-in) notehead, with a stem attached.

Next we'll see an example of a quarter rest (which also lasts for one beat).

Here's a notation example that uses some quarter notes and rests.

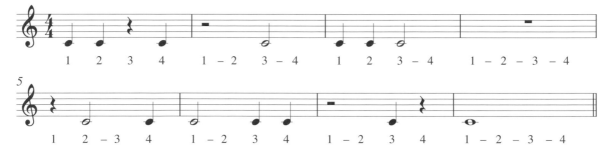

Note that the rhythmic sum of all the notes and rests in each measure agrees with the time signature (i.e., four beats in each 4/4 measure).

For information on other basic rhythmic values, see *Eighth Notes and Rests* (p. 55), *Half Notes and Rests* (p. 83), *Sixteenth Notes and Rests* (p. 167), and *Whole Notes and Rests* (p. 196).

R&B

R&B (rhythm and blues) is an American music style that emerged in the 1950s, and has flourished and developed up until the present day. R&B originally evolved from the jump blues styles made popular in the 1940s, and was an important precursor of the rock 'n' roll styles that emerged in the mid-1950s.

Nowadays the term R&B has come to encompass all black popular music, and therefore includes various sub-categories such as soul, funk, disco, dance-pop, hip-hop, neo-soul, and more. In this section we're going to spotlight two R&B sub-styles: Motown and neo-soul. Motown soul emerged in Detroit in the 1960s, fusing blues, gospel, and pop elements to create a uniquely commercial sound. This up-tempo Motown example has a swing-eighths rhythmic feel.

TRACK 125

Motown Soul

This simple rhythmic style anticipates beat 3 by an eighth note in both hands. Upper-structure triads are used in the right hand to create four-part chords, with some arpeggio embellishments beginning in measure 5. The left hand starts by playing the root of each chord, and then switches to root-seventh intervals (a device borrowed from jazz and blues styles) in measure 5.

Chord Voicing Tips

This Motown soul example uses upper-structure triad shapes as follows:

- The Amaj7 and Dmaj7 chords are voiced by building minor triads from the third: C#m/A and F#m/D.

- The Bm7 and C#m7 chords are voiced by building major triads from the third: D/B and E/C#.

- The E11 chord is voiced by building a major triad from the seventh: D/E.

Our next example is in a neo-soul style. Neo-soul is a 21st-century fusion of classic soul (from the 1960s–70s) and contemporary urban/hip-hop production. This example is a ballad, using 16th-note rhythmic subdivisions.

TRACK 126

This example has a more open feel at the beginning, with simple root-fifth and root-seventh intervals in the left hand, below the floating 5ths and 6ths of the right hand (as with most ballad styles, be sure to depress the sustain pedal for the duration of each chord). The energy then increases from measure 5 onward, with 16th-note rhythms and anticipations typical of R&B ballads, but with more sophisticated double-4th and cluster chord shapes being used.

Chord Voicing Tips

This neo-soul example uses intervals, upper-structure triads, and double-4th and cluster shapes as follows:

- On the Dm11 chord, the C-G, F-C, and D-A intervals provide the seventh-eleventh, third-seventh, and root-fifth of the chord. (These intervals all come from the D minor pentatonic scale).

- On the B♭6/9 chord, the same C-G, F-C, and D-A intervals provide the ninth-sixth, fifth-ninth, and third-seventh of the chord.

- On the Gm11 chord, the B♭-G, F-C, and D-A intervals provide the third-root, seventh-eleventh, and fifth-ninth of the chord.

- On the C11 chord, the B♭-G, F-C, D-A, C-G, and B♭-F intervals provide the seventh-fifth, eleventh-root, ninth-thirteenth, root-fifth, and seventh-eleventh of the chord.

- The B♭maj7 chord is voiced by building a minor triad from the third: Dm/B♭.

- The Fsus2/A chord is voiced by building a double-4th shape from the ninth (G-C-F).

- The Gm9 chord is voiced with a cluster voicing containing the ninth, third, and fifth (A-B♭-D). (I use the term "cluster" in my books to describe a three-note voicing consisting of a 3rd above a 2nd.)

- The E♭(add9) chord is voiced using a 9-1 resolution within an E♭ major triad.

- The Am7 chord is voiced with a "7-3" voicing (the seventh and third of the chord).

- The Gm7 chord is voiced by building a major triad from the third: B♭/G.

- The A♭sus2 chord is voiced with an inverted double-4th shape built from the ninth (B♭-E♭-A♭), preceded by a cluster voicing containing the root, ninth, and sharped eleventh (A♭-B♭-D).

- The D♭6/9(maj7) chord is voiced by building two double-4th shapes: from the seventh (C-F-B♭) and sixth (B♭-E♭-A♭).

- The C(add9) chord is voiced with an inverted double-4th shape built from the ninth (D-G-C).

Further Reading

For more information on the upper-structure, double-4th, and cluster shapes used in this neo-soul example, please check out my *Contemporary Music Theory: Level Three*, published by Hal Leonard LLC.

RELEASE

In a synthesizer, the **release** is the fourth or last stage of an envelope generator (see p. 58), which is a modifier normally applied to the filter (see p. 67) to control the timbre, or to the amplifier to control the volume. The release is the time taken for the envelope to close (return to zero amplitude) once the note has been released on the keyboard. Most commonly, release is used in the context of the amplifier envelope, representing the time taken for the sound to stop (or "die away") once the note is released.

The following musical example demonstrates some different release times applied to the amplifier envelope. This track uses a sawtooth/pulse wave combination from the ES2 softsynth (within Logic). This example is played three times in total, with different release times as noted below:

TRACK 127

- The first performance of this phrase has an amplifier envelope release time of zero. This results in a very abrupt, clipped ending to each note.

- The second has an amplifier envelope release time of 200 ms (milliseconds). You can hear that, compared to the first repetition, the ending of each note is less abrupt, and takes a little while to die away.

- The third has an amplifier envelope release time of 400 ms. Now the release sounds noticeably longer, making the 16th notes in the phrase run into one another.

Changing the release time and/or the attack time (see p. 19) of an amplifier envelope, are among the two most common edits that synth players have to do on the fly when dialing up a patch and tailoring it for use in a specific musical situation. Learn how to do this on your keyboard synthesizers and softsynths, because there'll probably be a time when you'll need to do it in a hurry, either at a live performance or in the recording studio.

REPERTOIRE

Most keyboard players need to be concerned with **repertoire** (that is, the quantity of tunes they know). If you're a jazz player, it's desirable to know the established jazz standards (and probably a selection of Latin/Brazilian tunes). On the other hand, if you play in classic rock cover bands, it would be handy to know the famous classic rock anthems from the '60s and '70s. If you aspire to play casual, wedding, or corporate gigs, a good repertoire across a range of styles is an indispensable asset. For tips on committing these songs to memory, see *Memorizing Songs* (p. 115).

As a good starting point for developing your repertoire, here is a list of songs in different styles that you should become familiar with. Get out those fake books and start playing!

Jazz Standards

All the Things You Are	Misty
Autumn Leaves	My Romance
Body and Soul	Night and Day
A Foggy Day	Our Love Is Here to Stay
On Green Dolphin Street	Stella by Starlight

Latin & Brazilian

Wave	The Girl from Ipanema
Desafinado	Triste
Black Orpheus	How Insensitive

R&B Classics

The Dock of the Bay	Through the Fire
In the Midnight Hour	What's Going On
Soul Man	After the Love Has Gone
When a Man Loves a Woman	Get Ready

'50s Pop

Rock Around the Clock	All Shook Up
Love Me Tender	Blue Suede Shoes
Long Tall Sally	

'60s Pop

Surfin' U.S.A.	Something
Hey Jude	Under the Boardwalk
Whiter Shade of Pale	

'70s Pop

    Imagine   Layla

    Crocodile Rock   Dancing Queen

    Baker Street

'80s Pop

    Every Breath You Take   Careless Whisper

    Sailing   Candle in the Wind

    Don't You Forget About Me

'90s Pop

    Power of Love   Mr. Jones

    Save the Best for Last   Losing My Religion

    Tears in Heaven

'00s Pop

    Fallin'   Love Song

    Smooth   I Gotta Feeling

    Fix You

RESONANCE

In a synthesizer, **resonance** is a function that boosts or reinforces the frequencies near the filter cut-off point (see p. 67). This can dramatically increase the effect of the filter, and is a very classic and recognizable analog synth sound, particularly when combined with an LFO modulation of the cutoff frequency. Technically, the width of the "resonant peak" of frequencies (i.e., how broad the frequency range being boosted) is a parameter called the "Q." However, the term Q is also more loosely used simply as a synonym for resonance, so these terms end up being used interchangeably.

The following musical example demonstrates different resonance settings applied to an analog synth bass sound, courtesy of the ES2 softsynth (within Logic). This is played three times, with different resonance settings as noted below:

TRACK 128

- The first performance of this phrase has a resonance setting of zero, so the filter and envelope are acting normally with no additional boosting of the frequencies.

- The second has a resonance setting of 25 percent, and you can hear (in comparison to the first repetition) that the frequencies around the cut-off are more pronounced.

- The third has a resonance setting of 50 percent, resulting in a more dramatic frequency boost on each note.

If you then increase the resonance setting beyond a certain point, the filter will go into self-oscillation, resulting in unusual (and sometimes rather tortured!) sounds being created. This can be useful in electronic styles such as industrial music, and also in sound effects production. Use the resonance parameter on your synth with care: it may bite back, so to speak!

RIBBON CONTROLLER

In a synthesizer, a **ribbon controller** is used to modulate (control) some aspect of the sound. It is most often used for pitch-bending, although it can be used to change other parameters such as filter cut-off frequency, amplifier volume, and so on. Unlike the modulation wheel controller (see p. 123), the ribbon controller has no moving parts. Instead, the player presses a finger down on the ribbon and then, maintaining contact with the ribbon, moves the finger along its length; the amount of movement then determines the degree of effect that is applied. Some ribbon controllers are also pressure-sensitive and/or velocity-sensitive, enabling further control over the sound.

The ribbon controller is actually similar in function to the touchpad found on laptop computers, in that it registers the motion and position of the user's fingers. However, ribbon controllers normally register only linear (i.e., one-dimensional) motion, unlike computer touchpads, which register in two dimensions. Perhaps the most famous exponent of the ribbon controller is the keyboardist Keith Emerson, who used it extensively on his Moog modular system during the early 1970s. One reason the Yamaha CS-80 is enduringly popular is its ribbon controller, which enables players to accomplish polyphonic glides and pitch-bends with ease. Ribbon controllers have also been implemented in several synths of the 1990s and 2000s, including Kurzweil's PC161, Alesis' Andromeda, and Yamaha's Motif XS series.

ROCK 'N' ROLL

Rock 'n' roll emerged onto the American music scene in the 1950s, combining elements of the blues, R&B, country, and gospel music at the time, and fusing them in a new way to create a highly rhythmic and danceable style.

A lot of early rock 'n' roll used a straight-eighths rhythmic feel, contrasting with the swing-eighths rhythms common in previous popular styles. Like the blues, a lot of rock 'n' roll tunes use a 12-measure progression or form consisting of three four-measure phrases, which start with the I, IV, and V chords of the key (chords built from the 1st, 4th, and 5th degrees), respectively. Most piano rock 'n' roll (again like the blues) uses driving left-hand patterns, as in the following straight-eighths example.

TRACK 129

Rock 'n' Roll

The right hand is using a mix of patterns derived from the C blues scale and the C and F Mixolydian modes, as well as some chromatically ascending and descending 6ths. The left hand is playing a driving, repetitive root-fifth and root-sixth pattern borrowed from piano blues and boogie styles.

Chord Voicing Tips

This rock 'n' roll example uses blues scales, Mixolydian modes, and patterns in 6ths, as follows:

- On the C7 chord in measures 1 and 11, and the F7 chord in measures 5 and 10, we are using the tonic of the C blues scale (C) as a drone (repeated top note) above the "♭5-5" (F♯-G) underneath.

- On the F7 chord in measures 2 and 6, and the G7 chord in measure 9, we are using the 7th of the C blues scale (B♭) as a drone above the "♭5-5" (F♯-G) underneath.

- On the C7 chord in measures 3, 7, and 11, we are using 3rds from the C Mixolydian mode (G-B♭, F-A, E-G), with some half-step approach tones or grace notes into the third and fifth of the chord.

- On the F7 chord in measure 10, we are using 3rds from the F Mixolydian mode (G-B♭, F-A, E♭-G).

- On the C7 chord in measures 4 and 12, we are using a descending pattern in 6ths (G-E, G♭-E♭, F-D, E-C) to connect the fifth and third of the chord (on beat 1) to the third and root (halfway through beat 2).

- On the C7 chord in measure 8, we are using an ascending pattern in 6ths (G-E, A♭-F, A-F♯, B♭-G) to connect the fifth and third of the chord (on beat 1) to the seventh and fifth (again halfway through beat 2).

Next we will look at a rock 'n' roll shuffle (swing-eighths) pattern. As we have seen, the swing-eighths rhythmic subdivision typically uses the first and third parts of the (implied) eighth-note triplet for each beat. However, in swing-eighths blues and rock 'n' roll styles we also have the option to use all three parts of the triplet, as shown in the following example.

Rock 'n' Roll Shuffle

This time the right hand is using 3rds and triads from the C and F Mixolydian modes, as well as some four-part upper structures for the busier eighth-note triplets.

Chord Voicing Tips

This rock 'n' roll shuffle example uses blues scales, Mixolydian modes and triads, upper-structure four-part chord shapes, and 6th patterns in the right hand, as follows:

- On the C7 chord in measures 1, 3, and 11, we are using 3rds from the C Mixolydian mode (G-B♭, F-A, E-G), with some half-step approach tones or grace notes into the third and fifth of the chord.

- On the F7 chord in measure 2, we are using 3rds from the F Mixolydian mode (G-B♭, F-A, E♭-G), with some half-step approach tones or grace notes into the seventh and ninth of the chord.

- The F7 chords in measures 5 and 10, the C7 chord in measure 7, and the G7 chord in measure 9 are all voiced (on beats 1–3) by building minor-seventh-flatted-fifth four-part shapes from the third: Am7♭5/F, Em7♭5/C, and Bm7♭5/G. These voicings upgrade all the chords to dominant ninths.

- On the F7 chord at the end of measure 5 leading into measure 6, and at the end of measure 10, we are using second-inversion triads from the F Mixolydian mode (Cm, B♭, Adim, Gm, F), with some half-step approach tones into the third of the chord. Similarly at the end of measure 9, the Bdim triad is derived from G Mixolydian.

- On the C7 chord at the end of measure 7 leading into measure 8, we are using second-inversion triads from the C Mixolydian mode (F, Edim, Dm, C), again with some half-step approach tones into the third of the chord.

- Elsewhere we are using embellishments from the C blues scale (at the end of measures 4 and 8) and patterns of descending 6ths (at the end of measure 3, and at the end of measure 11 leading into measure 12).

The left hand is using the same root-fifth and root-sixth pattern as in the previous example (adapted for the shuffle rhythm), with a chromatic walkup into the ending in measure 12.

Further Reading

For more info on rock 'n' roll and blues piano styles, please check out my *Blues Piano: The Complete Guide with Audio!*, published by Hal Leonard LLC.

SAWTOOTH WAVE

A **sawtooth wave** is a basic type of waveform (see p. 195), available on most synthesizers. Its name originates from its resemblance to the teeth of a saw blade:

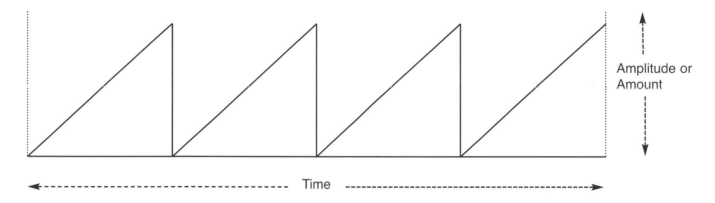

The sawtooth wave contains both even and odd harmonics (see p. 85) of the fundamental frequency. As a result, it has a harsh, buzzing sound quality. As all of these harmonics are present, this waveform is an ideal starting point for subtractive synthesis (see p. 171), for example, when synthesizing brass and string sounds.

The audio track demonstrates the sound of a sawtooth wave:

TRACK 131

This was produced from the ES2 softsynth, within Logic. No filtering (see p. 67) or envelope shaping (see p. 58) was used, so that you can hear the raw waveform. It sounds rather harsh in this setting, but this waveform is arguably the most important building block when you're constructing synthesized sounds.

SEQUENCER

A **sequencer** is a software program or hardware device that facilitates multitrack recording and playback. The first sequencers (in the 1980s) were essentially MIDI data recorders. Software sequencers (running on a Mac or PC) started out as MIDI-only, and then added digital audio capability in the 1990s (with the arrival of faster computers) to become digital audio workstations. Hardware sequencers (which could be used in live performance) also started out using MIDI data, and then added digital audio and sampling in the 1990s.

Modern hardware sequencers are stand-alone devices, typically with drum pads to facilitate the recording of drum and percussion parts. These are often referred to as "sampling groove workstations." Probably the most notable piece of equipment in this category is the Akai MPC60, which was instrumental in shaping today's hip-hop styles. Workstation keyboards usually contain on-board sequencers, and may also have sampling capability.

 Arranger keyboards also generally offer sequencing capability. These are functionally similar to workstation keyboards, but are primarily for the home market and for hobbyists (as opposed to workstation keyboards, which are used in live performance). Arranger keyboards normally have built-in speakers, on-board rhythm patterns, and automatic accompaniment features.

For summaries of leading equipment, see *Digital Audio Workstation* (p. 39) and *Workstation Keyboard* (p. 198). Here are some examples of other devices with sequencing capability.

Hardware sequencers/sampling groove workstations

> MPC Live 2, MPCX (Akai)
>
> DJS1000, ToraizSP-16 (Pioneer)
>
> Electribe Series (Korg)

Arranger keyboards

> PSR-S975, DGX-660, Genos (Yamaha)
>
> E-A7, BK-5 (Roland)
>
> PA4X, PA700 (Korg)

SEVENTH CHORDS

Seventh chords are four-note chords in which the highest extension is the seventh (the note that is a 7th above the root). Most four-note chords have a seventh, although some have a sixth instead. Here is a summary of the seventh chords found commonly in contemporary styles, with the addition of the widely used major sixth chord (which has a sixth instead of a seventh).

TRACK 132

These chords can be formed by building the following intervals above the root.

major seventh chord:	major 3rd, perfect 5th, major 7th (1-3-5-7)
major sixth chord:	major 3rd, perfect 5th, major 6th (1-3-5-6)
minor seventh chord:	minor 3rd, perfect 5th, minor 7th (1-♭3-5-♭7).
minor seventh-flatted fifth chord:	minor 3rd, diminished 5th, minor 7th (1-♭3-♭5-♭7)
dominant seventh chord:	major 3rd, perfect 5th, minor 7th (1-3-5-♭7)
diminished seventh chord:	minor 3rd, diminished 5th, diminished 7th (1-♭3-♭5-♭♭7)

Note that most of these chord qualities are found within a major scale, as diatonic seventh chords.

SINE WAVE

A **sine wave** is a basic type of waveform (see p. 195), available on most synthesizers. In fact, it is the most basic type of waveform, consisting only of a single frequency, with no harmonics or overtones:

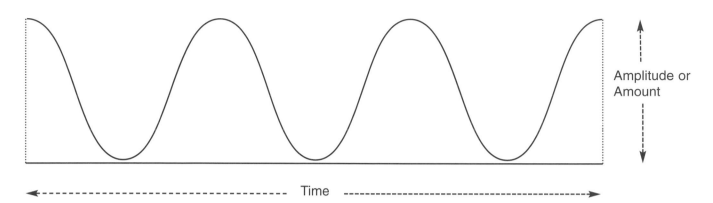

Amplitude or Amount

Time

To the human ear, a single sine wave sounds pure and clean, as no other overtones are present. The sounds made by whistling, or by striking a tuning fork, sound similar to a sine wave. All other waveforms, sometimes referred to as "composite" waveforms, can be thought of as combinations of sine waves added together. This is the principle behind additive synthesis, which combines sinusoidal waveforms together to produce complex waveforms and overtones.

The audio track demonstrates the sound of a sine wave:

TRACK 133

This was produced from the ES2 softsynth, within Logic. Again, no filtering or envelope shaping has been used, and you can hear the very mellow, rounded sound typical of a sine wave.

SIXTEENTH NOTES AND RESTS

A **16th note** lasts for a quarter of a beat. This is equivalent to a 16th of a measure in 4/4 time. Here is an example of some different ways that 16th notes can be written.

The rhythmic counting (1 e & a 2 e & a 3 e & a 4 e & a, etc.) is shown below the notes in this measure. The "e" and "a" subdivisions fall in between the eighth-note subdivisions.

The 16th note is written as a black (or filled-in) notehead, with a stem attached, and either two flags if the note is by itself (like the first four notes in the above example) or two beams if the note is joined to other notes (as in the remaining notes above). Sometimes the beams may join two 16th notes together within half a beat (as in the first two beamed pairs above), or the beams may join all of the 16th notes within one beat (as in the last two beats above).

Next we'll see an example of a 16th rest (which also lasts for a quarter of a beat).

Here's a notation example that combines some 16th notes and rests.

1 e & a 2 e & a 3 e & a 4 e & a   1 e & a 2 e & a 3 e & a 4 e & a

Note that the rhythmic sum of all the notes and rests in each measure agrees with the time signature (i.e., four beats for each 4/4 measure).

For information on other basic rhythmic values, see *Eighth Notes and Rests* (p. 55), *Quarter Notes and Rests* (p. 155), *Half Notes and Rests* (p. 83), and *Whole Notes and Rests* (p. 196).

SOLOING

Soloing normally involves improvising a single-note melodic line over a chord progression. There are various techniques available to you when soloing over chord changes, including arpeggios, neighbor tones, and target notes. Another useful technique when soloing is to use different scales, either on a chord-by-chord basis, or determined by the key of the song. In practice, these soloing techniques can be freely mixed. For example, you might use scale tones to connect between target notes. In this section we'll look at some soloing examples using scales, beginning with the following country/rock example.

TRACK 134

Country/Rock

This solo uses pentatonic scales built from the roots of the major chords, and from the thirds of the minor chords. For example, over the G major chords we are using notes from the G pentatonic scale (G-A-B-D-E), and over the A minor chords we are using notes from the C pentatonic scale (C-D-E-G-A), which is equivalent to the A minor pentatonic scale. Changing scales on a chord-by-chord basis like this is referred to as "playing *through* the changes" (and will make your solo sound more "inside" the chords).

The simple patterns in the first half of the above example are a good starting point for your own pentatonic improvisations. Notice that even if you just move up and down the pentatonic scale, the results will typically sound melodic and useful (this is due to the sequence of minor 3rds and whole steps in the scale). The second half of the example has some busier 16th-note figures, which are four-note pentatonic groups—like those in the scale exercise on Track 52 (p. 62). This type of figure is useful across a range of pop and rock styles.

In simple contemporary styles, the solo typically lands on a chord tone at the points of chord change (beat 1 of each measure in this case). In this example, the solo plays the root of the chord on beat 1 of measures 1 and 2, the 3rd of the chord on beat 1 of measures 3 and 4, and so on. These chord tones might also be target notes used as a framework around which the solo is developed.

Our next example is a more sophisticated jazz/blues, and uses the blues scale as a source of notes for the solo.

TRACK 135

This solo uses the blues scale built from the tonic of the key (the A blues scale in this case), playing it over all the chords in this 12-bar blues progression. This is referred to as "playing over the changes" (using one scale over the whole chord progression, rather than changing scales on a chord-by-chord basis). Some vertical dissonances may occur when doing this, but the character and linear strength of the blues scale normally makes the ear forgive these contradictions. Use this example as a springboard for your own blues solo ideas!

Further Reading

For more information on creating solos in jazz styles, please check out my *Smooth Jazz Piano: The Complete Guide with CD!* and *Jazz-Blues Piano: The Complete Guide with Audio!*, both published by Hal Leonard LLC.

SQUARE WAVE

A **square wave** is a basic type of waveform (see p. 195), available on most synthesizers. It has a symmetrical wave shape, which alternates instantaneously between two amplitude levels:

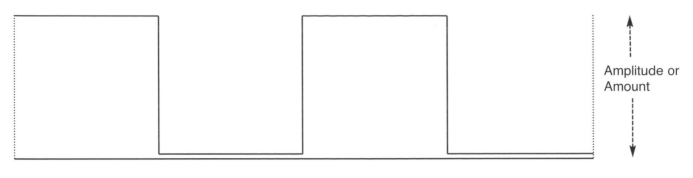

The square wave contains only odd integer harmonics of the fundamental frequency. Both square and pulse waves (see p. 153) are either "all the way on" or "all the way off," and the ratio of how much time the waveform spends on and off is known at the duty cycle. Since the square wave is a symmetrical shape, its duty cycle is always 50 percent. Square waveforms in general have a hollow-sounding characteristic, and are often used as a starting point for wind instrument sounds in conventional analog synthesis. Also, square waveforms can be useful when synthesizing overdriven electric guitar sounds. This is because guitar distortion effects tend to "clip" the outer parts of the waveform, which then more closely approximates a square wave as more distortion is applied.

The audio track demonstrates the sound of a square wave:

TRACK 136

This was produced from the ES2 softsynth, within Logic. Again, no filtering or envelope shaping has been used, and you can hear the very "hollow" sound typical of a square wave.

STACCATO

To play **staccato** means to play the notes in a short and separated style (as opposed to legato). **Staccato** playing is often needed in today's rock and funk styles, as shown in the following straight-eighths rock example.

TRACK 137

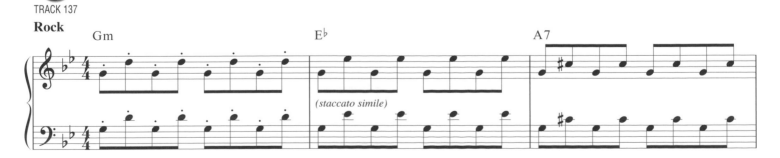

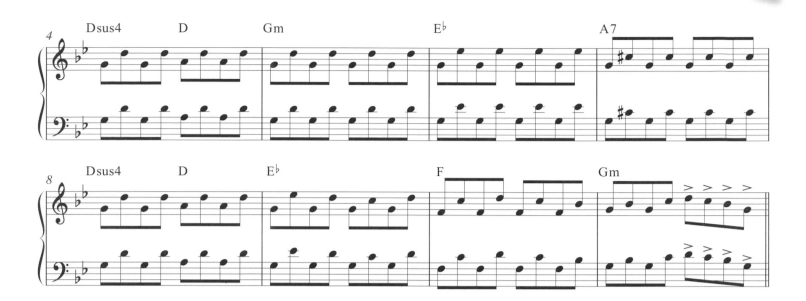

In this *staccato* rock style, the two hands are playing the same notes an octave apart, alternating between two chord tones on each chord. For example, on the Gm chord the root is alternating with the fifth, on the E♭ chord the third is alternating with the root, and so on. These chord tones are chosen to voice lead from left to right, to avoid unnecessary interval skips between chords. Starting in measure 9 the top note is varied to create some melodic interest, leading to an ending riff derived from the G minor pentatonic scale.

SUBTRACTIVE SYNTHESIS

Subtractive synthesis is a method of synthesis where harmonic content is subtracted from an oscillator waveform rich in harmonics by using a filter (see p. 67). This is the method of synthesis pioneered by the early analog synthesizers during the 1960s and 1970s. This can be compared to how the human voice works: the vocal cords (equivalent to an "oscillator") generate the raw sound, and the throat and mouth (equivalent to a "filter") shape the sound by removing (or attenuating) some of the frequencies.

A common subtractive synthesis technique is to take a sawtooth waveform (see p. 165) containing the fundamental frequency and all of the harmonics, and send it through a low-pass filter that attenuates the upper frequencies beyond a designated cut-off point. Resonance (see p. 160) may then be applied, to accentuate the frequencies around the cut-off point. In this way, the timbre of an acoustic instrument may be simulated, or an entirely electronic sound may be created.

In classic analog synthesizers, subtractive synthesis was applied to basic waveforms such as sawtooth (see p. 165), square (see p. 170), pulse (see p. 153), and triangle (see p. 183) waves. However, beginning in the late 1980s with groundbreaking synthesizer workstations such as Roland's D50 and Korg's M1 (see p. 113), sampled waveforms (digitally recorded fragments of real instruments) became available as raw material for subtractive synthesis, alongside the basic traditional waveforms. Nowadays hardware and software synthesizers can use many complex waveforms and samples as the starting point for subtractive synthesis.

Now we'll hear an example in a pop/rock style, which demonstrates the filtering inherent in analog synthesis. Here the featured instrument is a brassy analog synth, from the ES2 softsynth within Logic:

TRACK 138
Pop/Rock

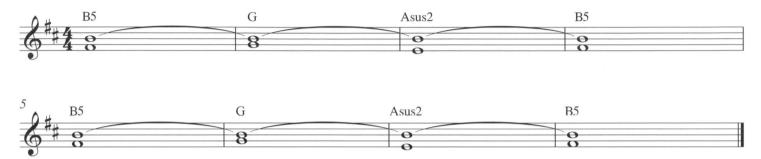

Listen to the track and you'll hear that the analog synth is on the right channel, with the rest of the band on the left channel. Note that during the first four measures, the synth has the bright, buzzy character typical of a sawtooth wave, as the filter is mostly open at this point. Beginning in measure 5 the filter then gradually closes, which subtracts (or attenuates) the frequencies above the cut-off point. This has the effect of progressively darkening the sound. The filter being used here is the conventional low-pass filter (see p. 67).

On the left channel, the backing band includes a fingered electric bass sample, courtesy of the EXS24 software sampler (again within Logic).

SUSPENDED CHORDS

A **suspended chord** is a chord in which the third has been replaced by another note, most often the fourth (the note that is a perfect 4th above the root). In mainstream styles, suspensions can be applied to triads (normally major), or seventh chords (normally dominant sevenths). Within a triad, the second (or ninth) can also replace the third of the chord. The following example shows suspensions applied to a C triad (first measure) and a C7 chord (second measure).

We can compare these suspensions to the original chords as follows:

- If we replace the third of the C major triad with the second (D is a major 2nd above C), we get the Csus2 chord.

- If we replace the third of the C major triad with the fourth (F is a perfect 4th above C), we get the Csus4 chord (if you see the symbol "Csus," then Csus4 is assumed).

- If we replace the third of the C7 chord with the fourth (F is a perfect 4th above C), we get the C7sus4 chord (if you see the symbol "C7sus," then C7sus4 is assumed).

We'll now make use of these triad and four-part sus4 chords in a style example. First, here are the chords we're going to use.

TRACK 139
Part 1

Now we arpeggiate and split these chords in various ways, creating a slow 16th-note rock groove.

TRACK 139
Part 2

Slow Rock

In the first four measures the suspended triads are arpeggiated, starting with the left hand and continuing with the right. In the second four measures the suspended dominant seventh chords are split into 4th and 5th intervals, over a root-to-fifth pattern in the left hand. Here the 16th-note rhythmic conversation between the hands is reminiscent of funk styles, but with more sustain and legato phrasing used.

SUSTAIN

In a synthesizer, the **sustain** is the third stage of a conventional envelope generator (see p. 58), which is a modifer normally applied to the filter (see p. 67) to control the timbre, or to the amplifier to control the volume. Unlike the attack, decay, and release envelope stages (see individual entries for these), the sustain is a level parameter, controlling the level or amplitude of the envelope for as long as the note is sustained (i.e., held down on the keyboard).

When sustain is used in the context of the filter envelope, it represents the brightness level of the sound after the attack and decay stages of the filter envelope have occurred. When sustain is used in the context of the amplifier envelope, it represents the volume level of the sound after the attack and decay stages of the amplifier envelope take place. Again it's important to bear in mind that these parameters are interconnected—for example, if the sustain level is too low in your amplifier envelope, you may not get to hear the brightness level that you expect from your filter envelope.

The following musical example demonstrates some different sustain levels applied to an amplifier envelope. This track uses an analog synth sound from the ES2 softsynth (within Logic). This example is played three times in total, each with the same attack, decay, and release times (0, 350 and 0 milliseconds respectively), and different sustain levels as noted below:

TRACK 140

- The first performance of this phrase has an amplifier envelope sustain level of zero. After the attack peak and (fairly short) decay time, the sound quickly dies away.

- The second has an amplifier envelope sustain level of 70 percent. After the attack and decay times, the volume adjusts to level a little lower than at the attack peak, for as long as the notes are held on the keyboard.

- The third has an amplifier envelope sustain level of 100 percent. After the attack and decay times, the volume stays at the maximum level for as long as the notes are held on the keyboard.

Changing the sustain level of an amplifier or filter envelope are common edits that synth players have to do "on the fly" when dialing up a patch and tailoring it for use in a specific musical situation such as a live performance or recording. Again, it's recommended that you learn how to do this on your keyboard synthesizers and softsynths.

SUSTAIN PEDAL

The **sustain** (or **damper**) **pedal** lifts all the dampers off the strings, enabling them to continue vibrating after the keys are released. On digital pianos and synthesizers, this effect is re-created electronically. Pedals for electronic instruments come in a variety of models, with two basic styles, one that is similar to the pedal on an acoustic piano, and another that is more of a plain small box (see photos below). On most digital pianos, the pedal is attached to the instrument, whereas with other keyboards and synthesizers, the pedal is something extra that gets plugged into a jack on the back (or sometimes the side) of the keyboard.

In contemporary music, the use of the pedal is style-dependent. For example, it is common to use the pedal in ballad styles, so that the notes from each chord all sound together, before the pedal is released at the point of chord change. However, the pedal is used sparingly (if at all) in up-tempo rock and funk styles, as it will detract from the rhythmic drive and/or syncopations used.

Here is a simple pop ballad comping example to demonstrate the use of the sustain pedal. The open-triad patterns in the left hand require the sustain pedal to be used for the duration of each chord. On the audio track, this example is first played without the sustain pedal; you can hear that it sounds rather dry and spare. The second time, however, the sustain pedal is added, allowing the notes of the left-hand arpeggios to blend together within each chord, creating a fuller effect.

TRACK 141

Pop Ballad

In this example the right hand is playing whole-note inverted triads, with voice leading.

SYNTH-POP

Synth-pop is a contemporary music style that emerged in the late 1970s and flourished and developed during the 1980s. Synthesizers are the dominant instrument in synth-pop, and they are mainly used to create synthetic and artifical textures (i.e., rather than to emulate the sound of acoustic instruments). In particular, the new and exciting sound of digital synths such as Yamaha's DX7 (see p. 50) were prominently featured on 1980s synth-pop songs, especially the rather over-used DX7 synth bells! Songs in this style are often very melodic, and for the most part use conventional (verse-chorus-bridge-etc.) song structures. Seminal synth-pop artists include Duran Duran, the Human League, Tears for Fears, Howard Jones, and the Thompson Twins.

Our first synth-pop example is in a style reminiscent of Howard Jones, and features a digital FM-style synth comping part courtesy of the ES2 softsynth (within Logic):

TRACK 142

Synth-pop

Listen to the track and you'll hear that the digital synth comping is on the right channel, with the rest of the band on the left channel. This synth comping part has a bright, digital sheen, using basic triads and arpeggios with some rhythmic anticipations, all typical of 1980s synth-pop. On the left channel, the backing band includes a light synth brass comping part and an analog pulse wave synth bass, both from the EXS24 software sampler within Logic.

The next synth-pop example is in a style reminiscent of the Thompson Twins, this time featuring a digital FM-style lead/melody synth part from the EXS24 software sampler:

TRACK 143

Synth-pop

Listen to the track and you'll hear that the digital synth lead/melody is on the right channel, with the rest of the band on the left channel. Again, this synth sound has a bright, digital quality typical of the style. On the left channel, the backing band includes an arpeggiated synth comping part and an analog synth bass (both from the EXS24 software sampler within Logic), as well as an electric guitar courtesy of MusicLab's RealStrat virtual guitar instrument.

Harmony/Theory Notes

A "target note" approach is used in this synth part. For example, we move from the 5th of the A chord (E) in measure 1, to the 5th and 3rd of the F#m7 chord (C# and A) in measure 3, to the 3rd of the G chord (B) in measure 5, and so on. The connecting tones in between are all from the A major scale.

TARGET NOTES

A **target note** is a note within a chord that is a desirable "landing point" for a solo (or melody) played over that chord. A series of target notes, therefore, gives us a framework around which a solo can be developed. In more basic contemporary styles, a target note might be just the root, third, or fifth of a triad. In styles using extended chords (i.e., jazz and R&B), target notes can be expanded to include sevenths, ninths, elevenths, and/or thirteenths. Also, in jazz styles we might make use of altered fifths and/or ninths, as these have a lot of color and character.

In practice, when soloing we might combine target notes with other techniques, such as arpeggios, neighbor tones, and the use of scales such as pentatonic or blues.

The first half of each solo in this section contains only the target notes to be used over each chord. Then in the second half of each example, we repeat the chord progression, creating a solo around the framework of these target notes. Our first example uses chord thirds and sevenths as target notes (a jazz staple), and is in a smooth jazz/funk style.

TRACK 144

Smooth Jazz/Funk

In the first measure, the target notes are B♭ and F (the third and seventh of the Gm7 chord), followed in the second measure by D and G (the seventh and third of the E♭maj7 chord), and so on. These target notes also occur in the solo over the last four measures, now with added connecting tones and rhythms in between. In this case the added notes are from the B♭ and F pentatonic scales. The rhythms are typical of funk and smooth jazz styles, with 16th-note subdivisions and anticipations.

The next example is in a more sophisticated jazz vein, and uses the flatted thirteenth (equivalent to the sharped fifth) as a target note on some dominant chords. Again we see just the target notes in the first half, and the full solo over the same chord changes in the second half.

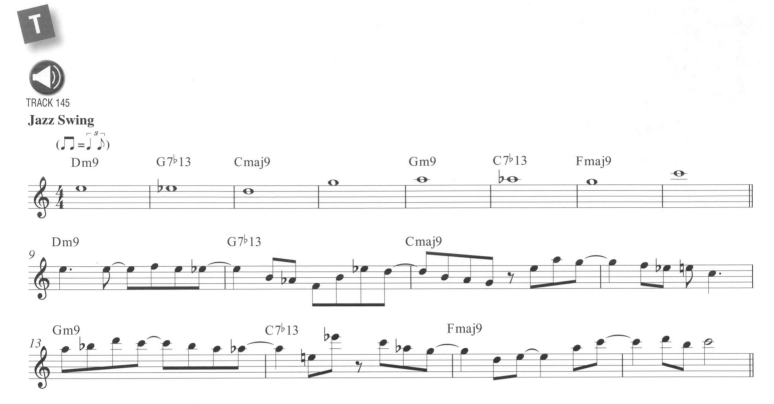

TRACK 145

Jazz Swing

Note that this solo example consists of two II-V-I progressions (chords built from the 2nd, 5th, and 1st degrees of a key—the two keys here being C major, then F major), which is a cornerstone of jazz harmony. The target notes over both keys create a "9-♭13-9" line over this progression: in measures 1–3 the target notes are E (the ninth of the Dm9 chord), E♭ (the flatted thirteenth of the G7♭13 chord), and D (the ninth of the Cmaj9 chord). The added notes in between the target notes are a mix of neighbor tones, arpeggiated chord tones, and pentatonic scales. Note the resulting solo phrases often start and/or end on an upbeat, which is common in mainstream jazz and blues styles.

Further Reading

For more information on using target notes to create solos and melodies in jazz styles, please check out my *Smooth Jazz Piano: The Complete Guide with Audio!* and *Jazz-Blues Piano: The Complete Guide with Audio!*, both published by Hal Leonard LLC.

TECHNO

Techno is an electronic dance music style that emerged in the mid-1980s and continues to evolve into the 21st century. Modern techno emphasizes synthetic and manipulated sounds, often with little or no harmonic structure, as opposed to trance (see p. 181). Like all electronic music styles, techno makes extensive use of samplers, sequencers, synthesizers and drum machines. Most techno tracks use fast tempos. (Around 135–155 beats per minute is typical.) Techno is a mostly instrumental style, and designed to be DJ-friendly so that successive tracks can be combined in a continuous DJ set.

The main unifying element in techno is the kick drum part (normally played on each beat) and the hi-hat pattern (on every second eighth-note, or upbeat). This is descended from house music (see p. 87), which is in turn descended from disco styles. Compared to these styles however, techno is much more synthetic-sounding and less organic.

Now we'll look at a couple of techno instrumental examples, and spotlight some synth parts on each. Our first example was created in Logic, and uses Logic's internal sounds and plug-ins (apart from a digital synth pad from Native Instruments' Massive softsynth). On this track we're featuring a staccato, percussive synth part.

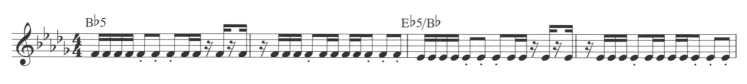

TRACK 146

Techno

Listen to the track and you'll hear that the staccato synth part is on the right channel, with the other instruments on the left channel. The analog synth bass (on the left channel) is also playing a busy octave pattern, with the filter cyclically opening and closing over time, a commonly used sound in techno styles.

Our next techno example was created in Reason, this time featuring an electronic string synth part:

TRACK 147

Techno

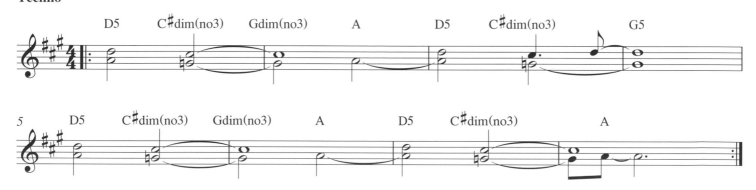

Listen to the track and you'll hear that the string synth is on the right channel, with the other instruments on the left channel. The string synth was produced using Thor, a softsynth included with Reason. On the left channel we have some more Reason softsynth sounds, including an aggressive, filtered synth bass from the "graintable" Malstrom synth, and (on the second repeat) a staccato analog synth figure from Subtractor.

Harmony/Theory Notes

Note the open, spacious quality of these two-note synth voicings, mostly using 4th and 5th intervals, with some tension due to the augmented 4th/diminished 5th intervals used over the diminished chords.

THUMB TURN

A **thumb turn** occurs when the thumb passes underneath the other fingers, or when the other fingers pass over the thumb. This normally happens when playing scales, arpeggios, or crossovers licks.

Let's see how thumb turns would be used when playing the C major scale. Fingering is shown for both hands.

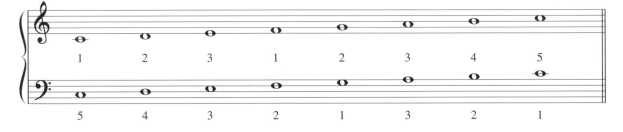

When playing the above scale with the right hand:

1) Ascending   After playing E with the third finger, the thumb passes under the fingers to play F.

2) Descending   After playing F with the thumb, the fingers pass over the thumb so that the third finger can play F.

When playing the above scale with the left hand:

1) Ascending   After playing G with the thumb, the fingers pass over the thumb so that the third finger can play A.

2) Descending   After playing A with the third finger, the thumb passes under the fingers to play G.

Always strive to keep the thumb mobile when executing these thumb turns: look ahead and move the thumb smoothly to its destination as soon as possible.

TIED NOTES

Tied notes are connected by a curved line in the music, indicating that the first note is to be played and then held for the combined duration of all the tied notes. The tie connects two or more notes of the same pitch. Here is an example incorporating tied notes.

The most common reason for using a tie is to extend a note's duration beyond the barline. In the first measure above, the only way to have a note landing on beat 4 last for two beats is to have a quarter note tied to another quarter note in the next measure. (If we wrote a half note starting on beat 4, we would have too many beats for a 4/4 measure.)

Another reason for using a tie is to show the start of beat 3 in a 4/4 measure, as a courtesy to musicians who are sightreading the music. In the first measure of the above example, the eighth note landing on the "and" of 2 is tied to the following quarter note. Technically we could have written a dotted quarter note, but this would have hidden beat 3 from view. Having the primary beats (1 and 3 in 4/4) visible is helpful, particularly if the music is being read at a fast tempo.

If your music contains 16th notes, it's considered good form to show the start of each beat (i.e., beats 2 and 4 as well as 1 and 3); again, using ties will help you do this. If you're writing music to be read by other players, they will thank you for it!

TRANCE

Trance is an electronic dance music style that emerged in the late 1980s, and is still going strong in the 21st century. Trance is derived from a combination of other styles such as house (see p. 87) and techno (see p. 178), as well as ambient electronic music. Like techno, trance features synthetic sounds, but with much more emphasis on melodic phrases and harmonic progressions, and favoring minor scales and arpeggios. Like all electronic music styles, trance makes extensive use of samplers, sequencers, synthesizers, and drum machines. Most trance tracks use fast tempos, typically 130–165 beats per minute.

Although many trance tracks are instrumental, a significant percentage of trance music makes heavy use of vocals. Because this style uses more melody and harmony than certain other electronic music styles, care is needed when blending from one track to the next, as would be the case in a typical DJ set. For this reason, trance tracks are normally constructed with sparser intros and outros. Trance records also make heavy use of effects (see p. 54) on the synthesizer parts, sometimes at extreme settings to create other-worldly sounds.

Like techno and house styles, trance tracks normally place a kick drum part on each beat and a hi-hat on every second eighth note. Snare drum rolls are used to transition between phrases, which are often 32 measures in length (or longer). Although early trance artists made extensive use of vintage analog synthesizers and equipment, these days most trance producers use digital audio workstations (DAWs, see p. 39) such as Reason and Live to create their tracks.

Now we'll look at a couple of trance instrumental examples, and spotlight some synth parts on each. Our first example was created in Logic, and uses Logic's internal sounds and plug-ins. On this track we're featuring an arpeggiated synthesizer part:

TRACK 148

Trance

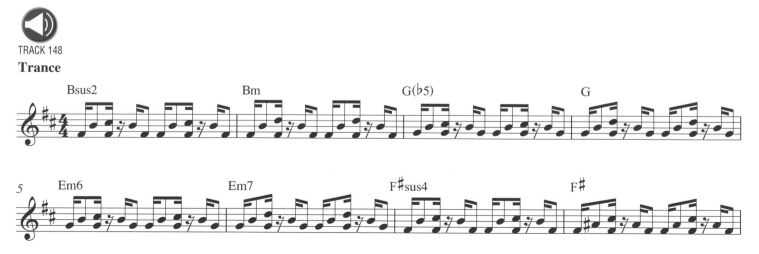

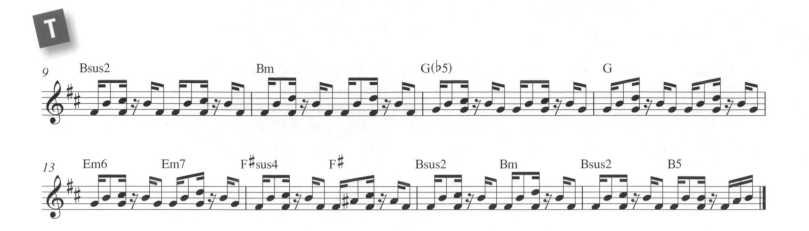

Listen to the track and you'll hear that the synth arpeggio part is on the right channel, with the other instruments on the left channel. This very bright, edgy synthesizer sound comes from the EXS24 software sampler, and is a signature trance music sound. On the left channel we have a fat Prophet-5-style analog synth bass, and an analog synth pad with an envelope applied to the filter (listen to its timbral change over time), courtesy of the ES2 softsynth.

Harmony/Theory Notes

Note this chord progression is in the key of B minor, and uses a i–♭VI–iv–V chord progression. This type of minor key progression is common in trance styles. The use of 16th-note syncopations in this figure (together with the fast tempo) creates a "busy" feel often heard in trance music. Also note the linear resolutions occuring in this part: for example, the C♯ in the Bsus2 chord (measure 1) moves to the D in the Bm chord (measure 2), the C♯ in the G(♭5) chord (measure 3) moves to the D in the G chord (measure 4), and so on.

Our next trance example was created in Reason, using its included softsynths Thor, Malstrom, and Subtractor. This time we're featuring a staccato synth comping part:

TRACK 149

Trance

Listen to the track and you'll hear that the staccato comping synth is on the right channel, with the other instruments on the left channel. The comping synth was produced using the "Epic Poly" sound from Thor, which has already found its way onto many electronic dance tracks. On the left channel we have an FM-style synth bass from Malstrom playing on all the 16th-note subdivisions, and a Jupiter-style analog synth comping pad from Subtractor.

Harmony/Theory Notes

This synth part is a very good example of using interior resolutions within triads. In measure 1, the 3rd of the Am chord (C) moves to the 9th or 2nd of the Asus2 chord (B) in measure 2, which then moves to the 4th of the Asus4 chord (D) later in measure 2, and so on. This makes the part much more interesting and melodic than if we had just used basic triads.

TRIADS

A **triad** is a three-note chord, consisting of a root, third, and fifth. There are four triads in common usage: major, minor, augmented, and diminished.

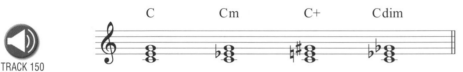

TRACK 150

These chords can be formed by building the following *intervals* above the root.

major triad:	major 3rd, perfect 5th (1-3-5)
minor triad:	minor 3rd, perfect 5th (1-♭3-5)
augmented triad:	major 3rd, augmented 5th (1-3-♯5)
diminished triad:	minor 3rd, diminished 5th (1-♭3-♭5)

Note that most of these triad qualities are found within a major scale, as diatonic triads.

TRIANGLE WAVE

A **triangle** wave is a basic type of waveform (see p. 195), available on most synthesizers. It has a symmetrical wave shape, which moves linearly between two amplitude levels:

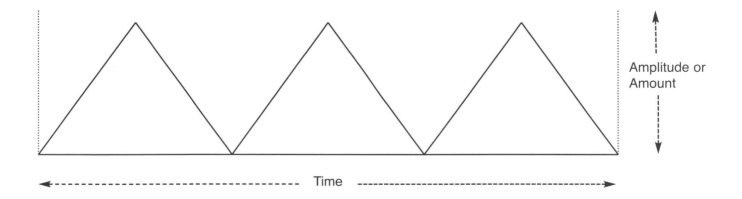

Like the square wave, the triangle wave contains only odd integer harmonics of the fundamental frequency. However, the higher harmonics "roll off" much faster than a square wave, resulting in a smoother, mellower sound that is actually closer to a sine wave. Although triangle waves sound unobtrusive by themselves, they can usefully add presence and reinforcement when layered with other sounds, such as harps and vocal samples.

The following audio track demonstrates the sound of a triangle wave:

TRACK 151

This was produced from the ES2 softsynth, within Logic. Again, no filtering or envelope shaping has been used, and you can hear the smooth sound typical of a triangle wave.

TRILL

In this book, we're referring to a **trill** as a rapid alternation between two notes. In classical or traditional circles, the term trill is used if the two notes are adjacent (i.e., a 2nd interval apart), but the term tremolo is used if the two notes are a 3rd (or larger) interval apart. Each of these situations is formally notated in its own way; we don't have the space to delve into that here. (Check out my *Blues Piano: The Complete Guide with Audio!* for examples of tremolo notation.) For today's synth players, it's okay to apply the term trill a bit more loosely, to cover 2nd, 3rd, 4th intervals and so on.

The notation below shows the result of executing a trill with an exact 16th-note rhythmic subdivision. Although this is quite feasible in practice, there will also be times when the rapid performance of a trill will not line up with commonly used rhythmic subdivisions. Don't worry about that— just use your ears! Also, don't confuse the above use of the term tremolo with the use of this term to describe a regular, repetitive change in volume.

For the synthesizer performer, trills are typically executed while the synth is in mono mode (see monophonic synthesizer, p. 124). This means that the lower note is held down while the upper note is rapidly and repeatedly played. This is an effective synth soloing technique, particularly when combined with pitch bend (see p. 143), which affects both notes of the trill simultaneously.

The following music example demonstrates this technique, using a Moog-like analog synth lead sound from the ES2 softsynth (within Logic):

TRACK 152

This example alternates between the notes E and G, which are a minor 3rd interval apart. This is a commonly used interval in synth solos. The audio track contains two repeats of the above phrase:

- On the first pass, no pitch bending is applied, so the phrase sounds exactly as written.

- On the second pass, an upward pitch bend is gradually applied after the phrase begins, with the pitchbend wheel then returning to the "center detent" position by the end of the phrase. You'll probably recognize this sound from some of your favorite synth solos— artists such as Jan Hammer, Edgar Winter, and Rick Wakeman come to mind.

UPBEATS

An **upbeat** falls in between the beats (i.e., halfway through beat 1, 2, 3, or 4 in a 4/4 measure)—as opposed to a downbeat, which falls on the beat. This is illustrated as follows.

When we count eighth-note rhythms this way (1 & 2 &, etc.), we can see that the downbeats fall on 1, 2, 3, and 4, and the upbeats fall on the &s in between (referred to as the "and-of-1," "and-of-2," etc.).

 Jazz swing styles often emphasize upbeats, as shown in the following comping example.

TRACK 153

This more sophisticated jazz example uses polychord (chord-over-chord) voicings, similar to the jazz/blues example on Track 77 (p. 96). Apart from the chords played on beat 1 of measures 1, 3, 5, and 7, note that all the other voicings land on upbeats, creating a syncopated effect that is common in mainstream jazz styles.

Chord Voicing Tips

This jazz swing example uses triads (with octave doubling) in the right hand, over double-4th shapes in the left hand. Double 4ths here include shapes with a diminished 4th (equal to a major 3rd) interval on top.

- The Em11 chord is voiced by building a major triad from the third in the right hand, over a double-4th shape (eleventh-seventh-third) built from the eleventh in the left hand.

- The A7(♯5,♯9) chord is voiced by building a major triad from the sharped fifth in the right hand, over a double-4th shape (seventh-third-sharped fifth) built from the seventh in the left hand.

- The A7(♭5,♭9) chord is voiced by building a major triad from the flatted fifth in the right hand, over the same double-4th shape (seventh-third-sharped fifth) built from the seventh in the left hand.

- The D$^{6/9}$(maj7) chord is voiced with various triads in the right hand: major triads built from the root and fifth, and a minor triad built from the sixth. These are all placed over a double-4th shape (third-sixth-ninth) built from the third in the left hand.

- The Am11 chord is voiced by building a major triad from the third in the right hand, over a double-4th shape (root-eleventh-seventh) built from the root in the left hand.

- The D9 chord is voiced by building a major triad from the root and a minor triad from the fifth in the right hand, over a double-4th shape (third-seventh-ninth) built from the third in the left hand.

- The G$^{6/9}$(maj7) chord is voiced by building minor triads from the third and sixth in the right hand, over a double-4th shape (sixth-ninth-fifth) built from the sixth in the left hand.

UPGRADING CHORDS

If you are faking a keyboard part, either working from a chart or from memory, some chord upgrading may be desirable. This means taking basic chord symbols (for example, triads) and adding upper extensions and/or alterations. The triad, seventh-chord, and double-4th upper-structure voicings we have used in this book offer a convenient and suitable way to upgrade chords in contemporary styles. In simpler pop/rock/R&B applications, we're unlikely to alter the chord (meaning flat or sharp the fifth and/or ninth by half step), and any extensions added (seventh, ninth, eleventh, thirteenth) will most often be diatonic (i.e., within the key of the song). By contrast, jazz musicians routinely add extensions and alterations to basic chord symbols—when playing a chart from a fake book, for example.

In this section we'll take a simple rock progression with basic triad chord symbols, and then upgrade these chords using upper-structure triad voicings. This will not only add extensions to the chords, but also impart that triad-over-root sound that is so appropriate for contemporary pop styles. Our starting point is a basic pop/rock groove using simple triads, as reflected in the chord symbols.

TRACK 154

Pop/Rock (Version 1)

Note that the right-hand voicings exactly match the chord symbols—no chord upgrading has occurred. We are still voice leading the triads from left to right, and anticipating beat 1 of each even-numbered measure by an eighth note—both standard pop/rock techniques. This would work fine for a simple song. But in the next version, we have upgraded the chords by using upper-structure triads, creating a more sophisticated sound.

TRACK 155

Pop/Rock (Version 2)

To help you to understand better how the chords have been upgraded, the chord symbols for version 2 have been changed to reflect the extensions added. However, in practice the experienced player would apply this upgrading in real time, working from the basic chord symbols shown for version 1. Here's how the chords were upgraded with upper-structure triads.

- On the minor chords Cm and Fm, we built major triads from the thirds: E♭/C and A♭/F, which upgraded the chords to minor sevenths. This upgrade of minor chords will work across a wide variety of pop styles (from the Beatles up until the present day).

- On the major chords E♭ and A♭, we built major triads from the fifths: B♭/E♭ and E♭/A♭, which upgraded the chords to major ninths (with the thirds omitted). This upgrade gives the major chord a bright and transparent sound, and is good for pop/rock, as well as contemporary jazz styles (in use from around the mid-1970s onwards).

- On the B♭ major chords, we built a major triad from the seventh (which is not even present in the original chord symbol): A♭/B♭. Note that this not a voicing for a major chord; instead we have created a suspended dominant chord (equivalent to a B♭11). In pop and rock songs, this chord quality often occurs on the 5th degree of a major key, and on the 7th degree of a minor key. In this case, the example is in C minor, of which B♭ is the 7th degree. So we took some liberties here by changing the chord from major to suspended dominant. You would not routinely do this in response to a "B♭" chord symbol, of course—but (melody and style permitting) it's a cool sound to drop in occasionally!

USED EQUIPMENT

In this section we'll cover some basic points about buying and selling musical equipment. Buying used equipment can make sense if you are looking for something that is not manufactured anymore, or if you are trying to save money in comparison to the cost of a new item. Selling used equipment typically occurs if you have something that you no longer need (because you've now upgraded to something better), or if you otherwise need to turn some equipment into money!

The main channels open to you for buying and selling equipment are:

Online: In addition to the familiar ebay.com and craigslist.com, there are other online classified ad sites (such as recycler.com), as well as dedicated musician sites (such as harmony-central.com). A lot of the equipment items on harmony-central.com are sold to out-of-state customers. So if you're selling, it's advisable to quote a price including shipping. And remember to insure the item(s) for the correct value when shipping.

Print ads: Check local papers and classified-ad papers (such as *Recycler*) in your area.

Stores: Music stores will often sell used equipment, including floor models or demo items. Check your local music dealer to find good deals.

Friends: Buying and selling equipment from/to friends and bandmates is another way to go. You are perhaps more likely to be confident about the item's history and reliability if you buy it from someone you know!

Here are some other things to be aware of if you are buying used equipment.

1) There are normally no warranties available on used equipment (unless you buy from a store), so do your best to evaluate the item(s) beforehand! If you know someone who's a gear expert, consider asking him or her to check the item(s) with you, provided that the seller is in your area.

2) If you are not a technical person, there are still things that you can check for (assuming you're able to try before you buy). If you're buying a keyboard, make sure it produces sound, and that you can activate the basic modes and functions. In the case of an amp, make sure that it produces sound when you plug your keyboard into it, without any noise or distortion (which could indicate problems with the amp and/or speaker). Do a visual check: make sure there are no missing or damaged keys, knobs, switches, etc. Above all, make sure that you like the sound that you're getting; if not, you should say: "No thanks!" Also, ask for any available original packaging; this can help when you are transporting the item (and it looks good if you end up re-selling it).

3) Be aware of the typical price range for the used equipment that you're interested in (by checking websites, publications, etc.). If you're being asked a top price for an item, make sure it's in excellent condition. With the exception of specialty and rare items, it's still generally a buyer's market out there, so feel free to make an offer below the asking price, especially if it's a cash sale!

VELOCITY

In the synthesizer and keyboard world, the term **velocity** is normally used in the context of **velocity sensitivity**. A velocity-sensitive keyboard is able to detect the velocity (or force) with which a key is played, and respond accordingly. For example, a grand piano has excellent velocity sensitivity, with a broad range of dynamic levels from very soft up to very loud. By contrast, a harpsichord has no velocity sensitivity, which is one of several reasons it was supplanted by the piano in the 18th century.

Most of today's electronic keyboards and synthesizers implement velocity sensitivity. Technically, this means they create a MIDI velocity message indicating how fast each note is "attacked." This is then used to control some aspect of the sound, either from the unit itself (if you are playing a keyboard synthesizer or workstation) or from another velocity-sensitive synthesizer or softsynth connected to your keyboard via a MIDI cable. Most often the velocity is used to control the volume of the sound, but other uses (changing filter cut-off point, for example) are also possible.

MIDI volume is expressed numerically as a range, from 1 to 127. When you record MIDI information using your favorite digital audio workstation (DAW), the MIDI volume is a very important component. Ideally, you want your controller keyboard to be transmitting MIDI volume uniformly across the whole range, and sometimes your controller's velocity curve may need adjusting to achieve this, depending on the physical feel of the keyboard (i.e., whether it has a light or heavy action) and your particular playing style (i.e., whether you tend to play lightly or more forcefully).

Here's an example of this concept in action: let's say you're playing Ivory (the virtual piano instrument, see p. 93) from a laptop computer on your next gig. A typical Ivory piano preset has 12 or more levels of samples for each note, triggered at various MIDI velocity levels (1 to 127). So if your controller keyboard is not transmitting volume data evenly across the range, you will not be accessing all of these velocity levels, which may detrimentally affect the realism and expression of your performance. This is where adjusting the keyboard's velocity curve may be helpful, to compensate for any issues regarding the keyboard feel and/or your physical playing style.

VIBRATO

On a synthesizer or electronic keyboard, **vibrato** is a regular, repetitive variation in pitch, normally caused by modulating the frequency of the note with a low-frequency oscillator. Vibrato is often confused with tremolo, which is a regular variation in volume. Synth players introduce vibrato by using different controller functions, such as aftertouch (see p. 8) or the modulation wheel (see p. 123). Some musicians subjectively describe vibrato as a "quivering" effect.

The two main variables relating to vibrato are the depth (the amount of pitch variation) and the speed (how fast the pitch is varied). Most synth players apply vibrato to single-note parts, for example when playing lead (see p. 105) or bass (see p. 21). Unless a more extreme or unusual effect is needed, you won't want to overdo the vibrato applied to lead and bass parts, because the results will not sound musical. Let your ears be the judge!

Now we'll hear an example of vibrato applied to a single, sustained synthesizer note:

TRACK 156

Listen to Track 156 to hear vibrato applied (via the modulation wheel) to an analog lead synth sound from Logic's ES2 softsynth. Note that the vibrato depth gradually increases, controlled by the amount of mod wheel movement. The vibrato speed is constant, and is determined by the pitch of the low-frequency oscillator within the ES2 softsynth.

VOICE LEADING

Voice leading occurs when some of the voicings in a chord progression are inverted, to ensure smooth movement between chords (i.e., movement without large interval skips). Most contemporary styles use voice leading to some degree. In this section we'll see two examples of a progression using basic triads, to be played in a pop ballad style. In the first example, the triads are just voiced in root position (i.e., no inversions or voice leading); you can hear that the motion from one chord to the next sounds rather disconnected. By contrast, the second example uses inversions to connect more smoothly between successive chords.

Each example contains four measures in which the chords are written as whole notes, followed by four measures of comping in a simple pop ballad style. In the comping pattern, the right hand is playing the triads as arpeggios, and the left hand is playing the root of each chord on beats 1 and 3, with an eighth-note pickup into beat 3. Here is the first example, with all the triads in root position.

TRACK 157

Pop Ballad (Version 1)

Now here's the second example, using triad inversions to voice lead between chords.

TRACK 158

Pop Ballad (Version 2)

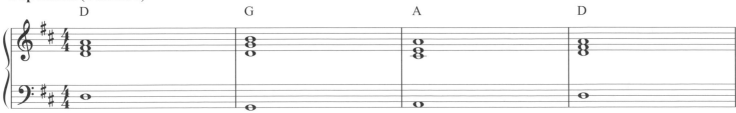

Note that the G triad in measure 2 is in second inversion, to voice lead more closely from the preceding root-position D triad. Similarly, the A triad in measure 3 is in first inversion to voice lead from the preceding G triad. This simple idea will make your comping sound much more musical!

VOICING

A **voicing** is an interpretation of a chord symbol by the pianist. At a simple level, this could be a decision on how to invert a chord, or how to distribute the notes between the hands. In a more advanced situation, this might involve upgrading a chord symbol by adding extensions and/or using upper structures appropriate for the style.

In this section we'll spotlight minor triads and minor seventh chords, and some of the upper-structure voicings available for them, as well as polychords (chord-over-chord voicings) where each hand is playing a chord shape. As a general rule, using a single upper structure over a root note is more typical in contemporary pop and R&B styles, whereas polychords are normally reserved for jazz applications. Here are some upper structure and polychord voicings available on a C minor chord.

TRACK 159

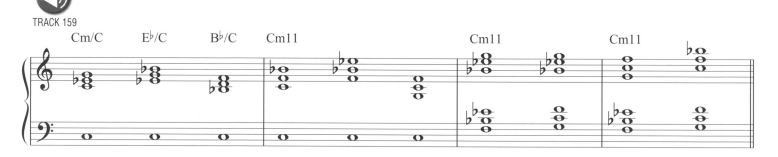

In the first measure, we have some triad-over-root upper-structure voicings. These are upper triads built from some part of the chord.

- The first voicing is a minor triad built from the root (Cm/C).

- The second voicing is a major triad built from the third (E♭/C), creating a minor seventh chord.

- The third voicing is a major triad built from the seventh (B♭/C), creating a less definitive minor eleventh chord (with the third and fifth omitted). In contemporary styles this voicing might alternate with the E♭/C above. This voicing also works for a suspended dominant ninth (a.k.a. dominant eleventh) chord.

In the second measure, we have some double-4th-over-root upper-structure voicings. These are upper double-4th shapes (consisting of two perfect 4ths stacked on top of one another) built from some part of the chord.

- The first voicing is a double 4th built from the root (C-F-B♭), giving us the root, eleventh, and seventh of the chord.

- The second voicing is a double 4th built from the eleventh (F-B♭-E♭), giving us the eleventh, seventh, and third of the chord.

- The third voicing is a double 4th built from the fifth (G-C-F), giving us the fifth, root, and eleventh of the chord.

In the third measure, we have some polychord voicings using triads in the right hand over double 4ths in the left hand. This is a classic jazz sound, pioneered by the legendary pianist Bill Evans in the 1950s. These voicings are sometimes referred to as "rootless," as the left hand is no longer playing the root on the bottom. These voicings use the major triad built from the third of the chord (E♭) in the right hand, over double 4ths built from the eleventh and from the fifth in the left hand. There are several possible combinations, of course!

In the last measure we have some more polychord voicings, with both hands now playing one of the above double-4th shapes, creating a very transparent quality. These are signature sounds in more contemporary and modal jazz styles.

 Next we'll put all these voicings to work in some style settings, beginning with an R&B/funk groove using a 12-bar minor blues progression.

TRACK 160

R&B/Funk

Here the 16th-note subdivisions and anticipations, with the rhythmic interplay between the hands, are typical of funk keyboard styles. The right-hand voicings are a mix of triad and double-4th upper structures.

Chord Voicing Tips

In this R&B/funk example the right hand is using upper-structure triads and double-4th shapes as follows:

- On the Em7 chords, we are alternating between major triads built from the third (G/E) and seventh (D/E), and between double-4th shapes built from the root (E-A-D), eleventh (A-D-G), and fifth (B-E-A).

- On the Am7 chords, we are alternating between major triads built from the third (C/A) and seventh (G/A), and between double-4th shapes built from the eleventh (D-G-C) and fifth (E-A-D).

- On the Bm7 chords, we are alternating between major triads built from the third (D/B) and seventh (A/B), and between double-4th shapes built from the eleventh (E-A-D) and fifth (F#-B-E).

The next example is in a modern jazz waltz style, and is typical of the more transparent modal jazz that emerged in the 1960s.

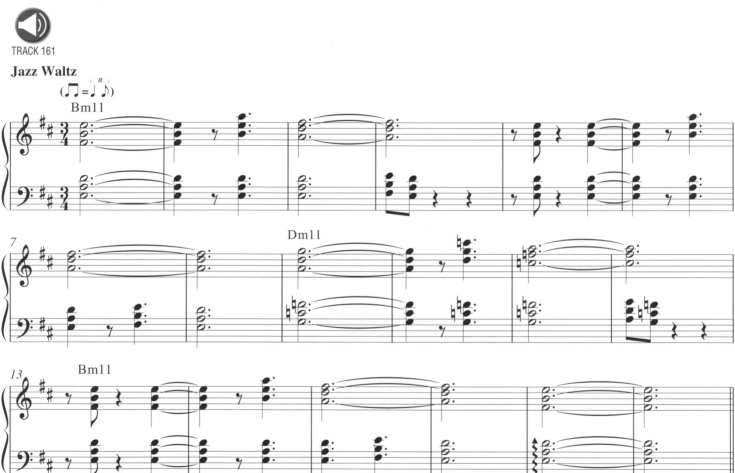

TRACK 161

The use of upbeats is similar to that in other jazz swing examples in this book, but adapted here to work in 3/4 time. For example, typical rhythmic figures land on the "and" of 1 and on beat 3 (measures 5 and 13), or on beat 1 and on the "and" of 2 (left hand in measures 7 and 15). The voicings are all polychords.

Chord Voicing Tips

This jazz waltz example uses double 4ths in the left hand, and triads and double 4ths in the right hand, as follows:

- The Bm11 chords are voiced with the following right-hand shapes: a major triad built from the third (D), and double 4ths built from the fifth (F♯-B-E) and from the root (B-E-A). These are placed over double-4th shapes built from the eleventh (E-A-D) and from the fifth (F♯-B-E) in the left hand.

- The Dm11 chords are voiced with the following right-hand shapes: a major triad built from the third (F), and double 4ths built from the fifth (A-D-G) and from the root (D-G-C). These are placed over double-4th shapes built from the eleventh (G-C-F) and from the fifth (A-D-G) in the left hand.

Further Reading

For much more information on chord voicings, polychords, and how to voice all types of chords using upper-structure triads and double-4th shapes, please check out my book *Contemporary Music Theory: Level Three*, published by Hal Leonard LLC.

WAVEFORM

A **waveform** is a two-dimensional representation of a sound signal, one dimension showing amplitude (sound pressure) and the other showing elapsed time. Waveforms such as sine, sawtooth, square, pulse, and triangle waves are the basic building blocks of sound synthesis. Here is a visual summary of these basic waveforms:

- *Sine Wave* (see p. 167)
  Fundamental frequency only (no harmonics). Pure, clean sound.

- *Sawtooth Wave* (see p. 165)
  Even and odd harmonics present. Bright, buzzing sound.

- *Square Wave* (see p. 170)
  Only odd harmonics present. Hollow sound.

- *Pulse Wave* (see p. 153)
  Thinner version of square wave. Some even harmonics added.

- *Triangle Wave* (see p. 183)
  Only odd harmonics present, with higher harmonics "rolling off" faster than the square wave. Mellow sound, like sine wave.

Most analog (and virtual analog) synthesizers have all of these waveforms available. For more information and audio examples, see individual entries for these waveforms.

WHOLE NOTES AND RESTS

A **whole note** lasts for four beats. This is equivalent to a whole measure in 4/4 time. Here is an example of how a whole note is written.

The rhythmic counting (1 2 3 4) is shown below the note in this measure.

The whole note is written as a white (or empty) notehead, with no stem attached.

Next we'll see an example of a whole rest (which also lasts for four beats).

Here's a notation example that uses a whole note and a whole note rest.

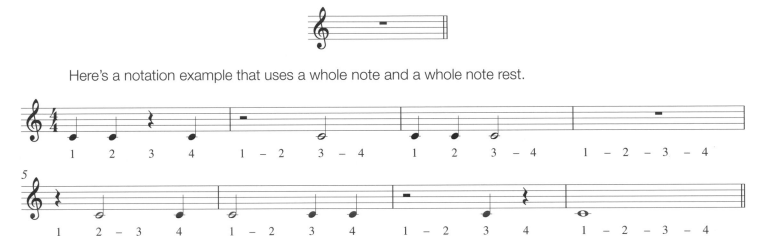

Note that the rhythmic sum of all the notes and rests in each measure agrees with the time signature (i.e., four beats in each 4/4 measure).

For information on other basic rhythmic values, see *Eighth Notes and Rests* (p. 55), *Half Notes and Rests* (p. 83), *Quarter Notes and Rests* (p. 155), and *Sixteenth Notes and Rests* (p. 167).

WHOLE STEP

The **whole step** is an interval double the size of the half step. If we move from any note on the keyboard to the nearest note on the right or left, and then again in the same direction to the next nearest note, this movement is a whole step. Here are some examples of whole steps.

Whole steps may occur between white keys and/or black keys as follows:

- The whole step C-D is between two white keys.
- The whole step E-F♯ is between a white key and a black key.
- The whole step G♯-A♯ is between two black keys.
- The whole step B♭-C is between a black key and a white key.

Whole steps and half steps are the most common building blocks used when creating scales. Another important relationship to know is that there are six whole steps per octave.

WHOLE-TONE SCALE

The **whole-tone scale** is a six-note scale that is built using consecutive whole steps. Here is an example of a G whole tone scale.

TRACK 162
Part 1

This scale has a uniquely "floating" and non-definitive character. Note that if we started the above scale on A, it would become an A whole-tone scale, but would contain the same notes; since the scale contains only whole steps, it can be named after any note within the scale. This means there are really only two whole-tone scales in existence: the above scale, and the whole-tone scale created from the six notes absent from the above scale (A♭-B♭-C-D-E-G♭).

In some contemporary situations we may use the whole-tone scale for embellishment over a dominant chord. The above scale contains the root (G), third (B), and seventh (F) of a G7 chord, which are the critical tones of the chord. If we use this scale over a G7 chord, we will also get the ninth (A), flatted fifth (D♭), and sharped fifth (E♭). Here is a mid-tempo pop/R&B groove, in the style of Stevie Wonder, that demonstrates this concept.

TRACK 162
Part 2

Pop/R&B

Note the G9(♭5,♯5) chord symbols; these have been upgraded (from the basic G7) to reflect the extensions added from the G whole-tone scale. The scale has been used in measures 3–4 and 7–8 in an ascending and descending pattern in 3rds. The left hand is playing a root-fifth-third open-triad pattern on the major chords, and a root-seventh-third pattern on the dominant chords.

Chord Voicing Tips

This pop/R&B example uses an upper-structure four-part chord shape as follows:

- The Cmaj9 chords are voiced by building minor-seventh four-part shapes from the third: Em7/C.

WORKSTATION KEYBOARD

A **workstation keyboard** is a self-contained keyboard/synthesizer, offering a range of different sounds (pianos, strings, brass, organ, bass, drums, etc.) and on-board sequencing/recording capability. You can go into the sequencer mode on the machine, record the piano part for your song (say on track 1) using one of the on-board sounds, and then go back and record a bass sound on track 2, drums on track 3, and so on, up to the limit of the number of tracks available in the unit (and the number of simultaneous notes that the unit will provide). Although the sound quality on these workstation keyboards is pretty good (and getting better all the time), it will generally not be quite as good as a computer-based recording solution (using a digital audio workstation), due to limitations in computer processing power and memory size.

Arranger keyboards are another category of electronic keyboard, which have a lot of the same functions as workstation keyboards, but are more oriented towards the home market and beginners/hobbyists. These machines have built-in speakers, as opposed to workstation keyboards that normally require external amplification. See *Sequencer* (p. 165) for more information on arranger keyboards.

Popular examples of workstation keyboards (manufacturers in parentheses) are:

Budget: Korg Kross
                Yamaha MX49

Mid-range: Korg Krome
                Yamaha MOXF8
                Roland FA08

High-end: Korg Kronos
                Yamaha Montage

Compared to personal digital studios and digital audio workstation software, the pros and cons of using a workstation keyboard are as follows:

Pros: Completely self-contained: nothing to hook up, no cables, etc. Can create entire song, from start to finish, on one piece of equipment. Learning curve typically faster than for computer-based systems.

Cons: Limited to the sounds, number of tracks, and number of simultaneous notes available in the machine. Limited editing functions and screen size compared to computer-based recording systems.

X-RAY YOUR PLAYING

You should always take time to evaluate your playing critically—to "x-ray" it—by recording it and then listening afterwards. You can learn a lot this way—things that might not have been apparent otherwise! Here are a few ways you can do this.

1) Record yourself while practicing.

You can do this while playing an acoustic or electric keyboard, and you can record with a portable digital recorder or a smartphone. Listen to your performance. Are you stumbling, or are you comfortable with the part? Are you rhythmically consistent? Are you articulating cleanly? Are you projecting the melody properly? Are you using dynamics correctly? And so on....

2) Record yourself into a sequencer or digital audio workstation.

All computer-based sequencers (or digital audio workstations) enable you to "view" your performance (i.e., the MIDI data) in various ways, including in a "piano roll" or graphic editing style. This is a great way to check on your rhythmic timing, as most sequencers these days are accurate down to at least 1/960th of a quarter note! I find it very interesting to look at the screen and see where I might have been a little ahead or behind the beat. This can be a humbling experience, but it's a great way to tell if you're "in the pocket" rhythmically.

3) Record your band while rehearsing or gigging.

Recording band rehearsals and gigs is very useful indeed. This not only helps you zero in on how your individual parts are working with the band, but also tells you how the band is sounding as a whole. In particular, recording rehearsals lets you iron out any trouble spots before the gig! Also, if you're in a cover or tribute band, you may want to record yourselves for comparison against the original artist's recordings (I have found this helpful for my Steely Dan tribute band here in Los Angeles). You don't want to obsess over small mistakes (which are not typically noticed by your adoring public), but you'll want to get an honest assessment of how you sound overall, and the recording doesn't lie!

YIELD

If you are in a band, you should take every opportunity to **yield**: to listen to the other members in your group, and genuinely to interact with them (rather than playing in your "own little world" without being aware of the others). I have taught a lot of ensemble classes, and this is a common problem that I see in beginning-level players.

More experienced players will always be aware of their roles in the group, and what the other players are doing. If it's time for one of your bandmates to take a solo, then you should play a supportive role, and let him or her step into the spotlight. I find that volume and dynamics are often a problem with less experienced players (particularly in rock bands). Make sure you're not playing so loud that you're drowning out the other band members (although this problem probably applies more to guitarists than to keyboard players...!).

If you're always aware of your role in your band, and how you can make the band sound better as a whole, then other musicians will enjoy playing with you, and everybody wins!

ZANY STUFF

One of the bands I perform with in the Los Angeles area is Doctor Wu, which is a fun Steely Dan tribute band. As you may know, Steely Dan (and in particular their keyboardist and main writer Donald Fagen) took elements of rock, jazz, and blues and forged a unique and identifiable style. Many of their keyboard parts are rather unconventional to say the least, so when I was thinking of ideas for this **Zany Stuff** section, I thought I would come up with a few grooves and phrases inspired by some famous Steely Dan and Donald Fagen songs. I hope you enjoy them!

TRACK 163
Part 1

"Greenflower Street"

This great fill consists of alternating B♭ major and E major triad arpeggios, over an E7 chord: not only a great lick, but a very good technical workout for the right hand!

TRACK 163
Part 2

"I Got the News" (1)

This fill is based on the C Mixolydian mode, used over a C7 chord. The first part uses Mixolydian triads, with 16th-note rhythms and syncopations. Then the triplet figure (alternating between a perfect 4th and a major 3rd) starts in bar 3, creating an interesting cross-rhythm against the left-hand part.

TRACK 163
Part 3

"I Got the News" (2)

This fill is based on the C eight-note dominant scale—introduced in *Eight-Note Scales* (p. 56). The 16th-note figure in the first measure (using octaves and minor 10ths between the hands) leads into a polychordal voicing in the second measure, with the right hand playing an E♭ minor triad (built from the sharped ninth of the C13 chord), over the left hand's double-4th shape E♮-B♭-E♭ ("3-7-♯9" of C13).

TRACK 163
Part 4

"Jack of Speed"

This pattern uses A major and E major triads over the F♯m7 chord (these triads are built from the third and seventh of the chord, respectively), within a funky 16th-note comping rhythm. At the end of the second measure, we have some rootless voicings for the E13 and G13 chords, with the left hand doubled an octave higher in the right.

TRACK 163
Part 5

"Babylon Sisters"

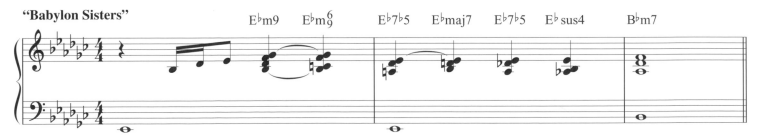

These chord voicings leading from the E♭m9 chord to the B♭m7 chord are quite unusual indeed! Check out the inner-voice motion by half steps as the chords move through the second measure.

TRACK 163
Part 6

"Kid Charlemagne"

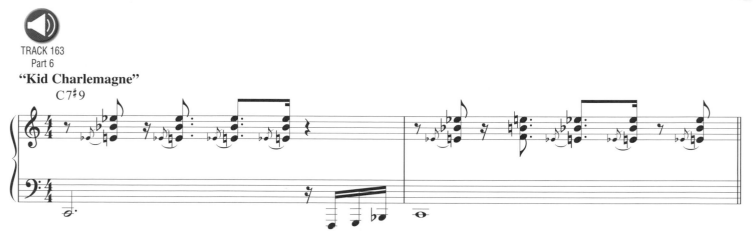

This comping groove on the C7♯9 chord uses the double-4th shape E♮-B♭-E♭ ("3-7-♯9" of the chord) in the right hand, with the grace note E♭ leading into the E♮. As an embellishment, this shape moves up by half step (to F-B-E) in the second measure. The left-hand 16th-note figure leading into the first beat of measure 2 comes from the C minor pentatonic scale.

TRACK 163
Part 7

"Josie"

This chord sequence is voiced using upper-structure four-part and double-4th shapes in the right hand as follows:

- On the Fmaj9 chord we build a four-part minor seventh chord from the third: Am7/F.

- On the F♯7♯9 chord we build a double-4th shape ("3-7-♯9") from the third.

- On the Gmaj9 chord we build a major triad from the fifth: D/G (with the root G also added in the right hand).

TRACK 163
Part 8

- On the A♭maj13 chord we build a double-4th shape ("7-3-13") from the seventh (and doubling the seventh on top). This shape is then played as an arpeggio from measure 2 into measure 3.

"My Old School"

In measures 1–2, the right hand is playing a cluster voicing (D-E-G) with the upper fingers while playing notes from the E blues scale underneath with the thumb. Then, in measure 3, we have whole steps and half steps (implying C major and C minor, respectively), leading into the unison octave riff derived from the G pentatonic/E blues scales in measures 4–5.

KEYBOARD STYLE SERIES

THE COMPLETE GUIDE!

These book/audio packs provide focused lessons that contain valuable how-to insight, essential playing tips, and beneficial information for all players. From comping to soloing, comprehensive treatment is given to each subject. The companion audio features many of the examples in the book performed either solo or with a full band.

BEBOP JAZZ PIANO
by John Valerio
This book provides detailed information for bebop and jazz keyboardists on: chords and voicings, harmony and chord progressions, scales and tonality, common melodic figures and patterns, comping, characteristic tunes, the styles of Bud Powell and Thelonious Monk, and more.
00290535 Book/CD Pack......................$18.99

BEGINNING ROCK KEYBOARD
by Mark Harrison
This comprehensive book/CD package will teach you the basic skills needed to play beginning rock keyboard. From comping to soloing, you'll learn the theory, the tools, and the techniques used by the pros. The accompanying CD demonstrates most of the music examples in the book.
00311922 Book/CD Pack......................$14.99

BLUES PIANO
by Mark Harrison
With this book/audio pack, you'll learn the theory, the tools, and even the tricks that the pros use to play the blues. Covers: scales and chords; left-hand patterns; walking bass; endings and turnarounds; right-hand techniques; how to solo with blues scales; crossover licks; and more.
00311007 Book/Online Audio $19.99

BOOGIE-WOOGIE PIANO
by Todd Lowry
From learning the basic chord progressions to inventing your own melodic riffs, you'll learn the theory, tools and techniques used by the genre's best practicioners.
00117067 Book/Online Audio $17.99

BRAZILIAN PIANO
by Robert Willey and Alfredo Cardim
Brazilian Piano teaches elements of some of the most appealing Brazilian musical styles: choro, samba, and bossa nova. It starts with rhythmic training to develop the fundamental groove of Brazilian music.
00311469 Book/Online Audio $19.99

CONTEMPORARY JAZZ PIANO
by Mark Harrison
From comping to soloing, you'll learn the theory, the tools, and the techniques used by the pros. The full band tracks on the audio feature the rhythm section on the left channel and the piano on the right channel, so that you can play along with the band.
00311848 Book/Online Audio $18.99

COUNTRY PIANO
by Mark Harrison
Learn the theory, the tools, and the tricks used by the pros to get that authentic country sound. This book/audio pack covers: scales and chords, walkup and walkdown patterns, comping in traditional and modern country, Nashville "fretted piano" techniques and more.
00311052 Book/Online Audio $19.99

GOSPEL PIANO
by Kurt Cowling
Discover the tools you need to play in a variety of authentic gospel styles, through a study of rhythmic devices, grooves, melodic and harmonic techniques, and formal design. The accompanying audio features over 90 tracks, including piano examples as well as the full gospel band.
00311327 Book/Online Adio $17.99

INTRO TO JAZZ PIANO
by Mark Harrison
From comping to soloing, you'll learn the theory, the tools, and the techniques used by the pros. The accompanying audio demonstrates most of the music examples in the book. The full band tracks feature the rhythm section on the left channel and the piano on the right channel, so that you can play along with the band.
00312088 Book/Online Audio $17.99

JAZZ-BLUES PIANO
by Mark Harrison
This comprehensive book will teach you the basic skills needed to play jazz-blues piano. Topics covered include: scales and chords • harmony and voicings • progressions and comping • melodies and soloing • characteristic stylings.
00311243 Book/Online Audio $17.99

JAZZ-ROCK KEYBOARD
by T. Lavitz
Learn what goes into mixing the power and drive of rock music with the artistic elements of jazz improvisation in this comprehensive book and CD package. This instructional tool delves into scales and modes, and how they can be used with various chord progressions to develop the best in soloing chops.
00290536 Book/CD Pack......................$17.95

LATIN JAZZ PIANO
by John Valerio
This book is divided into three sections. The first covers Afro-Cuban (Afro-Caribbean) jazz, the second section deals with Brazilian influenced jazz – Bossa Nova and Samba, and the third contains lead sheets of the tunes and instructions for the play-along audio.
00311345 Book/Online Audio $17.99

MODERN POP KEYBOARD
by Mark Harrison
From chordal comping to arpeggios and ostinatos, from grand piano to synth pads, you'll learn the theory, the tools, and the techniques used by the pros. The online audio demonstrates most of the music examples in the book.
00146596 Book/Online Audio $17.99

NEW AGE PIANO
by Todd Lowry
From melodic development to chord progressions to left-hand accompaniment patterns, you'll learn the theory, the tools and the techniques used by the pros. The accompanying 96-track CD demonstrates most of the music examples in the book.
00117322 Book/CD Pack......................$16.99

POST-BOP JAZZ PIANO
by John Valerio
This book/audio pack will teach you the basic skills needed to play post-bop jazz piano. Learn the theory, the tools, and the tricks used by the pros to play in the style of Bill Evans, Thelonious Monk, Herbie Hancock, McCoy Tyner, Chick Corea and others. Topics covered include: chord voicings, scales and tonality, modality, and more.
00311005 Book/Online Audio $17.99

PROGRESSIVE ROCK KEYBOARD
by Dan Maske
You'll learn how soloing techniques, form, rhythmic and metrical devices, harmony, and counterpoint all come together to make this style of rock the unique and exciting genre it is.
00311307 Book/Online Audio $19.99

R&B KEYBOARD
by Mark Harrison
From soul to funk to disco to pop, you'll learn the theory, the tools, and the tricks used by the pros with this book/audio pack. Topics covered include: scales and chords, harmony and voicings, progressions and comping, rhythmic concepts, characteristic stylings, the development of R&B, and more! Includes seven songs.
00310881 Book/Online Audio $19.99

ROCK KEYBOARD
by Scott Miller
Learn to comp or solo in any of your favorite rock styles. Listen to the audio to hear your parts fit in with the total groove of the band. Includes 99 tracks! Covers: classic rock, pop/rock, blues rock, Southern rock, hard rock, progressive rock, alternative rock and heavy metal.
00310823 Book/Online Audio $17.99

ROCK 'N' ROLL PIANO
by Andy Vinter
Take your place alongside Fats Domino, Jerry Lee Lewis, Little Richard, and other legendary players of the '50s and '60s! This book/audio pack covers: left-hand patterns; basic rock 'n' roll progressions; right-hand techniques; straight eighths vs. swing eighths; glisses, crushed notes, rolls, note clusters and more. Includes six complete tunes.
00310912 Book/Online Audio $18.99

SALSA PIANO
by Hector Martignon
From traditional Cuban music to the more modern Puerto Rican and New York styles, you'll learn the all-important rhythmic patterns of salsa and how to apply them to the piano. The book provides historical, geographical and cultural background info, and the 50+-tracks includes piano examples and a full salsa band percussion section.
00311049 Book/Online Audio $19.99

SMOOTH JAZZ PIANO
by Mark Harrison
Learn the skills you need to play smooth jazz piano – the theory, the tools, and the tricks used by the pros. Topics covered include: scales and chords; harmony and voicings; progressions and comping; rhythmic concepts; melodies and soloing; characteristic stylings; discussions on jazz evolution.
00311095 Book/Online Audio $19.99

STRIDE & SWING PIANO
by John Valerio
Learn the styles of the stride and swing piano masters, such as Scott Joplin, Jimmy Yancey, Pete Johnson, Jelly Roll Morton, James P. Johnson, Fats Waller, Teddy Wilson, and Art Tatum. This book/audio pack covers classic ragtime, early blues and boogie woogie, New Orleans jazz and more. Includes 14 songs.
00310882 Book/Online Audio $19.99

WORSHIP PIANO
by Bob Kauflin
From chord inversions to color tones, from rhythmic patterns to the Nashville Numbering System, you'll learn the tools and techniques needed to play piano or keyboard in a modern worship setting.
00311425 Book/Online Audio $17.99

HAL•LEONARD®

Prices, contents, and availability subject to change without notice.

www.halleonard.com

PLAY PIANO LIKE A PRO!

AMAZING PHRASING – KEYBOARD
50 Ways to Improve Your Improvisational Skills
by Debbie Denke

Amazing Phrasing is for any keyboard player interested in learning how to improvise and how to improve their creative phrasing. This method is divided into three parts: melody, harmony, and rhythm & style. The online audio contains 44 full-band demos for listening, as well as many play-along examples so you can practice improvising over various musical styles and progressions.

00842030 Book/Online Audio............................... $16.99

BEBOP LICKS FOR PIANO
A Dictionary of Melodic Ideas for Improvisation
by Les Wise

Written for the musician who is interested in acquiring a firm foundation for playing jazz, this unique book/audio pack presents over 800 licks. By building up a vocabulary of these licks, players can connect them together in endless possibilities to form larger phrases and complete solos. The book includes piano notation, and the online audio contains helpful note-for-note demos of every lick.

00311854 Book/Online Audio............................... $16.99

BOOGIE WOOGIE FOR BEGINNERS
by Frank Paparelli

A short easy method for learning to play boogie woogie, designed for the beginner and average pianist. Includes: exercises for developing left-hand bass • 25 popular boogie woogie bass patterns • arrangements of "Down the Road a Piece" and "Answer to the Prayer" by well-known pianists • a glossary of musical terms for dynamics, tempo and style.

00120517 .... $10.99

INTROS, ENDINGS & TURNAROUNDS FOR KEYBOARD
Essential Phrases for Swing, Latin, Jazz Waltz, and Blues Styles
by John Valerio

Learn the intros, endings and turnarounds that all of the pros know and use! This new keyboard instruction book by John Valerio covers swing styles, ballads, Latin tunes, jazz waltzes, blues, major and minor keys, vamps and pedal tones, and more.

00290525 .... $12.99

JAZZ PIANO TECHNIQUE
Exercises, Etudes & Ideas for Building Chops
by John Valerio

This one-of-a-kind book applies traditional technique exercises to specific jazz piano needs. Topics include: scales (major, minor, chromatic, pentatonic, etc.), arpeggios (triads, seventh chords, upper structures), finger independence exercises (static position, held notes, Hanon exercises), parallel interval scales and exercises (thirds, fourths, tritones, fifths, sixths, octaves), and more! The online audio includes 45 recorded examples.

00312059 Book/Online Audio............................... $19.99

JAZZ PIANO VOICINGS
An Essential Resource for Aspiring Jazz Musicians
by Rob Mullins

The jazz idiom can often appear mysterious and difficult for musicians who were trained to play other types of music. Long-time performer and educator Rob Mullins helps players enter the jazz world by providing voicings that will help the player develop skills in the jazz genre and start sounding professional right away – without years of study! Includes a "Numeric Voicing Chart," chord indexes in all 12 keys, info about what range of the instrument you can play chords in, and a beginning approach to bass lines.

00310914 .... $19.99

OSCAR PETERSON – JAZZ EXERCISES, MINUETS, ETUDES & PIECES FOR PIANO

Legendary jazz pianist Oscar Peterson has long been devoted to the education of piano students. In this book he offers dozens of pieces designed to empower the student, whether novice or classically trained, with the technique needed to become an accomplished jazz pianist.

00311225 .... $14.99

PIANO AEROBICS
by Wayne Hawkins

Piano Aerobics is a set of exercises that introduces students to many popular styles of music, including jazz, salsa, swing, rock, blues, new age, gospel, stride, and bossa nova. In addition, there is a online audio with accompaniment tracks featuring professional musicians playing in those styles.

00311863 Book/Online Audio $19.99

PIANO FITNESS
A Complete Workout
by Mark Harrison

This book will give you a thorough technical workout, while having fun at the same time! The accompanying online audio allows you to play along with a rhythm section as you practice your scales, arpeggios, and chords in all keys. Instead of avoiding technique exercises because they seem too tedious or difficult, you'll look forward to playing them. Various voicings and rhythmic settings, which are extremely useful in a variety of pop and jazz styles, are also introduced.

00311995 Book/Online Audio............................... $19.99

THE TOTAL KEYBOARD PLAYER
A Complete Guide to the Sounds, Styles & Sonic Spectrum
by Dave Adler

Do you play the keyboards in your sleep? Do you live for the feel of the keys beneath your fingers? If you answered in the affirmative, then read on, brave musical warrior! All you seek is here: the history, the tricks, the stops, the patches, the plays, the holds, the fingering, the dynamics, the exercises, the magic. Everything you always wanted to know about keyboards, all in one amazing key-centric compendium.

00311977 Book/CD Pack $19.99

HAL•LEONARD®
7777 W. Bluemound Rd. P.O. Box 13819
Milwaukee, Wisconsin 53213
www.halleonard.com

Prices, contents, and availability subject to change without notice.

1018
057

YOUR FAVORITE MUSIC
ARRANGED FOR PIANO SOLO

ADELE FOR PIANO SOLO – 2ND EDITION
This collection features 13 Adele favorites beautifully arranged for piano solo, including: Chasing Pavements • Hello • Rolling in the Deep • Set Fire to the Rain • Someone like You • Turning Tables • When We Were Young • and more.
00307585 ....$12.99

BATTLESTAR GALACTICA
by Bear McCreary
For this special collection, McCreary himself has translated the acclaimed orchestral score into fantastic solo piano arrangements at the intermediate to advanced level. Includes 19 selections in all, and as a bonus, simplified versions of "Roslin and Adama" and "Wander My Friends." Contains a note from McCreary, as well as a biography.
00313530 ....$17.99

THE BEST JAZZ PIANO SOLOS EVER
Over 300 pages of beautiful classic jazz piano solos featuring standards in any jazz artist's repertoire. Includes: Afternoon in Paris • Giant Steps • Moonlight in Vermont • Moten Swing • A Night in Tunisia • Night Train • On Green Dolphin Street • Song for My Father • West Coast Blues • Yardbird Suite • and more.
00312079 ....$19.99

CLASSICS WITH A TOUCH OF JAZZ
Arranged by Lee Evans
27 classical masterpieces arranged in a unique and accessible jazz style. Mr Evans also provides an audio recording of each piece. Titles include: Air from Suite No. 3 (Bach) • Barcarolle "June" (Tchaikovsky) • Pavane (Faure) • Piano Sonata No. 8 "Pathetique" (Beethoven) • Reverie (Debussy) • The Swan (Saint-Saens) • and more.
00151662 Book/Online Audio..........................$14.99

COLDPLAY FOR PIANO SOLO
Stellar solo arrangements of a dozen smash hits from Coldplay: Clocks • Fix You • In My Place • Lost! • Paradise • The Scientist • Speed of Sound • Trouble • Up in Flames • Viva La Vida • What If • Yellow.
00307637 ....$15.99

DISNEY SONGS
12 Disney favorites in beautiful piano solo arrangements, including: Bella Notte (This Is the Night) • Can I Have This Dance • Feed the Birds • He's a Tramp • I'm Late • The Medallion Calls • Once Upon a Dream • A Spoonful of Sugar • That's How You Know • We're All in This Together • You Are the Music in Me • You'll Be in My Heart (Pop Version).
00313527 ....$14.99

GREAT THEMES FOR PIANO SOLO
Nearly 30 rich arrangements of popular themes from movies and TV shows, including: Bella's Lullaby • Chariots of Fire • Cinema Paradiso • The Godfather (Love Theme) • Hawaii Five-O Theme • Theme from "Jaws" • Theme from "Jurassic Park" • Linus and Lucy • The Pink Panther • Twilight Zone Main Title • and more.
00312102 ....$14.99

PRIDE & PREJUDICE
12 piano pieces from the 2006 Oscar-nominated film, including: Another Dance • Darcy's Letter • Georgiana • Leaving Netherfield • Liz on Top of the World • Meryton Townhall • The Secret Life of Daydreams • Stars and Butterflies • and more.
00313327 ....$17.99

GEORGE GERSHWIN – RHAPSODY IN BLUE (ORIGINAL)
Alfred Publishing Co.
George Gershwin's own piano solo arrangement of his classic contemporary masterpiece for piano and orchestra. This masterful measure-for-measure two-hand adaptation of the complete modern concerto for piano and orchestra incorporates all orchestral parts and piano passages into two staves while retaining the clarity, sonority, and brilliance of the original.
00321589 ....$16.99

ROMANTIC FILM MUSIC
40 piano solo arrangements of beloved songs from the silver screen, including: Anyone at All • Come What May • Glory of Love • I See the Light • I Will Always Love You • Iris • It Had to Be You • Nobody Does It Better • She • Take My Breath Away (Love Theme) • A Thousand Years • Up Where We Belong • When You Love Someone • The Wind Beneath My Wings • and many more.
00122112 ....$17.99

STAR WARS: THE FORCE AWAKENS
Music from the soundtrack to the seventh installment of the Star Wars® franchise by John Williams is presented in this songbook, complete with artwork from the film throughout the whole book, including eight pages in full color! Titles include: The Scavenger • Rey Meets BB-8 • Rey's Theme • That Girl with the Staff • Finn's Confession • The Starkiller • March of the Resistance • Torn Apart • and more.
00154451 ....$17.99

TAYLOR SWIFT FOR PIANO SOLO – 2ND EDITION
This updated second edition features 15 of Taylor's biggest hits from her self-titled first album all the way through her pop breakthrough album, *1989*. Includes: Back to December • Blank Space • Fifteen • I Knew You Were Trouble • Love Story • Mean • Mine • Picture to Burn • Shake It Off • Teardrops on My Guitar • 22 • We Are Never Ever Getting Back Together • White Horse • Wildest Dreams • You Belong with Me.
00307375 ....$16.99

UP
Music by Michael Giacchino
Piano solo arrangements of 13 pieces from Pixar's mammoth animated hit: Carl Goes Up • It's Just a House • Kevin Beak'n • Married Life • Memories Can Weigh You Down • The Nickel Tour • Paradise Found • The Small Mailman Returns • The Spirit of Adventure • Stuff We Did • We're in the Club Now • and more, plus a special section of full-color artwork from the film!
00313471 ....$16.99

Prices, content, and availability subject to change without notice.
Disney Characters and Artwork TM & © 2018 Disney

HAL•LEONARD®

7777 W. BLUEMOUND RD. P.O. BOX 13819 MILWAUKEE, WI 53213

www.halleonard.com